The
Mortgage
Wars

*Inside Fannie Mae, Big-Money Politics,
and the Collapse of the American Dream*

Timothy Howard

Mc
Graw
Hill
Education

New York Chicago San Francisco Athens London Madrid
Mexico City Milan New Delhi Singapore Sydney Toronto

1 2 3 4 5 6 7 8 9 0   DOC/DOC   1 8 7 6 5 4 3

ISBN: 978-0-07-182109-4
MHID: 0-07-182109-0

e-ISBN: 978-0-07-182110-0
e-MHID: 0-07-182110-4

McGraw-Hill Education books are available at special quantity discounts to use as premiums and sales promotions, or for use in corporate training programs. To contact a representative, please visit the Contact Us page at www.mhprofessional.com.

This book is printed on acid-free paper.

*For my wife, Debbie
and my daughters, Julia and Lauren*

Contents

CONTENTS

Principal Players in the Mortgage Wars Story

Hank Paulsen, secretary of the Treasury, 2006 to 2009. His decision to nationalize Fannie Mae and Freddie Mac in September 2008 arguably triggered the bankruptcy of Lehman Brothers, which ignited the financial crisis. Along with Ben Bernanke, he worked tirelessly in the fall and winter of 2008 to contain the effects of the meltdown.

Ben Bernanke, chairman of the Federal Reserve, 2005 to 2013. After being slow to recognize the extent of the problems in the mortgage market, he led the Fed's response to the rapidly deteriorating financial crisis, adding massive amounts of liquidity to the system to keep it functioning.

David Maxwell, chairman and CEO of Fannie Mae, 1981 to 1991. He took over a Fannie Mae in dire financial difficulty in 1981 and transformed it into a financially strong entity that became the dominant institution in the U.S. mortgage market in the 1990s.

Paul Volcker, chairman of the Federal Reserve, 1979 to 1987. After leaving the Fed, he worked with Fannie Mae in 1989 and 1990 to develop the risk-based capital standard that was incorporated into regulatory and capital legislation in 1992 and laid the foundation for the company's subsequent rapid business growth.

Jim Johnson, Fannie Mae chairman and CEO from 1991 to 1999. He greatly expanded Fannie Mae's affordable housing efforts with his Trillion Dollar Commitment in 1994, and he made the company a formidable force politically.

Frank Raines, vice chairman of Fannie Mae from 1991 to 1996, chairman and CEO from 1999 to 2004. He became CEO shortly before the anti–Fannie Mae lobbying group FM Watch was formed. In December 2004 he was forced to resign over allegations by Fannie Mae's regulator of accounting fraud, later proven to have been false.

Richard Baker, congressman from Louisiana and chairman of the Capital Markets Subcommittee of the House Financial Services Committee (formerly the Banking and Financial Services Committee) from 1995 through 2007. He led congressional opposition to Fannie Mae beginning in 1999.

Larry Summers, deputy secretary of the Treasury, 1995 to 1999, and secretary of the Treasury 1999 to 2001. In 2000 he lent Treasury Department support to efforts by Richard Baker to restrain Fannie Mae by removing elements of the company's charter.

Alan Greenspan, chairman of the Federal Reserve from 1987 to 2006. A committed advocate of free-market financial principles, he was a staunch opponent of Fannie Mae's mortgage portfolio business. He proposed federally mandated limits on the size of the portfolio in 2004.

Gary Gensler, undersecretary of the Treasury for domestic finance under Larry Summers. At Summers' request, he testified in March 2000 in favor of legislation adverse to Fannie Mae.

Lou Ranieri, executive of Salomon Brothers in the 1970s and 1980s. A pioneer of the mortgage-backed securities (MBS) business, he helped draft the Secondary Mortgage Market Enhancement Act of

1984, increasing the marketability of private-label MBS. In 1986 he sought unsuccessfully to prevent Fannie Mae and Freddie Mac from obtaining authority to issue multiclass REMIC securities.

Paul O'Neill, secretary of the Treasury under President George W. Bush in 2001 and 2002. He declined to participate in the Fannie Mae reform initiatives advanced by Richard Baker, impeding Alan Greenspan's participation in these issues during O'Neill's term as secretary.

Armando Falcon, director, Office of Federal Housing Enterprises Oversight (OFHEO), 1999 to 2005. He was appointed OFHEO director shortly after the formation of FM Watch. In a special examination of Fannie Mae in 2004, he made accusations of accounting fraud that led to the forced retirement of CEO Frank Raines and the resignation of CFO Timothy Howard (the author of this book) at the end of that year.

Steve Blumenthal, key deputy to Armando Falcon at OFHEO. Hired in July 2002 as counsel to the director, he also served as deputy director and acting director before leaving in 2006. He advocated and pursued a much more aggressive approach by OFHEO to Fannie Mae regulation.

John Snow succeeded Paul O'Neill as Treasury secretary under George W. Bush, serving from 2003 through 2005. He collaborated with Frank Raines on the details of regulatory legislation in 2003, but then joined other members of the Bush administration to pursue changes to the legislation contrary to Fannie Mae's interests.

Wayne Abernathy, sworn in as assistant secretary for financial institutions at Treasury in December 2002. When the Bush administration switched from being a supporter of Fannie Mae to an opponent in the fall of 2003, he became the public spokesperson for the Treasury Department on Fannie Mae issues.

Leland Brendsel, chief executive officer of Freddie Mac, 1987 to 2003. He resigned in June 2003 in the wake of accounting irregularities discovered by the company's new auditor, PriceWaterhouseCoopers, and an outside law firm, Baker Botts.

Richard Syron, appointed CEO of Freddie Mac in December 2003, during a period of extensive executive turnover at the company. Lacking direct mortgage credit experience, he permitted the acquisition of a large number of high-risk mortgages during his tenure.

Don Nicoliasen, chief accountant of the Securities and Exchange Commission from 2003 to 2005. In December 2004, he ruled that Fannie Mae's implementation of a complex standard for accounting for derivatives, FAS 133, did not comply with generally accepted accounting principles and required the company to restate its earnings.

Warren Buffett, chairman of Berkshire Hathaway. He began but then aborted a significant investment in Fannie Mae in 1988. In December 2004, he offered to place enough preferred stock with Fannie Mae to keep it in compliance with its minimum capital standard.

James Lockhart, succeeded Armando Falcon as director of OFHEO in 2005 and became director of the successor agency to OFHEO, the Federal Housing Finance Agency, in 2008. After classifying Fannie Mae and Freddie Mac as adequately capitalized in August 2008, he gave in to pressures from Hank Paulsen to put the companies into conservatorship the following month.

Dan Mudd, vice chairman and chief operating officer of Fannie Mae between 2000 and 2004, president and CEO of Fannie Mae from 2005 to 2008. As CEO, he lowered Fannie Mae's credit standards to compete with private-label securities for market share, causing the company to report losses in 2007 and 2008.

Preface

For almost 20 years I was the most senior risk management executive at Fannie Mae. At its peak, Fannie Mae was responsible for financing more than one out of every four home loans in the United States and was the cornerstone of the most successful mortgage finance system in the world. But in the mid-2000s, that system broke down catastrophically. Credit standards weakened dramatically, and highly risky loans made to borrowers with little ability to repay them fueled a boom in the mortgage and housing markets that sped to a spectacular collapse, triggering a global financial crisis and the worst U.S. recession in modern times.

The mortgage meltdown was the culmination of a decade-long fight for control of the U.S. mortgage finance system, the largest credit market in the world. Fannie Mae was at the center of that fight, which I call the mortgage wars. From my top-level position at Fannie Mae—not in government affairs or public relations, but in finance and risk management—I had a unique inside perspective on the mortgage wars: how they began, why they escalated, and how and why they ultimately spun out of control, irrevocably altering the lives of tens of millions of families.

This book tells that story. It is a fascinating story in its own right but one that is especially relevant today as Congress considers reforms for the mortgage finance system of the future. If we fail to understand or acknowledge the true causes of the wrenching mortgage and financial crises we have just gone through and do not learn the right lessons from them, we will greatly increase the odds of repeating that experience.

I was a bank economist before I joined Fannie Mae, serving as senior financial economist at Wells Fargo Bank in San Francisco between 1976 and 1982. While there I wrote a weekly financial market newsletter called *Money and Credit Markets*, which was widely read by fixed-income investors across the country and frequently quoted in financial market columns and stories in the *Wall Street Journal*, *New York Times* and other national and regional media. At Wells I also wrote several articles on banking industry profitability for the *ABA Banking Journal*; did extensive consulting with the bank's commercial, real estate, and mortgage banking clients; and worked with Wells Fargo's Investment Advisors division to investigate what then was an emerging fixed-income asset class—mortgage-backed securities.

I was recruited to Fannie Mae as chief economist in March of 1982, when it was losing a million dollars a day. I knew the company might not survive but was willing to move from a stable job in San Francisco to an uncertain situation in Washington, D.C., because of my conviction—based on my meetings with research teams from Salomon Brothers and First Boston in the Investment Advisors conference rooms—that if Fannie Mae did turn itself around, it would be ideally situated to thrive in a mortgage market about to be revolutionized by securitization and the participation of capital-markets investors and Wall Street.

Once at Fannie Mae, I quickly became engaged on the business side. In 1985 I was put in charge of developing interest rate risk management strategies for the company's mortgage portfolio, the source of its near-failure a few years earlier, and that same year I set up and managed a group to do credit pricing for its mortgage-backed securities business. Fannie Mae's chairman, David Maxwell, decided to combine all key mortgage portfolio management responsibilities into one executive position in 1987, and he asked me to take it. I did.

In 1990 I was appointed Fannie Mae's chief financial officer and at that time added the traditional CFO functions of treasury, business planning, accounting, and investor relations to my existing duties as head of the mortgage portfolio and supervisor of the credit risk analysis group. A corporate reorganization made me the company's de facto chief risk officer in 2000, and in 2003 I was elected vice chairman of the board.

I left Fannie Mae at the end of 2004, along with Fannie Mae's chairman and CEO Frank Raines, in the wake of allegations by the company's regulator that we had deliberately falsified its financial reports. We denied the allegations, which became the basis of a civil suit naming Raines, Fannie Mae's former controller, and me as individual defendants.

The suit dragged on for over eight years. During that time, nearly 67 million pages of documents were reviewed, and testimony was taken from 123 fact witnesses and 35 expert witnesses. Through all this fact finding, no direct evidence emerged to support the regulator's contentions of wrongdoing. Raines, the former controller, and I filed motions for summary judgment in our favor, and in the fall of 2012, the federal district court judge presiding in the case granted them, dismissing us.

I had virtually no contact with the media while the civil suit was in process. This book, for the first time, tells the full story of the mortgage wars and of my experience at Fannie Mae.

Acknowledgments

Countless people suggested that I write this book. For nearly eight years after being asked to leave Fannie Mae at the end of 2004, I was advised by my personal counsel not to speak publicly about my experience at the company because of pending litigation. When I talked about it privately with friends and acquaintances, however—whether to explain how in just five years Fannie Mae could have gone from being one of the most successful companies in the country to being put into conservatorship, or to give them the back story on the accounting allegations leveled by its regulator—they invariably had the same reaction: "You *have* to write a book about that!"

I didn't think I ever would, but three things happened to change my mind. First, more and more was written about Fannie Mae and the financial crisis, and the story that was told about the company bore little resemblance to what I knew and had lived through first-hand. Second, in late August 2011, lawyers in the Fannie Mae civil suit in which I was named as a defendant filed a series of motions with the presiding judge that contained important information about the regulatory assault on the company not disclosed previously. Because these motions were made public, I would be able to refer to their contents in anything I wrote.

I began work on the book shortly after the motions were filed, but I did not definitely decide to go ahead with it until October

2012, when the judge emphatically dismissed me from the civil suit. That dismissal allowed me to write more freely about the mortgage wars and also, by restoring my public identity as a career financial executive and risk manager rather than as the suspected architect of an accounting fraud, gave me a much more credible platform from which to do so.

I have written numerous papers, presentations, and speeches during my business career, but a full-length book is a very different matter. Early on in the project, a former Fannie Mae colleague who also is a published author, John Buckley, put me in contact with an agent at Folio Literary Management in New York, Scott Hoffman. Scott is the reason this book exists. As a first-time author, my earliest drafts of a story outline fell well short of what most publishers look for, but rather than reject them, Scott made valuable suggestions for reshaping and refining them to the point where I finally had something he could send to editors. Tom Miller at McGraw-Hill saw the potential in the book, made an offer to publish it, and we were off and running.

Writing, I found, is a full-time and solitary job. The book took much longer to write than I expected it to, and during that time I could not have asked for more or better support than I received from my wife, Debbie. If she ever got tired of hearing me say, "I can't do that now; I have to work on the book," she never let on. For that I am deeply in her debt. I am also grateful to our many friends who indulged our requests to be allowed to drop off their radar screens for extended periods of time while I toiled away at my new vocation.

As the book was being written, I sent working drafts of chapters and sections to a number of people for their review and comments. I specifically want to thank Frank Raines, Bill Maloni, Tom Lawler, Jonathan Boyles, and Barry Zigas for the time they took to go over the material and for the very helpful comments they offered and the corrections they made. After the initial draft was finished, my editor, Tom Miller, made several useful suggestions on organization and presentation that significantly improved the final product. That product may bear my name, but it reflects the support, assistance, and indulgence of a great many people of whom I am enormously appreciative.

PART ONE

The Mortgage Wars
and the
Financial Crisis

CHAPTER 1

The Financial
Market Wildfire

ON SEPTEMBER 16, 2008, THE CONSEQUENCES OF FIVE YEARS' worth of unchecked lending excesses in the U.S. residential mortgage market flared up to ignite the worst financial crisis in modern history.

Barely a week earlier, the Treasury Department had put the mortgage giants Fannie Mae and Freddie Mac into conservatorship—effectively nationalizing them—expecting that this would contain the spreading effects of the mortgage market collapse. It did not.

The investment bank Lehman Brothers came under pressure almost immediately. Treasury and the Federal Reserve worked feverishly to find a buyer for Lehman, but having already put taxpayer money at risk in the rescue of another investment bank, Bear Stearns, six months earlier, and having just committed taxpayer money in the takeover of Fannie Mae and Freddie Mac, they were insistent that any acquisition be done without government assistance. London-based Barclays came close to an agreement on a deal for Lehman but pulled out when their regulator refused to approve it for fear of worsening the United Kingdom's financial problems.

Lehman filed for bankruptcy at 1:45 a.m. on Monday, September 15. That same day, Merrill Lynch announced it had agreed to be acquired by Bank of America.

The situation worsened quickly. The insurance firm AIG, with over $1 trillion in assets, was running out of money. A subsidiary of AIG, AIG Financial Products, had used complex derivatives to insure huge amounts of high-risk mortgages under the assumption that it would experience few if any losses on them, and that bet had gone horribly wrong. Counterparties to AIG were asking it to post collateral against the mounting value of its likely mortgage losses, and AIG did not have that collateral and was unable to borrow to obtain it. AIG had come to the Federal Reserve to ask for help. The Fed was inclined to give AIG a loan—both because the Fed believed AIG had enough value in its insurance subsidiaries to ultimately repay it, and because the Fed feared the repercussions of an AIG failure. The amount AIG was asking for was staggering: $85 billion.

As the Fed was considering the request, the financial markets were reeling from the Lehman bankruptcy. The Dow Jones average had fallen more than 500 points, and trading in the short-term commercial paper markets had come close to a halt.

Tuesday, September 16, was when everything fell apart. That morning Lehman's bankruptcy administrator in the United Kingdom froze all of Lehman's assets in the U.K. This was completely unanticipated, as it was contrary to how customer assets were treated in a U.S. bankruptcy. Fearing that the failure of any investment bank would lead to a freezing of assets, hedge funds responded by removing tens of billions of dollars of their custody accounts from Morgan Stanley, Goldman Sachs, and even Merrill Lynch. For similar reasons, institutional investors stopped lending securities to one another through what was called the repurchase market, which provided liquidity essential to the smooth trading of bonds and stocks.

After the stock market closed, the Reserve Primary Fund, a $62 billion money market mutual fund with over half its assets in commercial paper ($785 million from Lehman Brothers), announced that its net asset value had fallen below $1 per share. In mutual fund parlance, it had "broken the buck," meaning that its investors would not get all of their money back.

Then, at 9 p.m. that evening, the Federal Reserve announced that it had made a two-year, $85 billion emergency loan to AIG, a company most people never had heard of, to keep it from failing.

A financial system cannot function without the confidence of its participants, and in just two days confidence in almost every major U.S. financial institution had evaporated. Very few companies had walled themselves off from the problems in the mortgage sector, and after the Lehman bankruptcy, everyone feared there might be no government assistance forthcoming for many of the firms that could fail in the coming days and weeks. Investors and creditors did not want to try to guess which would be saved and which would not. They wanted out of all of them, and they fled corporate debt in droves for the safety of short-term Treasuries. Overwhelming demand for these securities pulled their yields down to almost zero.

It was not just companies that were in danger of failing—it was entire markets. Money market mutual funds had $2.7 trillion invested in them, $1.5 trillion of it by individuals. Outstanding commercial paper—a critical source of financing for large U.S. corporations—totaled $1.8 trillion. And according to the Bank for International Settlements, an incomprehensibly large $600 trillion worth of assets worldwide were used as the basis for contracts in over-the-counter derivatives. AIG's activities and operations coursed throughout that unregulated market in ways few understood, which was why rescuing AIG had been imperative.

In the wake of the news from the Prime Reserve Fund, all money market funds, not just those with exposure to Lehman, were hit with unprecedented requests for redemption, and even the highest-quality corporations were unable to sell their commercial paper. In response to both problems, the Fed and Treasury announced two new programs on Friday, September 19. Treasury said they would guarantee a $1 net asset value for money market funds, for a fee paid by them, and the Fed said it would make loans to depository institutions for use in purchasing high-quality commercial paper from these funds. Together, the actions stopped the runs on money market funds, gave support to the commercial paper market, and bought the Fed and Treasury precious time to address the urgent liquidity and capital problems of the large investment and commercial banks.

On Thursday evening, September 18, Treasury Secretary Hank Paulson and Fed Chairman Ben Bernanke had gone to Capitol Hill to brief congressional leaders on the financial crisis and tell them they would be requesting "hundreds of billions of dollars" to recapitalize the banks by purchasing toxic assets. It was a high-stakes gamble on their part. Seven weeks before a presidential election, the secretary of the Treasury and the chairman of the Federal Reserve were asking Congress to authorize a massive bailout of Wall Street at taxpayer expense. If Congress turned them down, the crisis could spin out of control. But they felt they had no choice. The Fed could make loans to stave off liquidity problems, but neither it nor Treasury could put capital into failing firms. For that they needed Congressional permission.

As Paulson and Bernanke sought broader powers, the crisis continued unabated. Investors picked Morgan Stanley as the next investment bank likely to fail and Washington Mutual (WAMU) as the next depository institution. Morgan Stanley's immediate problem was liquidity. The Fed could deal with that for the moment, but ultimately the firm would need either a buyer or a major infusion of capital. WAMU's problem was capital. They had been one of the most aggressive mortgage lenders—specializing in a very risky form of adjustable-rate mortgage called the "pay-option" ARM—and were paying the price. In the week following the Lehman bankruptcy, depositors pulled over $15 billion from WAMU, putting them on the verge of collapse.

On September 25 the government seized WAMU, and on the same day JP Morgan agreed to acquire WAMU's banking operations from their receiver, the Federal Deposit Insurance Corporation (FDIC), for $1.9 billion.

The FDIC was obligated to cover any losses of WAMU's insured depositors, but it did not agree to cover the losses of their uninsured creditors. That gave unsecured depositors at other troubled financial institutions a strong incentive to flee them. The next depository institution in the domino line was Wachovia, the nation's fourth largest bank by assets and the third largest by deposits. Like WAMU, they held large concentrations of pay-option ARMs. The run on Wachovia began the day after WAMU was seized.

Wachovia would not have been able to survive on its own. In a quick policy reversal, the FDIC agreed to use its funds to protect Wachovia's uninsured creditors by invoking for the first time what was called the "systemic risk exception" under the FDIC Improvement Act.

With expanded FDIC assistance, Wells Fargo and Citigroup both made bids for Wachovia. The FDIC deemed Citigroup's bid to pose less risk to its insurance fund, and early on Monday, September 29, it announced that Citigroup would acquire Wachovia.

The good news from that event did not last even a day. Treasury and the Fed had put together a formal proposal to Congress for their Troubled Assets Relief Program (TARP), which now had a price tag of $700 billion. Negotiations over TARP had been arduous. With an eye on the political campaign, members of Congress had insisted on a host of provisions and restrictions, including limits on executive compensation for companies receiving TARP money. Those issues finally were worked out, and on the afternoon of September 29, a bill was brought to the floor of the House for a vote. Both presidential candidates, Barack Obama and John McCain, pushed for passage of the bill, but it failed, 228–205.

That failure was a devastating blow. In reaction, the Dow Jones average fell a record 778 points, its largest one-day fall ever, wiping out more than $1 trillion in stock market value.

The stock market's reaction, together with modest changes to the proposal, seemed to make a difference. Two days later, the Senate passed a revised TARP proposal, 74–25, and on Friday, October 3, the House passed it by a vote of 263–171.

But the markets continued to fall. Treasury had congressional authority to spend the money, but they did not yet have a program for buying troubled assets, and it was not clear when they would develop one. In fact, they never did.

Shortly after TARP passed, Treasury changed their strategy. Rather than recapitalize banks by buying their bad assets, they would try to shore up investor confidence by putting capital into the banks directly. On Columbus Day, October 13, Paulson summoned to Washington the heads of nine major financial institutions—four banks (Bank of America, Citigroup, JP Morgan, and Wells Fargo), the three remaining large investment banks (Morgan Stanley and Goldman Sachs, which on September 21 had become bank holding companies, and Merrill Lynch, which Bank of America had agreed to acquire), and two important clearing banks (State Street and BNY Mellon).

Paulson told them he wanted them all to accept equity from the government. To avoid the perception of nationalization, he did not make the capital mandatory, and to encourage participation, he sought to make its terms attractive. Treasury would purchase preferred stock that would pay a 5 percent dividend for five years (before stepping up to 9 percent to encourage repayment), although at the insistence of Congress, participating companies would have to agree to restrictions on their executive compensation and corporate governance.

Not all of the bankers believed they needed the capital, but they understood the importance of the signal Treasury was trying to send, and all agreed to take it. In a further attempt to bolster confidence, the FDIC at the same time temporarily guaranteed new issues of unsecured debt by bank holding companies and also guaranteed non-interest-bearing deposits at insured financial institutions. And later that week, Treasury made TARP funds available to a broad group of financial institutions on the same favorable terms given to the nine large banks.

At this point, Treasury, the Fed, and the FDIC had done everything they could think of to prevent the financial system from collapsing. In addition to TARP, they had put in place more than two dozen emergency financing or guaranty programs, totaling trillions of dollars. Still, it had not been enough. Investors were setting their sights on the most iconic bank in the world: Citigroup.

Citigroup had stayed under the radar earlier in the crisis, mainly because other banks seemed like easier targets. Ironically, it was the resolution of the Wachovia situation that put the focus on them. Three days after Wachovia had accepted Citigroup's takeover offer, Wells Fargo used a favorable tax ruling made by the IRS two days earlier to come back with an offer that not only gave a higher price to Wachovia but also posed less risk to the FDIC.

With the FDIC's approval and over Citigroup's objections, Wachovia accepted the Wells offer. Losing the Wachovia deal meant Citigroup would not be acquiring that bank's very large base of depositors and would remain heavily dependent on purchased money for funding. Of the largest three remaining U.S. banks—Bank of America, Citigroup, and JP Morgan—Citigroup's reliance on this "hot" money, combined with their greater exposure to high-risk mortgages, made them the most vulnerable.

By the middle of November, short sellers succeeded in driving the price of Citigroup stock into the single digits, and depositors were rapidly withdrawing funds from the bank. It was clear to everyone that if the government did not do something, Citigroup would fail.

On Sunday, November 23, the Fed, Treasury, and FDIC put together a rescue package for the bank whose key components were a loss-sharing agreement between Citigroup and the government that effectively guaranteed a pool of $306 billion in high-risk assets and a further injection of $20 billion in TARP money in exchange for preferred stock paying an 8 percent dividend. Regulators held their breath, waiting for the stock market's reaction on Monday. The market liked what it saw, and Citigroup's stock rose almost 60 percent.

It had been a very close call, but the financial system had survived. The American home buyer and the U.S. economy, in contrast, fared much worse. Millions of people lost their homes to foreclosure, and the economy was plunged into an 18-month recession that was deeper than any since the Depression, from which the country still is struggling to recover.

The financial crisis began in the U.S. mortgage market. It had spread so quickly and so intensely because, like a wildfire, it had found so much tinder to burn. That tinder, of course, was the hundreds of billions of dollars in high-risk home mortgages made over the previous five years that were sitting on the balance sheets of virtually every major financial institution in the country. Many of these mortgages were unlikely ever to be repaid, and most of them never should have been made.

This was the great irony of the financial crisis. The policies and the regulatory stances of the "heroes" of that crisis, the Federal Reserve and the Treasury, were among the principal reasons such a tremendous number of toxic home mortgages existed in the first place.

CHAPTER 2

The Largest Credit Market in the World

A MILLION DOLLARS IS A LOT OF MONEY. ELEVEN *TRILLION* DOL-lars is an unfathomable amount of money. By way of comparison, a million seconds is about a week and a half; eleven trillion seconds is almost 350,000 years.

Just before it collapsed in 2008, the U.S. home mortgage market exceeded $11 trillion in size. It was the largest credit market anywhere. The dollar value of outstanding U.S. home mortgages was 20 percent greater than the country's national debt.

The crisis that almost brought down the global financial system had its origins in a no-holds-barred political fight among giant financial companies and their regulators over who would have the dominant position in this market—and the profits that went along with it.

As the top risk management executive at one of the principal combatants, Fannie Mae, I witnessed that fight firsthand. I ran Fannie Mae's largest and most controversial business—its mortgage investment portfolio—for 15 years and for over a dozen years was responsible for evaluating and pricing the company's mortgage credit risk.

The mortgage fight was rooted in a fundamental disagreement over the role of the government in housing. Supporters of the government-sponsored enterprises (GSEs), Fannie Mae and Freddie Mac, argued that housing was sufficiently important to society that the government should sponsor special-purpose institutions to provide low-cost financing to home buyers on an advantaged basis. The GSEs' opponents argued that their activities distorted capital flows and subjected taxpayers to unnecessary financial risk. The disagreement was ideological, but what fueled it was money. At issue was whether the GSEs or fully private firms—principally commercial banks and bank-owned mortgage companies—should be allowed to control the largest single credit market in the world.

Supporters and opponents of the GSEs had been having this dispute from the time Fannie Mae was created in 1938, but its intensity ramped up markedly in the late 1990s when three developments in combination greatly raised its stakes.

First, Fannie Mae supplanted the thrift industry as the dominant provider of mortgage financing, either owning or guaranteeing more than one in every four home loans in the country.

Second, at around the same time, Fannie Mae built seemingly unassailable congressional support for the role it had assumed.

And third, nearly two decades of deregulation in the financial services industry led to the emergence of very large and politically powerful lenders, who viewed Fannie Mae as an obstacle to their ambitions in the residential mortgage market.

Fannie Mae nearly failed when interest rates rose sharply in the late 1970s and early 1980s, but it was able to restructure its business and become financially strong. GSE regulatory and capital legislation passed by Congress in 1992 in response to the thrift crisis then laid the foundation for Fannie Mae's rapid growth over the balance of the decade. Drawing on the work of former Federal Reserve chairman Paul Volcker, Congress tied the company's required capital to the amount of interest rate and credit risk it took. Provided it kept those risks low, which benefited taxpayers, Fannie Mae would be allowed to hold relatively low amounts of minimum capital and could price its mortgage purchases and credit guarantees attractively, which benefited home buyers.

This was sound public policy, but it gave Fannie Mae a competitive advantage over fully private lenders, which made it harder for the private lenders to achieve their profitability goals.

Fannie Mae's market success and the highly ambitious affordable housing initiatives it launched in 1994 strengthened its political support. In an attempt to counter that support and further their own agenda, in 1999 four large lenders and two major mortgage insurers formed a Washington trade group called FM Watch, whose purpose was to lobby Congress to level the playing field by removing many of Fannie Mae's charter benefits. Fannie Mae fought to maintain the status quo, and the mortgage wars began.

In the late 1990s, Fannie Mae was providing record amounts of low-cost, fixed-rate financing to home buyers at minimal risk to taxpayers, as studies by the Treasury Department, the General Accounting Office, and other government agencies confirmed. Convincing Congress to reduce Fannie Mae's role in the market required its competitors and adversaries to overcome this fact. The strategy they chose to try to do so was an unprecedented disinformation campaign, carried out through the media, in which they put out a great deal of deliberately inaccurate information mischaracterizing the company's business, exaggerating its risks, and understating its benefits. This campaign was highly effective at creating a public image of Fannie Mae that bore little resemblance to the company that actually existed, and it greatly complicated the task of policy makers trying to determine the true facts in the fight they were being asked to referee.

The Federal Reserve and the Treasury were powerful allies of private lenders and FM Watch in their battle against the GSEs. Historically, both had opposed the GSEs for ideological and regulatory reasons, and following the lead of Fed chairman Alan Greenspan, they actively were seeking to substitute free-market principles, mechanisms, and disciplines for government involvement and regulation wherever they could.

In 2000, Treasury secretary Larry Summers sent a senior Treasury official to testify in favor of a bill introduced by Congressman Richard Baker that would remove some of the GSEs' charter attributes. The bill went nowhere, but Treasury's support of it signaled their intent to try to restrict the GSEs' activities.

The efforts of Fannie Mae's competitors and opponents to replace GSE mortgage financing with private-market financing fell into two broad categories: advocating legislative and regulatory actions that would raise GSE debt costs or limit the size of their mortgage portfolios and developing new mortgage products and financing methods that did not involve the GSEs.

Subprime mortgages were the private-market alternatives to loans financed by the GSEs, and what were called "private-label" mortgage-backed securities (MBS) were the alternatives to GSE-guaranteed mortgage-backed securities. To help foster both, the Federal Reserve and the Treasury allowed each to function with minimal federal regulation. The Fed and Treasury also pushed for and obtained bank capital requirements for AAA- and AA-rated private-label MBS that were equal to GSE mortgage-backed securities, indicating to investors that the two types of securities were equivalent in credit quality, which they were not. The spectacular collapse of the manufactured housing market in the early 2000s provided a clear demonstration of the risks of private-label MBS financing, but the banking regulators ignored it.

In the spring of 2003, rising tensions between Fannie Mae and its larger lenders led the company's CEO, Frank Raines, to try to achieve peace in the mortgage wars by working with Treasury Secretary John Snow on legislation that would address many of the lenders' concerns. Just before the legislation was introduced, however, the Bush administration insisted on changes that Fannie Mae believed would be harmful to it. When the legislation stalled, the administration launched a coordinated regulatory assault on the company dubbed "Operation Noriega," whose goal was to impose through regulation restrictions on Fannie Mae that could not be achieved legislatively. Fannie Mae's safety and soundness regulator, the Office of Federal Housing Enterprises Oversight (OFHEO), was an active participant in this assault.

The dual efforts of Fannie Mae's adversaries to increase the role of private-market mortgage-lending mechanisms and to constrain the GSEs bore fruit simultaneously. In 2004 the issuance of private-label mortgage-backed securities exceeded the issuance of GSE mortgage-backed securities for the first time, causing the GSEs to lose the role of prime mortgage standard-setter they had held since their inception. That same year, OFHEO used claims of accounting fraud—subsequently proved to have no basis in fact—to oust Fannie Mae's top management and to force an overhaul of its risk management.

Together these developments were catastrophic. Private-label MBS issuers put no practical limit on the riskiness of the mortgages they financed, and financial regulators refused to. In the absence of external credit discipline, lenders who were not retaining the risk of the loans they made engaged in a "race to the bottom" for market share and profits. Because the lowest-quality mortgages were the most profitable to finance through private-label securitization, the credit quality of prime home mortgages fell precipitously. Fannie Mae had adopted disciplines intended to protect it from credit excesses, but with new management and a radically different risk organization, the company abandoned these disciplines and switched from resisting the lending frenzy to joining it, making the ultimate boom and bust that much more severe.

Home sales peaked in the summer of 2005, and home prices peaked a year later. It took longer for the lending bubble to burst, but by the end of 2007, defaults on private-label securities had risen so high that the private-label mortgage-backed securities market shut down entirely. The GSEs were the only major sources of financing left.

Treasury, the Fed, and the Bush administration needed GSE financing to keep the housing market from complete collapse, but they opposed the GSEs having an expanded role as shareholder-owned companies. Treasury resolved their dilemma. Citing concerns about the quality of their capital, in September 2008 Treasury put Fannie Mae and Freddie Mac into conservatorship in spite of the fact that both companies met their statutory capital requirements at the time.

The mortgage wars were over. None of the principal combatants survived them, and the immense damage done to the battlefield on which they had been fought left almost all of the nation's financial institutions vulnerable to the crisis that quickly engulfed everyone.

The U.S. financial crisis was the direct result of a pitched battle between supporters and opponents of the GSEs for control of the $11 trillion residential mortgage market. Previous accounts of the crisis have almost completely missed this fact—ironically because they have had to rely on materials produced to gain political advantage in that battle, which are deliberately inaccurate and almost impossible for outsiders to decipher or disentangle. Fannie Mae and Freddie Mac's opponents waged an aggressive media campaign to convince opinion lenders, policy makers, and the general public that the two GSEs were dangerously risky companies that were able to maintain their positions of market prominence only because of bare-knuckled lobbying prowess. The widespread perception that this was true—and it was not—completely obscured the fact that the private-market financing mechanisms advocated by the GSEs' opponents were where the real risks lay.

The mortgage wars were never about protecting home buyers from risk; they were about who would control the flow of profits from the largest credit market in the world. And in this fight over money, risk was not a constraint; it was a weapon.

With the help of financial regulators and the credit rating agencies—whose AAA and AA ratings gave investors a false sense of confidence in the credit quality of complex mortgage securities they had no ability to evaluate on their own—lenders were able to decouple the rewards of mortgage risk-taking from its consequences to the point they could profit by making loans a borrower never could repay. Once that occurred, a mortgage boom and bust was virtually inevitable.

Homeowners never had a chance.

PART TWO

Fannie Mae's Rise
to Prominence

CHAPTER 3

Birth, Trial,
and Turnaround

THREE CONSISTENT THREADS RUN THROUGHOUT THE HISTORY OF U.S. mortgage finance over the past century: a high degree of risk, heavy involvement by the government in determining how the system operates, and—not unrelated to the first two—periodic and spectacular failures. Although the mortgage market collapse of 2008 was by far the most cataclysmic of these failures, it was not the first, and its roots reached far back in time.

A System in Transition

At the beginning of the 1920s, the main sources of U.S. mortgage finance were small, mutually owned building and loan societies. Along with mutual savings banks, they were known as thrift institutions. Commercial banks and life insurance companies did some mortgage lending but together accounted for less than half the mortgage holdings of thrifts. By far the most common types of mortgage were three- and five-year balloon loans, which had to be repaid or refinanced at maturity, although some building and loan societies made amortizing loans that with level monthly payments would be fully repaid in 10 to 12 years.

Neither the mortgage institutions nor the instruments of the 1920s could withstand the stresses of the Great Depression. Rising unemployment led some members of building and loan societies to redeem their savings and left others unable to repay their mortgages. That was a deadly combination for these member-owned entities, and a large number of them were forced to liquidate. Home owners with maturing balloon loans from banks faced their own set of challenges. Many found it difficult if not impossible to obtain new mortgages when their existing ones came due, often because the value of their homes had fallen, or they had lost their jobs, but in some cases because the banks or thrifts to which they turned simply had no money to lend. The abrupt withdrawal of credit caused home price declines to feed on themselves, and as prices continued to spiral downward, mortgage delinquencies and home foreclosures climbed sharply.

The government's initial response to the housing and mortgage crisis of the 1930s—as it was in the most recent one—was aimed at helping existing lenders. In the summer of 1932, Congress passed the Federal Home Loan Bank Act, creating the Federal Home Loan Bank Board and a set of 12 regional Federal Home Loan Banks (FHLBs), whose purpose was to make secured loans, called advances, to their member thrifts with the proceeds of bonds sold to the public. After President Roosevelt took office in 1933, the new administration and Congress turned to the task of devising a more robust mortgage finance system for the future. The National Housing Act of 1934 was the result. One of its principal features was the creation of a new housing agency, the Federal Housing Administration (FHA). A second key feature was an FHA program that offered insurance against default on 30-year fully amortizing fixed-rate mortgages with low down payments, provided they were made by qualified lenders and met the FHA's underwriting standards.

Included in the National Housing Act was a provision called Title III, authorizing the creation of a system of privately owned, federally chartered national mortgage associations. The idea behind these associations was to provide a reliable market for the new FHA-insured 30-year fixed-rate mortgage, which lenders were reluctant to originate. But in the three years after national mortgage associations were authorized, not a single one was set up. To demonstrate the viability of the concept, the FHA authorized the Reconstruction Finance Corporation to organize the National Mortgage Association of Washington in February 1938. Three months later, this institution was renamed the Federal National Mortgage Association, and its initials, FNMA, gave rise to the nickname "Fannie Mae" by which the entity would come to be known. (The Federal National Mortgage Association formally changed its name to Fannie Mae in 1997.)

Fannie Mae was the only national mortgage association ever created, and it was government-owned, not private. During its first 10 years of operation—much of which was during wartime—it did only a moderate amount of business. In 1948, however, it received authorization to purchase loans insured by the Veterans Administration (VA). VA loans were extremely popular among returning World War II soldiers as they formed families and were buying homes. Spurred by its new VA loan authority, Fannie Mae acquired over 130,000 loans in 1950, nearly double the amount of business it had done over its entire previous history.

Fannie Mae's sudden expansion caught the attention of critics and competitors, who worried that the government was playing too prominent a role in the housing market. The administration of President Eisenhower was sympathetic to those concerns, and in response to them Congress passed the Federal National Mortgage Association Charter Act in 1954, making Fannie Mae a mixed-ownership corporation. The U.S. Treasury was issued nonvoting preferred stock in Fannie Mae, and nonvoting common stock was made available to lenders, who were required to own it to sell loans to the company. The Charter Act included a provision for the gradual retirement of Treasury's preferred stock and stated that once it was repaid, legislation would be submitted to Congress to transform Fannie Mae into an entity fully owned by its private shareholders.

That moment came in 1968. The national debt was approaching $100 billion, a threshold President Lyndon Johnson desperately did not wish to exceed (it is now over $16 trillion). Pressures were growing to include Fannie Mae's then $2.5 billion in borrowings in the debt totals. Johnson's advisors told him that if Fannie Mae were made a private company, its debt could be kept off the government's books, creating more room for borrowing to finance the Vietnam War or his Great Society programs before the $100 billion federal debt level was breached.

Johnson embraced the idea, and the Housing and Urban Development Act of 1968 was the vehicle chosen to accomplish it. The act split Fannie Mae into two entities. The first was a stockholder-owned company with the same name and secondary mortgage market role as the original Fannie Mae and a revised federal charter. The second was a new agency called the Government National Mortgage Association (GNMA, or "Ginnie Mae"). Ginnie Mae was given the special assistance purposes that had been added in Fannie Mae's 1954 Charter Act, including the securitization of FHA and VA mortgages. Ginnie Mae was kept within the government and made part of the Department of Housing and Urban Development (HUD), and HUD became the new Fannie Mae's regulator.

The thrift industry did not sit idly by while Fannie Mae was being rechartered and Ginnie Mae created. It pushed for its own secondary market institution and got it. In the Emergency Home Finance Act of 1970, Congress created the Federal Home Loan Mortgage Corporation (FHLMC). The FHLMC was owned and regulated by the Federal Home Loan Banks, with the purpose of providing a secondary market for the conventional, or nongovernment insured, mortgages made by their member thrift institutions. (The 1970 act gave Fannie Mae the same conventional loan purchase authority.) The act did have one noticeable shortcoming: it did not produce a pronounceable acronym for its new offspring. The closest phonetic equivalent to FHLMC, "Flummox," was out of the question as a nickname. It became known as "Freddie Mac" instead.

New Institutions with Old Problems

Under the Federal Home Loan Bank Board, the thrift industry transformed itself from a large number of small, poorly managed building and loan societies into a smaller number of larger, professionally managed savings and loan associations. The industry grew rapidly in the 1950s and 1960s, and when total home mortgages outstanding crossed the half-trillion dollar mark in the mid-1970s, thrifts held nearly 60 percent of them, more than triple the share of commercial banks and over 10 times the holdings of Fannie Mae.

Thrifts and Fannie Mae each specialized in financing fixed-rate mortgages, but their business models were different. Fannie Mae sold commitments to buy fixed-rate mortgages to mortgage bankers and other lenders and then funded the resulting purchases with a mix of short-, intermediate-, and long-term debt issued in the capital markets. Thrifts took in short-maturity time deposits from savers and then made long-term fixed-rate mortgage loans to borrowers. The thrift model was built on a maturity mismatch between its loans and deposits and required stability in short-term interest rates to be successful. Rates did remain stable through the early 1960s, but then in the mid-1960s, they moved briefly but sharply higher. To keep thrifts from losing money, Congress imposed interest rate ceilings on thrift time deposits in 1966. (Commercial banks had had interest rate ceilings on their savings deposits since 1933.)

Deposit ceilings held off market forces for about a decade. By the mid-1970s, however, other types of financial institutions were offering market-rate products such as money market mutual funds as alternatives to regulated-rate deposits. Banks and thrifts still had federal deposit insurance in their favor—money market funds were uninsured—but there would come a point at which the difference between the regulated rates allowed on deposits and the market rates available on competing instruments would become too large for bank and thrift customers to ignore. October 6, 1979, marked that moment. On that day, Federal Reserve Chairman Paul Volcker announced that the Fed would raise short-term interest rates to whatever level was necessary to subdue inflation, which at the time was running at an annual rate of more than 11 percent. The short-term interest rate the Fed controlled, called the federal funds rate, already was at 10 percent, and in six months it had risen to over 17 percent. It ultimately exceeded 19 percent in early 1981. Federal funds rates at these levels caused all market interest rates—both short and long term—to spike dramatically.

As short-term interest rates rose to record levels, banks and thrifts suffered unprecedented deposit outflows. Banks held many types of assets that had variable interest rates, and they could afford to replace most of their lost consumer deposits with market-rate funding. Thrifts could not. For them, it no longer was possible to pretend that there was any simple solution to the structural flaw that had characterized their industry from the beginning of its existence.

Sharply rising interest rates also exposed the flaws in Fannie Mae's business model. In the mid-1970s, the company had begun to sell what were called "long-term optional purchase commitments." Lenders purchasing them could deliver mortgages to Fannie Mae at a preset price at any time prior to the commitments' expiration—which could be a year or more—but were not obligated to do so if they could get a better price elsewhere. The terms of these commitments meant that when interest rates fell, their holders would sell their loans to buyers who could pay a higher price than Fannie Mae had agreed to, and when interest rates rose, they would deliver their now below-market-rate loans to Fannie Mae.

Mortgage rates began rising in 1977, and they continued to go up in 1978. As they did, more and more of the optional commitments Fannie Mae sold turned into deliveries. The problem, of course, was that the note rates on the loans being delivered had been set many months earlier, and the cost of the debt required to fund them had risen in the interim. In an attempt to maintain a positive funding spread on the new mortgages, Fannie Mae's management financed them with shorter-term debt. This strategy, however, would work only if interest rates did not rise further. If they did, the company would have to continually reissue its short-term debt at even higher costs, while the yields on its mortgages remained the same.

October 1979 had the same effect on Fannie Mae as it did on the thrift industry. The company barely broke even in 1980. Rolling over maturing debt at much higher market rates—as it was forced to do—was causing Fannie Mae's interest expense to rise rapidly, while the interest income from its mortgages barely rose at all. Furthermore, lenders were continuing to exercise their options to deliver mortgages originated many months earlier at interest rates far below the company's current cost of debt. Fannie Mae certainly would begin losing money in 1981; the only questions were how large those losses would be and how long it would take for them to exhaust the company's capital.

Fannie Mae's president at that time was Oakley Hunter, who had been appointed to his position by President Nixon in 1970, just before Fannie Mae became a public company. Hunter was having heart problems in 1980, and with the now shareholder-owned company in great financial difficulty, its board of directors retained a search firm to find a successor. The board's choice was a man named David Maxwell, a former HUD general counsel who was then running a mortgage insurance company in Los Angeles called Ticor. Maxwell became Fannie Mae's chairman and CEO in May of 1981.

The Maxwell Turnaround

Rapidly rising interest rates had put both the thrift industry and Fannie Mae in dire jeopardy. However, the approach taken by the government to the problems of the thrifts and the approach taken by Maxwell to the problems of Fannie Mae could not have been more different.

The government's response to the worsening plight of the thrifts—beginning under President Carter and continuing under President Reagan—had been to comprehensively deregulate the industry through both legislative and regulatory actions. In 1980 Congress eliminated thrift deposit ceilings. Regulators authorized thrifts to make adjustable-rate and other forms of shorter-term mortgages in 1981, and in 1982 the Garn–St. Germain Depository Institutions Act gave thrifts sweeping new powers to invest in a variety of nonmortgage asset types while greatly increasing the percentage of commercial real estate assets they could hold. In concert, through a combination of legislated and regulatory authorities, the Federal Home Loan Bank Board took a series of steps intended to give money-losing thrifts time to regain their financial health, if they could. These included reducing thrift capital requirements from 5 percent to 3 percent of assets, greatly expanding the definition of what could qualify as regulatory capital, and allowing thrifts selling low-rate mortgages to spread their losses on those sales over a 10-year period.

Maxwell knew he could not count on any help from the Reagan administration. Key administration officials made clear that they strongly favored private market solutions to the thrift crisis and had taken the position early in 1981 that Fannie Mae's charter benefits should be eliminated as soon as it was feasible to do so. It would be all Maxwell could do to preserve the charter he had; enhancements to it that could help the company escape its financial peril were out of the question. Fannie Mae would have to be fixed as Maxwell inherited it.

He faced daunting challenges. The company was losing a million dollars a day. It had nearly $50 billion in mortgages with note rates far below the current market rate—which Maxwell referred to as the "block of granite"—and a three-year mismatch between the expected lives of those low-rate mortgages and the average maturity of the high-cost debt funding them. Fannie Mae had an antiquated and unworkable business model, and the single product to which it was limited by statute—U.S. residential mortgages offered for sale in the secondary market—was mired in a severe slump in the midst of record high interest rates.

Maxwell was a lawyer by training. He attended Yale Law School and upon graduation practiced law for several years. He took an early interest in politics, running for Congress at the age of 30 (he lost) and then, after working to help elect Raymond Shafer governor of Pennsylvania, became Pennsylvania's state insurance commissioner. It was in this job that Maxwell discovered he had a talent for management. The insurance commission was a disaster, and Maxwell was able to straighten it out. He then served at HUD during the Nixon administration and following that accepted the offer from a title insurance company named Ticor to start up a mortgage insurance subsidiary in California. By the time he came to Fannie Mae, Maxwell considered himself a businessman rather than a lawyer.

Maxwell understood instinctively that to change the results at Fannie Mae, he had to change the company's culture, and that meant changing its people. He filled the company's top positions with individuals he knew and trusted, and they in turn brought in a new group of executives with a broad range of skill sets and experience. By the time I came to Fannie Mae in March of 1982, Maxwell's turnaround team was largely in place and already had identified most of the critical strategies they would follow. They were a mix of actions designed to quickly generate income in the short term while building a solid foundation for stability over the long term.

The first key decision Maxwell made was to stop selling optional purchase commitments in favor of mandatory commitments that required lenders to deliver their mortgages to us or pay a penalty for not doing so. The president of the Mortgage Bankers Association objected strenuously to the change, telling Maxwell, "You have no purpose if you do this." Maxwell's response was that Fannie Mae could not afford to offer a product whose risk was not manageable.

What we most needed from our customers was more mortgages to buy, and in the early 1980s, finding them was not easy. The economy was in deep recession, mortgage rates were in the mid-teens, and relatively few of the product types Fannie Mae traditionally purchased—conventional and FHA-insured 30-year fixed-rate mortgages—were being originated or offered for sale. Fortunately the Federal Home Loan Bank Board allowed savings and loans to begin offering adjustable-rate mortgages (ARMs) in 1981, and the Office of the Comptroller of the Currency soon gave the same authority to banks. To make ARMs more attractive to borrowers, almost all had "teaser rates"—initial payment amounts well below the fully indexed payment—as well as caps on how much their monthly payments could increase each year. These features made ARMs almost as difficult to manage as fixed-rate loans, but we nonetheless bought many different types of them.

Purchasing the volume and variety of mortgages we were seeking required changes in our business processes. We had to abandon what we called our prior approval approach—in which we underwrote all our loan purchases ourselves—and instead rely on lenders to warrant the creditworthiness of the loans they were selling us. We also had to relax many of our credit standards and in some cases acquire new types of loans without a firm idea of whether their credit performance would be acceptable. (One such initiative got the nickname "cash for trash.") We knew these steps carried risk but felt we had to take them. We needed the income. If the new mortgages available for us to buy had more credit risk than we bargained for—or if it turned out we were delegating too much credit authority to the lenders selling us these loans—we would have to deal with that later.

Higher fee income was the fourth component of Maxwell's turnaround strategy. We averaged over $200 million per year in commitment fees from 1982 to 1984, more than triple the annual fees in the last two years under Hunter. Most of the increase came from greater business volumes, although some reflected higher fee rates on the riskier loan types we were acquiring. Our decision in 1981 to begin guaranteeing loans as mortgage-backed securities (MBS) gave us a second major source of fee income. Fees were not the main reason we entered this business—it diversified our risk profile and enabled us to serve more borrowers in fulfillment of our mission—but by 1985 our MBS guaranty fee income had passed the $100 million per year mark.

Mismatching the company's mortgages and debt is what had gotten Fannie Mae into trouble in the first place. The goal we set here was to eliminate our mismatch in two stages. We would begin by match-funding our new mortgage purchases and then—if and when interest rates declined—extend debt maturities on the existing portfolio. That turned out to be too ambitious. We soon realized that if we exactly matched the mortgage and debt maturities on our new purchases, we would not generate enough income to offset the losses from our low-rate "block of granite" loans. So we tried to strike a balance. Between 1982 and 1984, the debt we issued against our new mortgage purchases had an average maturity about one year shorter than the expected lives of the mortgages we bought. It wasn't perfect, but it was the best we felt we could do under the circumstances. Similar to our approach to credit risk, we would work to achieve further reductions in the portfolio's mismatch once we were in a less precarious financial state.

, With everything we were able to do in the first three years of Maxwell's chairmanship—the switch to mandatory commitments, a much larger volume and wider variety of products purchased, changed business processes, significantly higher fee income, and a closer maturity match on our new business—interest rates still had to come down for us to survive. We kept track of the relationship between the projected income on our new business and the losses on our existing portfolio using what we called our "months to go" chart, which indicated how long our capital would last without further declines in interest rates.

Fortunately, rates began falling in the second half of 1982, and they continued to fall through the middle of 1983. They shot back up again through the middle of 1984—causing us some anxious moments—but then embarked on an irregular but sustained decline through the end of 1986. With this seesaw interest rate pattern, Fannie Mae reported a small ($75 million) profit in 1983 and lost money again in 1984. We returned solidly into the black in 1985, and by the end of 1986, there was no doubt in anyone's mind that we had definitely turned the corner.

One afternoon at the beginning of 1988, I looked out the door of my office into Fannie Mae's executive waiting area and saw someone I recognized. It was Warren Buffett, the well-known investor and chairman of Berkshire Hathaway. He was there to see Maxwell. Buffett reported on what happened next in his 1991 annual report to shareholders:

In early 1988, we decided to buy 30 million shares (adjusted for a subsequent split) of Federal National Mortgage Association (Fannie Mae), which would have been a $350–$400 million investment. We had owned the stock some years earlier and understood the company's business. Furthermore, it was clear to us that David Maxwell, Fannie Mae's CEO, had dealt superbly with some problems that he had inherited and had established the company as a financial powerhouse—with the best yet to come. I visited David in Washington and confirmed that he would not be uncomfortable if we were to take a large position. After we bought about 7 million shares, the price began to climb. In frustration, I stopped buying . . . In an even sillier move, I surrendered to my distaste for holding small positions and sold the 7 million shares we owned. I wish I could give you a halfway rational explanation for my amateurish behavior vis-à-vis Fannie Mae. But there isn't one. What I *can* give you is an estimate as of year end 1991 of the approximate gain that Berkshire *didn't* make because of your Chairman's mistake: about $1.4 billion.

The turnaround engineered by Maxwell had been a remarkable success. The outcome for the thrift industry would be far different.

CHAPTER 4

Managing Risk

As DAVID MAXWELL LIKED TO SAY, "FANNIE MAE WAS POLITIcal to its bone marrow." It hardly could have been otherwise. It had the benefit of a special congressional charter that gave it valuable advantages over purely private companies, and it operated in a mammoth financial market—residential mortgages—whose smooth functioning was vital to the health of the American economy. If that weren't enough, it was located in Washington, D.C.

A Unique and Controversial Charter

Fannie Mae's 1954 charter, as amended in 1968, gave it the mission "to provide supplementary assistance to the secondary market for home mortgages by providing a degree of liquidity for mortgage investments, thereby improving the distribution of investment capital available for home mortgage financing." To ensure that its efforts were focused on low- and moderate-income home buyers, it was limited to the purchase or guaranty of U.S. residential mortgages below a certain dollar amount (an amount that in 1981 was allowed to increase each year, based on the change in an index of national home prices). It could participate only in the resale or secondary mortgage market, with a primary market lender—typically a bank, thrift, or mortgage bank—that chose to do business with it. And it had to maintain a presence in all parts of the country, in bad times as well as good.

Balancing these restrictions—and to enable the company to attract the private capital necessary to carry out its mission—the charter contained benefits that fell into two broad categories: those that created the perception of a special relationship with the U.S. government and those that lowered the cost or increased the marketability of the company's securities. Charter attributes falling into the first category included authorization for the secretary of the Treasury to purchase up to $2.25 billion of Fannie Mae debt at Treasury's discretion, an exemption from state and local income taxes, and the appointment by the president of the United States of five members to Fannie Mae's board of directors. Charter attributes that benefitted the company's securities included the facts that they were eligible to be purchased or sold by the Federal Reserve in open market operations, were eligible for unlimited investment by national banks and most state banks and thrift institutions, and were considered government securities for purposes of the Securities Act of 1933 and the Securities Exchange Act of 1934 and were therefore exempt from SEC registration requirements. All of these benefits were intentional, and collectively they enabled Fannie Mae to do business on a scale and at a cost that would not have been possible without them.

From the time it became a shareholder-owned company, Fannie Mae faced criticism and pressures from three main sources: free-market advocates, actual and potential competitors, and the two principal bank regulators, the Federal Reserve and the Treasury. Free-market advocates opposed Fannie Mae on ideological grounds, because it used government-provided advantages to channel more funds into housing than would have been available otherwise. Actual and potential competitors of Fannie Mae were concerned about the company's market power; they found it in their commercial best interest to ally with the free-market viewpoint and did. The Federal Reserve and Treasury were mistrustful of a profit-making entity with the implied backing of the government but not controlled by it, and they felt Fannie Mae's government sponsorship gave it the ability to expand its business at will (to the disadvantage of the competitive position of the banks they regulated) as well as an incentive to take excessive risk.

Each of these groups of critics sought something different. The free-market ideologues wanted Fannie Mae not to exist at all or to be "fully privatized." Most of Fannie Mae's competitors wanted the company to be more tightly regulated and its business powers to be limited and strictly defined (though a few favored full privatization). And the Fed and Treasury, at least initially, were focused on constraining Fannie Mae's size and risk taking. Any of the company's critics or opponents seeking changes to its role in the market, risk, or regulation in a manner that advanced their interests came to Washington to try to get them.

Maxwell became Fannie Mae chairman seven months after Ronald Reagan's election as president and after Reagan had filled key positions at Treasury, the Office of Management and Budget (OMB), and the Council of Economic Advisers with committed free-market conservatives. The philosophy of the Reagan administration toward both the rescue of the thrifts and the plight of Fannie Mae was made clear in the Report of the President's Commission on Housing, published in 1982. That report said, "The Commission foresees a future in which government should be a participant in housing finance only in those areas where the private sector cannot provide needed services at a reasonable cost to borrowers." The report left no doubt about the role envisioned for Fannie Mae and Freddie Mac in that future: "after FNMA's [Fannie Mae's] financial condition clearly has stabilized," it said, the two GSEs "should become entirely private corporations."

The policies of the Reagan administration toward Fannie Mae were based purely on ideology. No one on Wall Street or in the commercial banking industry was yet asking for any restraints to be put on us or for any of our agency attributes to be pared back (that would come later). Wall Street in fact was quite happy with us. They underwrote and made markets in the debt we issued, and we were in the process of initiating a new mortgage-backed securities program they would profit from as well.

We were fortunate that in the early stages of Reagan's first term, proposals to cut back Fannie Mae's agency attributes were not high policy priorities. Had we been in their gun sights, we may well not have survived. A crucial element of our turnaround was quickly doing more types of profitable new business, much of which required HUD approval. HUD was considered a backwater in the administration. The administration paid little attention to the department, and the new HUD secretary, Sam Pierce, paid little attention to us. We had a good friend and ally in HUD's undersecretary, Don Hovde, who had been president of the National Association of Realtors and knew us well. We would bring our proposals for new programs—ranging from adjustable-rate mortgage purchases to multifamily investments to our new mortgage-backed securities business—to Hovde, who would put them in front of Pierce and ask Pierce to sign them. He invariably did. It was more than a little ironic that while the heads of Treasury and the OMB privately were telling Maxwell that Fannie Mae should be done away with, we were walking through the front door at HUD and obtaining the administration's permission to expand.

Fannie Mae barely turned profitable in 1983, and to our critics within the administration, this was a signal that it was safe to come after us (notwithstanding the fact that a subsequent rebound in interest rates pushed us back into the red in 1984).

The assault started with the Office of Management and Budget and its director, David Stockman. A three-term congressman from Michigan before being tapped to run the OMB at the age of 35, Stockman was a close ally of Jack Kemp, a leading supply-side economist and coauthor of the Kemp-Roth tax cuts that were the centerpiece of the Reagan economic platform. Stockman's preferred policy objective for Fannie Mae was full privatization immediately, but he knew Congress would not support that idea and so instead proposed to charge a "user fee" on the debt we issued to fund our mortgage purchases. The theory behind user fees was that because our charter benefits enabled us to borrow more cheaply in the capital markets than fully private firms, the government ought to be entitled to attach a fee to our debt as compensation for those benefits. Once put in place, the user fee could be raised over time to a level where eventually the cost of our debt and the debt issued by our competitors would be equal.

We took our case against user fees to our allies and Congress. Our best argument was a purely economic one: any fees added to our debt would cause us to raise the yield requirements on the mortgages we purchased, and as such it would be home owners who ultimately would bear the cost. To make that point clear, we called user fees a "home ownership tax." That proved to be very effective labeling, and we were able to defeat user fees on Capitol Hill. But it was a constant battle. User fees were proposed every year, in varying amounts and with varying rationales. For us it was the vampire issue; we never could definitively kill it.

A second political problem for Fannie Mae in the mid-1980s was the increasingly vocal opposition of the California savings and loans. The S&L industry had been granted significantly broader asset powers in the Garn–St. Germain Act, but the large California S&Ls elected to stay concentrated in residential mortgage lending. They considered a healthy Fannie Mae a serious threat to their business. The executives who engaged most actively against us were Jim Montgomery, CEO of Great Western Financial, and Herb and Marion Sandler, co-CEOs of Golden West Financial. They argued that we had outlived our business purpose because the two conditions we had been chartered to alleviate—credit-driven housing cycles and regional mismatches between the need for and the supply of mortgage credit—had been addressed by thrift deregulation. They seconded the administration's contention that our charter gave us unfair advantages over fully private firms, and they maintained that our portfolio exposed the U.S. taxpayer to excessive risk. They also aggressively supported user fees.

Full Privatization Gets Full Consideration

Fierce opposition to our charter from the Reagan administration and the California thrifts, along with the growing realization that there were no obvious ways to make this opposition disappear, led Maxwell to seriously investigate full Fannie Mae privatization in 1987.

We had looked at privatization before. In 1983 we had hired Lazard Frères to help us investigate privatization alternatives for discussion with our board, in an effort we called Project One. Project One took place while we still were struggling to return to profitability, however, and even with Lazard's help we were unable to come up with any practical version of a fully private Fannie Mae worth recommending to our directors. We shelved Project One in the fall of 1984.

Three years later, several things were different. We were solidly profitable and had growing confidence in our future prospects. We had just raised over $100 million in fresh capital in February of 1987, selling six million shares of stock in the United States and two million shares in Europe. And we were strongly motivated by a desire to escape the political pressures we were facing. Maxwell hired Shearson Lehman Brothers to be the consultant on the new privatization study, largely because he wanted the assistance of the head of their Washington, D.C., office, Jim Johnson. Johnson had accompanied Maxwell and me on the road show for our European equity issue, and I had gotten to know him then. I was appointed Fannie Mae's lead on the project shortly after it began.

Applied to Fannie Mae, the term "privatization" was a misnomer. Technically, we *were* private: we were owned by our shareholders. What our opponents and critics meant by Fannie Mae privatization was giving up some or all of the benefits of our federal charter while retaining our business restrictions. That would have been suicidal. The one conclusion we did come to in Project One was that a Fannie Mae bereft of agency attributes but limited to the residential mortgage business would not have been able to survive. For all of the talk by the California S&Ls about Fannie Mae's "unfair advantages," thrifts had their own federal benefit—federal deposit insurance—along with two captive federal agencies, the Federal Home Loan Banks and Freddie Mac, both under the wing of a supportive regulator, the Federal Home Loan Bank Board. Commercial banks had similar federal ties. It might have been expedient for thrifts and banks to ignore their federal benefits when referring to themselves as "private" and pressing their cases in the political arena, but for us to have ignored them when putting together a privatization business plan would have been foolhardy.

What we called the Shearson study had three components: developing versions of our existing businesses that could operate without the implicit support of the federal government, identifying new asset powers that would give us business and risk diversification while drawing on expertise we either already had or believed we could acquire, and outlining a feasible path of transition from the government-sponsored Fannie Mae to the new private company.

I took the lead on the non-government-sponsored enterprise versions of our portfolio investment and credit guaranty business. We and the Shearson team concluded that if a private Fannie Mae had a portfolio business at all, it would have to be far smaller than the $90 billion we then held, and that it would be more difficult to manage and be able to operate only in certain favorable market environments. The credit guaranty business of a private Fannie Mae would be smaller as well, because it would provide less value to lenders. Investors would not be willing to pay as much for mortgage-backed securities guaranteed by a private Fannie Mae, and the higher capital a private Fannie Mae would have to hold would raise the guaranty fees it charged.

The virtual certainty of having much smaller existing businesses in a non-GSE Fannie Mae raised the stakes for finding new products to offer, new businesses to enter, and new corporate forms of operation as a private company. Together with the Shearson staff, we investigated a number of possibilities, many of which seemed promising. But when we looked at implementation issues, we understood what we were up against.

Any proposal for Fannie Mae privatization required legislation to replace our existing charter with a new one. We believed it would be possible to find support for giving up our government-sponsored enterprise status, although the Realtors and the National Association of Home Builders—and probably the Mortgage Bankers Association—would fight it because we would be replacing a GSE Fannie Mae that was very valuable to their business with one that would do much less for them. But we became convinced that there was little chance of getting backing from anyone for any reasonable form of new business powers, for fear we might become competitors with them. Further, there were daunting transitional challenges involved in an orderly liquidation of the GSE Fannie Mae as the new private entity was trying to establish itself. Advocates of Fannie Mae privatization already were talking about imposing an exit fee on the new non-GSE Fannie Mae to prevent the transfer of any monetary value we may have received and retained as a result of our federal charter.

All of these uncertainties and imponderables proved too much to overcome. Once we took a privatization proposal to Congress, we would have no control over the outcome. We had a fiduciary duty to our shareholders to safeguard their interests and could not in good faith initiate a privatization process we had come to believe had so little chance of success. After a year and a half of work, we shut the Shearson study down. It had led us to precisely the same place as Project One: a realization that the status quo for Fannie Mae was preferable to any alternative we or anyone else had been able to come up with.

Our work on privatization crystallized the situation we faced. There was no realistic possibility of changing Fannie Mae in a manner that would appease our ideological critics and competitors and at the same time maintain our value to home buyers and our shareholders. Whether we liked it or not, political opposition would be a permanent aspect of our existence. To fulfill our charter mission, we would have to be able to both run our business successfully and defend ourselves in Washington against attempts to make running that business more difficult.

Congress had not seemed particularly receptive to the argument of the California S&Ls that we had unfair advantages over thrifts and banks that needed to be pared back, and it certainly didn't agree with our ideological opponents that the government should not be involved in mortgage finance at all. But Congress did take seriously the notion that the benefits we provided to home buyers might not be worth the risks our activities posed to taxpayers. Fannie Mae's near-failure already had given Maxwell an economic reason to make the company world class in managing our two principal business risks, interest rate and credit risk. Increasingly, we came to understand that to maintain strong and bipartisan support in Congress, we had a compelling political reason to do exactly the same thing.

Rethinking Interest Rate Risk

Interest rate risk was our most difficult challenge. Fannie Mae had been created to serve as a secondary market purchaser of the 30-year fixed-rate mortgage (30-year FRM), which was the government's solution to the problems borrowers had with short-term balloon mortgages during the Depression. Thirty-year FRMs are extremely consumer friendly. Borrowers with a 30-year FRM who make a fixed monthly payment for 30 years can pay off their mortgage entirely, but the loan includes an option that allows them to prepay it at any time without penalty (although they do have to pay certain fees to obtain a new loan). When interest rates go up, borrowers can hold onto the loans they have—which at that point have below-market interest rates—and when interest rates go down, they can pay them off and take out new ones that cost less. It's a terrific deal, which is why since adjustable-rate mortgages became widely offered in the early 1980s, U.S. home owners have preferred FRMs to ARMs by more than three to one.

The prepayment option that makes a 30-year FRM so attractive to borrowers is what makes managing its risk so difficult for lenders. The most comprehensive measure of the life of a fixed-income security, or bond, is its *duration*. While a bond's *maturity* measures only the date on which the final repayment of principal is received, its duration incorporates all of the interest and principal payments from that security and weights them by when they occur. Large payments made early in the life of a bond shorten its duration, and large payments made late lengthen it. For most bonds, the duration calculation is straightforward, but for 30-year FRMs, it is complicated by the fact that very few mortgages remain outstanding for their entire lives. Typically, they get repaid—either when the borrowers sell their homes, or when interest rates fall and they refinance. And exactly *when* the mortgage gets repaid has a huge impact on its duration, because that repayment is by far the largest single cash flow from the mortgage that takes place.

The challenge of managing a group of fixed-rate mortgages is, in a nutshell, that their durations are not knowable. Mortgage durations depend on interest rates, which can't be reliably predicted. Managers of fixed-rate mortgages therefore need to be able to protect themselves from changes in mortgage durations by reacting to their effects as they occur. If they are unable to do so—as was the case with Fannie Mae and the thrifts in the late 1970s and early 1980s— serious problems can ensue.

Ideally, the durations of a company's assets and debt should be equal. When Maxwell became chairman of Fannie Mae, the company had a mismatch, or "gap," of three years between the average duration of its mortgages (five years and two months) and the average duration of its debt (only *two* years and two months). We set a goal of reducing the portfolio's duration gap to less than one year as quickly as market conditions permitted. We made relatively little progress through the end of 1984, but when mortgage rates fell in 1985 and 1986, we finally were able to get the duration gap down to under a year. Once there, our strategy was to initiate a series of "rebalancing" actions—adding fixed-rate or adjustable-rate mortgages and shorter- or longer-term debt—in response to future interest rate changes to keep the duration gap below one year, with a goal of eventually achieving a match.

I had joined Fannie Mae in 1982 as chief economist but began working with the company's senior business officers on strategic and financial management issues almost immediately. In 1985 I was given responsibility for recommending interest rate risk management strategies for the portfolio. Then, in late 1987, Maxwell decided to put a single executive in charge of all aspects of the portfolio business—determining what types and amounts of mortgages to buy, when to buy them, how to fund the purchases initially, and when and how to rebalance the portfolio as interest rates changed. He asked me to take that position, and I did.

Having a dedicated portfolio group enabled us to take a fresh look at all aspects of the business. We kept coming back to its structure. Active rebalancing could keep the portfolio's risk within acceptable limits, but it was not particularly efficient and could be very expensive if interest rates were volatile. Borrowers of fixed-rate mortgages had the advantage of a powerful option to repay or not repay the loan at their discretion. The fixed-term debt that we issued, in contrast, would stay on our books until it matured or we repurchased it.

The solution to this asymmetry turned out to be the obvious one. Since there were options embedded in the fixed-rate mortgages we bought, we needed to have options embedded in at least some of the debt we used to finance those mortgages. Option-based, or "callable," debt in fact existed; it had been common in the corporate bond market for decades. Callable debt has a stated final maturity but also a specified earlier date on or after which the issuer can redeem, or "call" it. Callable debt would be more expensive to issue initially, but over time it had the potential to lower our rebalancing costs by an even larger amount and to greatly reduce the sensitivity of the portfolio's net income to interest rate changes. Callable debt, however, had not been used to any significant extent by Fannie Mae or any other government-sponsored agency. In order to make it the foundation of our new portfolio strategy, we would have to reinvent the agency debt market.

Fannie Mae had a selling group of about 20 Wall Street firms, each of which had an "agency desk" specializing in the sales and trading of our and other government agencies' securities. The traders and salespeople staffing these desks were highly effective at selling our noncallable (or "bullet") debt. But callable debt involved options, which involved mathematics and quantitative analysis, and we had to give the staff on our dealers' agency desks both the tools and the training to sell it. As we did that, we experimented with their corporate finance departments on different combinations of final maturities and call dates to find out which best met our risk management needs while appealing to the broadest range of investors.

On the investor front, we got a serendipitous break from Michael Milken, the pioneer of the junk bond phenomenon of the mid-1980s. It had not been uncommon during that time for holders of highly rated corporate bonds to see their bonds suddenly downgraded—and have their prices drop sharply—after the company that issued them fell victim to a hostile takeover by a junk-bond financed acquirer. This "downgrade risk" had caused new issuance of callable corporate bonds to all but dry up. Just as we were starting our callable agency debt program, we stumbled upon this large base of traditional corporate debt investors thrilled to be offered an alternative callable security from a high-quality issuer with negligible risk of falling prey to a leveraged buyout.

While developing our callable debt issuance capability, we worked to define specific risk management objectives that incorporated callable debt funding. As a shareholder-owned company, we did intend to take *some* interest rate risk, but we also believed that equity investors would reward us for a steady pattern of earnings growth. We made two important decisions. First, we determined that financing the portfolio with a roughly equal mix of callable debt and bullet debt would give us the best chance of achieving the combination of strong earnings growth, high returns, and low earnings volatility we sought. Second, we set strict internal guidelines for rebalancing the portfolio, linked to changes in its duration gap. As long as our duration gap remained within a range of plus or minus six months, we would not rebalance. (Mortgage durations longer than debt durations made the duration gap positive; the reverse was a negative gap.) When the duration gap was between 6 and 12 months—positive or negative—we would undertake actions to bring it back to 6 months or less, but with no set time limit in order to accomplish the rebalancing as cost effectively as possible. And if our duration gap ever exceeded 12 months, we would conduct immediate rebalancing to bring it back to 12 months or less by the next monthly reporting period, irrespective of cost. These guidelines would remain in effect for over a decade.

Devising standardized callable debt structures, developing a callable debt investor base, and reorienting our dealers to be able to distribute callables through their agency desks and to make active markets in them afterwards took us over two years. But by the beginning of 1990, we had done it. In 1990, 70 percent of the long-term debt we issued was callable, and soon the callable market was broad and deep enough to finance rapid portfolio growth. We were able to grow our portfolio by 50 percent during 1992 and 1993. At the end of 1993, the portfolio was $190 billion in size, its duration gap was a negative two months—very close to a match—and over half of it was financed by callable debt.

The portfolio business had been transformed completely from what it was when Maxwell first came to the company. In his bestselling book *Good to Great*, noted business author Jim Collins said:

> Fannie Mae had no choice but to become the best capital markets player in the world at managing mortgage interest risk . . . Step by step, day by day, month by month, the Fannie Mae team rebuilt the entire business model around risk management and reshaped the corporate culture into a high-performance machine that rivaled anything on Wall Street . . .

With the use of callable debt, defined risk management objectives, and disciplined rebalancing guidelines, we now could legitimately claim that Fannie Mae was far better able to manage the risk of holding fixed-rate mortgages in portfolio than any other financial institution, including commercial banks and thrifts. In defending ourselves against our critics and detractors in Congress, this would be an invaluable advantage.

Credit Has Its Price

It was an irony of Fannie Mae's charter restrictions—which limited us to dealing in residential mortgages—that Maxwell's sole alternative for saving his company from the effects of excessive interest rate risk was to buy ARMs and other higher-risk products that significantly increased the amount of credit risk we took. Fannie Mae's credit losses rose from a negligible $5 million in 1981 to $170 million in 1985. In just four years, loans acquired to give ourselves enough time and income to fix our interest rate risk problems were causing serious problems with credit risk. But the strategy worked. In 1985 the portfolio's net interest income—the interest income on our mortgages less the interest expense on our debt—finally turned positive. Together with our growing fee income, positive net interest income enabled us to report a profit in 1985, even with our sharply higher credit losses. That year we made a thorough study of the company's defaults to determine which risk factors were primarily responsible for them. Our analysis identified some obvious culprits, and in August 1985 we announced a sweeping set of revisions to our underwriting guidelines to address them.

Underwriting was one aspect of our credit risk management we needed to address; pricing was the other. When we purchased a loan for portfolio, our pricing theoretically included compensation for credit risk as well as interest rate risk, but the credit risk amount was nowhere calculated or specified. While we might have been able to get away with this in the portfolio, we could not with our credit guaranty business, where we were paid a monthly fee for guaranteeing the timely payment of interest and principal on the loans that went into our mortgage-backed securities. Initially we picked guaranty fees that were deliberately conservative, but we knew that at some point we would need a way to determine those fees with more precision.

I took the lead on that task. In 1985 I set up a financial analysis group and staffed it with individuals with expertise and experience in mortgage credit analysis and financial modeling. Fannie Mae's size, national presence, and longevity gave us enormous amounts of historical information on single-family loan performance by product and risk type (which we had used to determine where and how to tighten our underwriting standards). We set out to use this information to assess how economic and financial variables affected the credit performance of the different types and characteristics of mortgages we would be guaranteeing.

The mechanics of credit guaranty pricing are straightforward. You make estimates of the incidence of default and the severity of loss on the loans that go bad (which constitute your losses) and projections of prepayment rates on the loans that stay good (which produce your income), and then you determine a fee that is high enough to cover your expected losses, prepayments, and administrative costs while providing a market return on your invested capital. As we approached this task, however, we faced a complication. Fannie Mae was not in the mortgage-backed securities business when the company was privatized in 1968 and HUD was designated as its regulator. We had a statutory capital requirement for our portfolio investments, which were held as assets on our balance sheet, but no capital requirement for MBS guarantees, which were not. Before we could determine how to price our credit guarantees, we first had to figure out how much capital to put behind them.

Having just survived a brush with insolvency from excessive interest rate risk—and having also seen how quickly our credit losses could rise—our goal was to devise a capitalization framework for our single-family guaranty business that could withstand a defined level of worst-case, or "stress," credit losses. To quantify that loss amount, we generated several hundred random paths for future interest rates and home prices, and then we employed the results of our loan performance analyses to project mortgage prepayments, defaults, and loss severities in each of the individual scenarios. We defined the stress loss amount as the one that was just worse than 99 percent of all the other loss amounts produced by this exercise. Put differently, the capital that would back our mortgage-backed securities guarantees would come from a loss scenario our analytic group estimated had only a 1 percent chance of occurring.

Once we had our methodology for setting capital requirements for our credit guarantees, pricing them became simple. There was only one combination of initial capital and guaranty fee that simultaneously would produce exactly our target return on capital in the loss scenario our credit pricing model assessed to be most likely, and also was just sufficient to cover the credit losses in the 1 percent probability stress scenario we wished to protect ourselves against. That was the amount of capital we would hold and the guaranty fee we would seek to charge.

Defaults from loans made before we tightened our underwriting standards in 1985 continued to drive our credit losses higher through 1988, when they peaked at $315 million, or 11 basis points as a percentage of our combined portfolio and mortgage-backed securities outstanding. From that point, however, our credit losses declined, both absolutely and as a percentage of our book of business. By 1993 our total credit losses had fallen to $244 million, or only four basis points as a percent of our book, which by then had grown to two and a half times the size of our 1988 book. That same year our average single-family MBS guaranty fee rate was 21 basis points. Our underwriting was solid, our guaranty fee pricing was comfortably covering our credit losses, and the capital we held to back our credit guarantee business was growing rapidly. As was the case with our management of interest rate risk, in 1993 we could credibly claim in Congress and elsewhere that our management of mortgage credit risk was second to none.

CHAPTER 5

The Volcker Standard Gives Fannie Mae an Edge

Just as Fannie Mae and the thrift industry took starkly different paths in response to their common financial problems stemming from mismatched mortgage portfolios, they produced starkly different results. In 1989 Fannie Mae was well on the way to creating a new type of funding tool, agency callable debt, that would allow us to profitably finance 30-year fixed-rate mortgages with manageable levels of interest rate risk. We had reduced our portfolio's duration gap from three years to six months. We had added risk diversification by entering the MBS guaranty business, and by 1989 we were prudently underwriting, conservatively capitalizing, and properly pricing these guarantees. After losing a million dollars a day in 1982, Fannie Mae was poised to earn a billion dollars in 1990. And the thrift industry? In 1989 it was about to require a massive taxpayer bailout and to be so fundamentally restructured through congressional action that it would cease to be a meaningful source of home financing by the end of the coming decade.

Thrift Failures Put the Focus on Fannie Mae

The story of the failure of the thrift industry is well known. The deregulation of deposit rates and asset powers between 1980 and

1982 led to a flood of new money into both existing and new savings and loan institutions, whose charters now allowed a wide range of investment activities. In 1980, 80 percent of S&L assets were in residential mortgages; by 1986 that percentage had plunged to 56 percent. While S&Ls invested in a variety of exotic asset types—ranging from junk bonds to casinos to windmill farms—the bulk of their new investments went into commercial and residential real estate development and construction lending, fueling severe overinvestment in all of these areas. The S&Ls making these investments often were owned by developers themselves.

The cure for the thrift industry proved worse than the disease. The free market philosophy of the Reagan administration meant that S&Ls' new powers came with few restrictions and little regulation. Easy access to federally insured deposits, broad new asset powers, and minimal supervision were a powerful recipe for incompetent management as well as outright fraud. By the mid-1980s, hundreds of S&Ls were insolvent. The Federal Home Bank Board attempted to crack down on abuses and close insolvent thrifts, but its efforts were fiercely opposed by the industry, the administration, and members of Congress, who adamantly opposed any government expenditures to resolve the crisis and resisted closing failed institutions for fear it would undermine public confidence. It was not until after the election of the first President Bush that the new administration and Congress finally faced up to the severity of the problem and accepted that it would not be resolved without a forceful government response.

At President Bush's initiative, in 1989 Congress passed the Financial Institutions Reform, Recovery, and Enforcement Act (FIRREA). FIRREA abolished the Federal Home Loan Bank Board and created a limited-life entity, the Resolution Trust Company, to liquidate the assets of failed thrifts. The act created a new Office of Thrift Supervision (OTS) to charter, supervise, and regulate savings institutions, and a new Federal Housing Finance Board to supervise the Federal Home Loan Banks. Regulation of Freddie Mac was moved from the abolished FHLB Board to HUD. Following passage of FIRREA, the OTS moved aggressively to close failed thrifts at an ultimate cost to taxpayers of more than $130 billion and to supervise existing S&Ls much more closely.

The costly experience of allowing the thrift crisis to develop and build unaddressed prompted Congress to turn its attention to the business practices, regulation, and capital adequacy of the eight government-sponsored enterprises it had created. Collectively the GSEs had over $800 billion in assets in 1989, even more than the thrift industry. Fannie Mae and Freddie Mac were the two largest GSEs, and the government closely supervised neither.

In FIRREA Congress mandated two studies of the GSEs' risk and capital by the General Accounting Office (GAO) and directed Treasury to conduct studies of the GSEs' safety and soundness and "the impact of GSE operations on federal borrowing." It later requested the Congressional Budget Office (CBO) to do a study covering the same subjects as the GAO and Treasury, adding an analysis of alternative models for GSE oversight. There was little doubt that when all these studies were completed, there would be legislation addressing the regulation, capital, and possibly the business powers of Fannie Mae and Freddie Mac.

Much was at stake. Thrifts' share of the mortgage market had fallen sharply during the previous decade, and FIRREA virtually guaranteed that thrifts would continue to recede as providers of mortgage credit in the decade to come. The largest credit market in the world was wide open, and a congressional review of Fannie Mae's charter offered our opponents and critics a rare and valuable opportunity to remove or restrict some of the benefits that made us a competitive force. We anticipated a fierce assault.

We were particularly vulnerable on capital. Together Fannie Mae and Freddie Mac financed half a trillion dollars in mortgages, but we had less required capital as a percentage of our assets than a typical savings and loan. And we had no capital requirement at all for our credit guaranty businesses. The capital requirement for Fannie Mae's on-balance sheet assets was set and enforced by HUD, which was not a safety and soundness regulator, and the recent problems with our portfolio were fresh in everyone's mind. We had been insolvent on a market value basis earlier in the decade, and we could have run through all our capital had interest rates not come down when they did.

Our competitors and critics took the position that we should be required to hold the same percentage of capital as commercial banks, citing both safety and soundness and fairness considerations. But bank-like capital standards for Fannie Mae would have been anything but fair. Capital needs to be related to risk, and we had a much lower risk profile than a bank. Our charter permitted us to take interest rate and credit risk on just one high-quality asset type, residential mortgages, and only in the United States. Banks' charters permitted them to take multiple types of risk in a wide variety of asset types, including very risky ones, in countries throughout the world. Bank-like capital standards without bank-like asset powers would have put Fannie Mae and Freddie Mac at a crippling competitive disadvantage—which was precisely our opponents' objective.

Being against bank-like capital standards wasn't going to be sufficient, however. We had to have an alternative, and we had to be able to convince Congress of its merits in the face of intense opposition from our critics.

I became involved in developing that alternative by happenstance. In 1989 my primary job was running the portfolio business. In July of that year, I attended a meeting with Maxwell, soon-to-be vice chairman Jim Johnson, and others to discuss and agree on an approach to Fannie Mae capitalization that we could present to the GAO, Treasury, and the CBO. When none of the ideas presented by members of our finance team met with Maxwell and Johnson's approval, I drew on my experience in risk management to make a suggestion. A unique attribute of each of our two businesses, I pointed out, was that they had measurable risks. In the credit guaranty business, we used a worst-case default rate and loss severity by loan type to set our capital internally. A statutory capital standard could work the same way. And we could use a comparable approach to capitalize the portfolio business: devise some standard of extreme and sustained movements in interest rates that we would be required to be able to protect against through a combination of initial capital and sufficiently strong hedging strategies.

Maxwell and Johnson were intrigued by the concept of a risk-based capital standard and asked me to develop it further. I did, and the result met with their approval. We next made a decision that proved to be crucial. No matter how good an idea a risk-based standard might have been, if proposed by us it would have been seen as self-serving and faced long odds of being considered seriously, let alone adopted. To give the concept credibility, we needed the endorsement of an independent and respected third party. As we discussed the credentials we were looking for in a reviewer, one name kept coming up as far superior to anyone else for the task we envisioned: former Federal Reserve Board chairman Paul Volcker.

The Volcker Letter

Volcker was an iconic figure, universally thought to have unassailable independence and integrity. While at the Fed, he had used punishingly high interest rates to end the persistently high rates of inflation that had taken hold in the economy in the 1970s and early 1980s. He had impeccable credentials as a bank regulator. Prior to being tapped as Fed chairman by President Carter in August 1979, Volcker had worked at Chase Manhattan Bank, been an undersecretary at Treasury, and served as president of the New York Federal Reserve. Volcker had left the Federal Reserve Board in August 1987 and was teaching at Princeton when in early 1988 he agreed to join the small firm of James D. Wolfensohn Inc. as chairman. Jim Wolfensohn had been an investment banker at Schroders and Salomon Brothers before opening up his own boutique advisory operation in 1981. Hiring Volcker was a coup for him.

Maxwell and Volcker knew each other from Volcker's days as Fed chairman, when Fannie Mae was fighting for its life. We understood that he was not a fan of the GSEs, but we thought that worked to our advantage: even our worst critics would not suspect him of bias in our favor. What remained to be seen was whether he would take the assignment we had in mind.

Although I did not yet know him, I believed he would. Risk-based capital was the Holy Grail of international bank regulators, but large multinational banks had such broad asset powers that it had not been possible to devise capital standards that reflected their actual economic risk. Volcker's interest in risk-based capital as a concept, together with his institutional mistrust of GSEs' incentives to properly manage their risks, made it seem likely to me that he would see in our project an opportunity to help devise for Fannie Mae the type of true risk-based capital scheme he greatly would have wished to impose on the banks he regulated as Fed chairman.

As a firm, Wolfensohn normally worked with clients on an annual retainer. We wanted Volcker for a special project, so we needed both Volcker and Jim Wolfensohn to give it the green light. I met with members of Wolfensohn's Financial Institutions Group to walk them through our risk-based capital framework, and they then reviewed it with Volcker. Two weeks later, Fannie Mae's President Roger Birk and I met with both Jim Wolfensohn and Volcker to formally ask them to take the assignment. Our request was for Volcker to work with us to refine the risk-based capital concept to where it potentially could serve as the basis for a capital standard for Fannie Mae and Freddie Mac in legislation. Were that effort to be successful, the end product would be a letter from Volcker to Maxwell describing and discussing the standard and containing Volcker's views on its merits. Volcker and Wolfensohn agreed to work with us on those terms.

We began immediately. To assist him, Volcker selected one of Wolfensohn's top bankers, Jeffrey Goldstein, and two members of its Financial Institutions Group, Eldad Coppens and Tom Kang. I was the lead, and often the only, person from Fannie Mae on the project, which took seven months to complete.

While the focus of Fannie Mae's critics was almost exclusively on our interest rate risk, Volcker spent most of his time and effort determining how to properly capitalize for credit risk. The most critical aspect of the credit standard was picking the level of loss to protect against. Volcker believed it was possible to err on both sides: too little required capital and the company (and the taxpayer) would not be adequately protected, too much required capital and the business would not be economic to conduct. Volcker wanted to avoid either extreme.

For the regulatory credit standard, I originally had proposed loss rates derived from Fannie Mae's analytical models. Volcker wanted to have historical reference points. Coppens, Kang, and I tried mightily to find reliable default and loss severity data from the Depression, but we were unable to find anything Volcker could get comfortable with. As an alternative, we hit on the idea of looking at Fannie Mae's own historical data in a region, state, or metropolitan area for experiences that were severe enough to be usable as a standard that could be applied more broadly. We reviewed a number of different geographic areas and time periods before finally coming up with what came to be called the "Texas stress test." The original version of that test took Fannie Mae's lifetime default rates and loss severities on loans originated in 1981 and 1982 in Texas, and it applied them to all of the company's business, from every state and every year.

The Texas stress test had two essential attributes of a good credit standard: it was unquestionably rigorous, and it had a great story behind it. The rigor was enough for Volcker; the story would help sell the standard to legislators. In the early 1980s, the U.S. economy was in severe recession, but one region was doing much better than others: the oil patch, including Texas. Oil prices were at record highs, and the industry was booming. People were leaving the industrial Midwest in droves to come to Texas to work in the oil fields, and they needed a place to live. In the first half of 1982, one out of every seven housing starts in the country was in Harris County, Texas (an area surrounding Houston). Home prices soared along with the new demand. But by 1986, the economy had recovered, and more significantly for Texas, oil prices had come down dramatically. The oil industry went into a slump, and many of the people who had come to Texas in the early 1980s left. Home prices in some areas fell by 50 percent, and in certain markets there were more homes than residents to live in them. Mortgage defaults spiked, as did loss severities.

Our experience with 30-year fixed-rate mortgages from Texas made in 1981 and 1982 was acceptable to Volcker as a reference point. The Wolfensohn team and I used more recent data to develop multiples of the 30-year fixed-rate experience to apply to other products such as ARMs, intermediate-term loans, and second mortgages, and to risk factors such as investor properties or loan seasoning. Everything needed to be submitted to Volcker for his review and amendment or approval. It took several months of work, but we finally had a full Texas stress test that met his standards.

Devising an interest rate stress test did not take nearly so long. Our initial idea was simply to repeat the path 10-year Treasury rates took in the five years between 1978 and 1982. But when we ran our current portfolio through that test—even with the relatively small amount of callable debt we had at the time—we passed it easily. As an alternative, we created a test where interest rates would rise or fall over a one-year period by an amount that depended on their starting point but could be as much as six percentage points, and then they would remain there for an additional four years. We would run the portfolio against both rising and falling interest rates, with the scenario that produced the greatest capital requirement being the binding one. That, too, met Volcker's standard of an extreme test.

Volcker insisted on an additional component we had not included in our framework: minimum amounts of capital we would have to hold no matter how little risk we took. We went back and forth on the appropriate amounts for these minimums. Volcker finally agreed to figures of 250 basis points (2.5 percent) of capital for on-balance sheet mortgages and other assets and 50 basis points of capital for our MBS guarantees and other off-balance sheet items. Applied to our assets and mortgage-backed securities outstanding at the end of 1989, these minimums produced a capital requirement of $4.25 billion. At the time, our capital was less than $3 billion. We would have our work cut out for us to get to a level of capitalization that Volcker would characterize as adequate.

Volcker completed his work in February 1990, and on March 6 he wrote Maxwell a letter summarizing its results. Volcker explicitly recommended against imposing bank-like capital ratios on Fannie Mae and Freddie Mac. Instead, he endorsed a standard subjecting us to stringent stress tests run against our two businesses simultaneously. We would be required to hold enough capital to pass those tests or the amount produced by application of the proposed minimum capital ratios, whichever was greater. Volcker's letter explained the risk-based capital stress tests he had helped us devise, and it discussed their rationale. He concluded by saying, "With [Fannie Mae's] current business practices and assuming it reaches its proposed capital standards, the Company would be in a position to maintain its solvency in the face of difficulties in the housing markets and an interest rate environment significantly more adverse than any experienced in the post-World War II period." He added that if we met those standards, the risk of taxpayer loss from our activities would be "remote."

Landmark Legislation

We received the Volcker letter while the General Accounting Office and Treasury were in the midst of their studies of government-sponsored enterprise regulation and capital, and we provided them with copies. We already had been meeting with their staffs to explain the evolution of our risk management strategies since the beginning of Maxwell's chairmanship. Volcker's letter reinforced our claims of the effectiveness of these strategies, and we believed his endorsement of a risk-based capital standard would be hard for Treasury, the GAO, or the Congressional Budget Office to ignore.

Treasury, however, had their own idea. In the first of their two GSE reports, published in May 1990, Treasury objectively described and analyzed our proposed risk-based capital standard—already known as the "Volcker standard"—but did not endorse it. Instead, in a concluding segment oddly detached from the rest of their report, they stated:

We believe that the approach used to evaluate and monitor risks in private markets can and should be used to evaluate GSE risk ... Treasury recommends that GSEs be required to obtain a rating equivalent to triple-A, absent any implicit Government guarantee, from at least two of the nationally recognized credit rating agencies ... Should a GSE be rated below triple-A, it would be required to submit, and adhere to, an acceptable business plan describing the actions it plans to take to achieve a triple-A rating within five years from the date of enactment of the legislation, or lose its ties to the Federal Government.

This was a thinly disguised prescription for an old ideological staple at Treasury—full GSE privatization—coupled with a new idea to which they would return in the future: reliance on rating agencies to perform duties normally left to regulators.

Neither the GAO nor the CBO endorsed Treasury's recommendation. The CBO discussed it along with other alternatives for GSE regulation and capital in its April 1991 report but made no judgments about any of them. The GAO did. In its May 1991 report, it called both bank-like capital ratios and the use of rating agency ratings "less than satisfactory" approaches. It noted that rating agencies "base their decisions on the subjective judgment of those performing the evaluation, without stating specifically the capital levels needed to obtain a given rating," and added, "We are not ready to delegate to rating agencies ... inherently governmental functions." The GAO recommended a combination of stress tests and a minimum capital requirement for Fannie Mae and Freddie Mac, just as Volcker had done.

The Volcker letter was invaluable in convincing members and staff of the House Banking Committee to make stress tests the basis for the capital standard in the government-sponsored enterprise legislation they were drafting, H.R. 2900. Texas Democrat and Banking Committee Chairman Henry Gonzalez sponsored the bill, which was introduced in July 1991. Key provisions addressed the supervision, regulation, and capitalization of Fannie Mae and Freddie Mac. The bill created a new safety and soundness regulator for the two companies as an independent entity within HUD, and it required the secretary of HUD, who remained our program regulator, to determine the percentage of business we did with low- and moderate-income borrowers. It also mandated that the director of the new safety and soundness agency "establish by regulation a risk-based capital test for the enterprises." H.R. 2900 passed overwhelmingly in September.

We were highly supportive of the capital provisions of H.R. 2900, which we had helped design. Our opponents and critics, including Treasury, were not, and when the bill went to the Senate, they sought to change them. With no chance of removing stress tests as the basis for our capital requirement, they concentrated on making the structure of those tests as onerous as possible and on giving our new safety and soundness regulator maximum discretion to change the tests' parameters and also to raise our minimum capital requirement. We were willing to accept a very tough capital standard, but in exchange we insisted on certainty once it was agreed upon. Our great fear was that if a safety and soundness regulator sharing the ideological perspective of Treasury were given discretion over our capital requirements, they would ratchet them up for reasons having nothing to do with risk in order to raise our costs, reduce our competitiveness, and limit the amount of business we could do. We wanted to prevent that if we possibly could.

We held the line on regulatory discretion, but to get a final bill passed, we agreed to a number of changes to the stress test in H.R. 2900 that made it more difficult. The most significant were the addition of a 30 percent surcharge to the risk-based capital requirement to cover management and operations risk—far more than was justified by the risks involved—and an assumption that we did no additional business from the time the test began. A test that had been good enough to satisfy Paul Volcker had to be substantially toughened to get through the Senate.

In contrast, the Senate actually reduced our minimum capital requirement. After the passage of H.R. 2900, Freddie Mac realized they would not be able to meet its minimum capital ratios with the amount of capital they then had. We had been well short of those same ratios when Volcker first proposed them in 1989, and we simply pledged to make up the shortfall in the future. Freddie Mac insisted they could not accept any capital standard they did not meet at the time it became law. The Senate chose to accommodate their concern by reducing the minimum capital requirement for MBS guarantees—at the time Freddie Mac's main business—from an even 50 basis points to an otherwise inexplicable 45 basis points, permitting Freddie Mac to be just within capital compliance when the bill was passed. It was Freddie Mac's reward for being the "good GSE" during the capital debates. Fannie Mae never had been a serious contender for that designation.

The Federal Housing Enterprises Financial Safety and Soundness Act of 1992 was signed into law in October of that year. It created a new safety and soundness regulator for Fannie Mae and Freddie Mac—the Office of Federal Housing Enterprises Oversight, or OFHEO—as an independent agency within HUD. It put in place a capital regime requiring us to hold capital equal to the greater of the risk-based amount sufficient to pass interest rate and credit stress tests imposed upon us by OFHEO, plus 30 percent, or the amount produced by application of our minimum capital ratios. And it required that 30 percent of Fannie Mae and Freddie Mac's business be done with low- and moderate-income borrowers and in what were termed "underserved" housing areas, while giving the HUD secretary authority to change both the definitions and the percentages of our housing goals in the future.

Since Fannie Mae became a shareholder-owned company in 1968, the most powerful argument that could be made against us was that our activities posed risks to taxpayers that outweighed the benefits we provided to home buyers. Now there was a statutory framework that permitted this assessment to be made on an objective basis. HUD would set housing goals on the mission side. We either would meet those goals or not—and seek to do more than that to advance the cause of affordable housing, which also would be measurable. And our new risk-based capital standard would force us to keep our interest rate and credit risks at very low levels or else hold enough capital that the risks we did take would be borne by our shareholders and not taxpayers.

From a public policy standpoint, it was a win-win outcome: less risk for taxpayers and greater mortgage availability and lower mortgage rates for the home buyers we were chartered to serve. The fact that our minimum capital requirement took effect only if we kept our interest rate and credit risks below a certain threshold gave us a powerful incentive to manage those risks in a way that protected taxpayers. And if we did keep our risks low, we could base the pricing of our portfolio purchases and MBS guarantees on our minimum capital requirements, making our services more competitive and benefiting home buyers in the form of lower guaranty fees, lower rates on our mortgage purchases, and greater volumes of business.

The acceptance by Congress of a risk-based approach to determining Fannie Mae and Freddie Mac's required capital flowed directly from Paul Volcker's decision in 1989 to review the risk-based capital standard we presented to him. Consistent with his character and reputation, Volcker's evaluation and ultimate endorsement of this standard was based solely on its merits; at no time during our engagement did he ever consider any political or competitive implications his work might have. Two and a half years later, the ironic result was that, in return for accepting strict risk disciplines, two companies Volcker had not supported as Fed chairman were able to gain a significant minimum capital advantage over the banks he once regulated.

The 1992 act was landmark legislation. It transformed Fannie Mae's capital from a political liability into an economic asset, and it laid the foundation for the explosion in business growth and profitability we would experience over the next dozen years. In so doing, however, it also sowed the seeds of the mortgage wars.

OFHEO Disables the Standard

Other than opposing Treasury, during legislative discussions about a new safety and soundness regulator, we did not take a position on who the regulator should be or where it should be located. We did, however, make it a top priority to try to ensure that the powers and authorities of this regulator be limited and strictly defined. We felt very strongly that any action affecting our fate as a business should come through open deliberations in Congress rather than through closed-door rulings by a regulator. We had many difficult battles in the Senate over this issue but prevailed on the most important of them. The major parameters of the risk-based capital standard were specified in statute rather than left up to OFHEO. They could not raise our minimum capital unless we fell short of the amount of capital the statute directed us to hold. And although the cost of running OFHEO was paid for by assessments of Fannie Mae and Freddie Mac, they had to submit their annual budgets to the House and Senate Appropriations Committees as a check against regulatory excess.

Important as these objectives were to achieve, they did not come without costs. The congressional and Treasury staff who had fought to invest our new safety and soundness regulator with more discretionary powers were bitterly disappointed they did not succeed. Several left for senior positions at OFHEO when the agency became operational, with a goal of using the regulatory process to constrain us in a way that had eluded them in the legislative process. The resentments and ideological biases of these staffers made Fannie Mae's relationship with OFHEO unavoidably adversarial from the moment they opened their doors.

The mistrust between senior OFHEO officials and Fannie Mae's executives had an immediate consequence. OFHEO had responsibility for implementing the stress tests in our risk-based capital standard. We strongly advised them to use the financial models we and Freddie Mac employed for assessing and pricing our portfolio purchases and MBS guarantees, which OFHEO would have the right to audit, as the basis for the tests. Under this "supervisory" approach, OFHEO would add their own assumptions for variables not specified in statute that defined the stress environment, and we would run the tests under the supervision of their examiners. Two important benefits of this approach were that it would establish a direct link between our actual interest rate and credit risk and our required capital, and that it would allow us to remain in capital compliance as we evaluated and priced new business. We already had built our own version of the "Volcker standard" into our interest rate and credit risk-assessment models for precisely these reasons.

OFHEO refused to go this route. Instead, they insisted on building their own proprietary models of our businesses, with the intention of running the stress tests with these models and sending us the results. Replicating our businesses from scratch was an extraordinarily difficult if not impossible task, and even attempting it fatally compromised the integrity of the standard. A risk-based standard could be effective only if it captured the true economic risks Fannie Mae and Freddie Mac were running, not some abstraction of those risks. We believed OFHEO's approach was destined to fail from the outset, but we could not talk them out of it. At the time, we speculated that their senior officials might have thought, mistakenly, that by having their own stress test models, they could somehow exert control over our business decisions through the way the tests were constructed and run.

Irrespective of OFHEO's motives, their results were disastrous. The act directed them to publish a final risk-based capital regulation by January 1, 1994. Their decision to use proprietary models delayed publication of the final regulation for nearly seven years, and when it finally became effective in September 2002, it was hopelessly flawed. As we feared, the results the OFHEO tests produced were driven primarily by the quirks in their models, not by the risks in our business. We managed the risk-based capital requirement as a separate exercise, keeping our calculated risk-based capital amount below our statutory minimum by making small changes in our business that were important to the OFHEO models but had little effect on our true risk position or profitability. For our actual risk assessment and risk management, we relied exclusively on our own analytical tools.

The risk-based standard was designed to give our safety and soundness regulator a real-time indication of changes in our financial risks and to trigger automatic increases in our required capital whenever those risks rose. That was why Volcker had endorsed it. OFHEO's politicized implementation of that standard, however, disabled it, leaving Fannie Mae and Freddie Mac essentially self-regulated for risk taking. Self-regulation could work, but only if the leadership of both companies had the ability and the experience to measure and manage the interest rate and credit risks inherent in their businesses. While that may have been the case when the risk-based standard first took effect in 2002, the time was not far off when it would not be—and the mortgage crisis would deepen as a consequence.

CHAPTER 6

Fannie Mae's Opponents
Change Tactics

I N 1989 DAVID MAXWELL HAD BEEN CHAIRMAN OF FANNIE MAE for almost nine years. He had accomplished all he had set out to do. Fannie Mae had been pulled back from the brink and transformed into a healthy and sophisticated financial institution with a leadership culture focused on its housing mission. Maxwell found himself giving the same speeches to the same groups. He was beginning to get bored. It was time to think about stepping down and putting the company in the hands of a successor.

A New Chairman for New Times

His choice was Jim Johnson. Maxwell had met Johnson at a dinner party in the mid-1980s and been extremely impressed by him. Johnson held a master's degree in public policy from Princeton. He had worked in the political campaigns of Eugene McCarthy, George McGovern, and Jimmy Carter and during the Carter presidency had been executive assistant to Vice President Walter Mondale. He ran Mondale's 1984 presidential campaign against Reagan, which did not end well; Mondale carried only his home state of Minnesota and the District of Columbia. Johnson then returned to the advisory firm Public Strategies, which he had founded in 1981 with the diplomat

Richard Holbrooke. Shearson Lehman Brothers acquired Public Strategies in 1985, so when Maxwell met him, Johnson was an investment banker with solid political credentials. That combination led Maxwell to select him, and Shearson Lehman, as outside advisors for the Fannie Mae privatization study we were about to embark upon in the spring of 1987.

Maxwell got to know Johnson well during the Shearson study (as did I), and by the time we finished it at the end of 1988, he had settled on him as the company's next chairman. Looking ahead as far as he could see, Maxwell was convinced that his successor's biggest threats would be political. We now were financially strong, and our investors expected us to capitalize on that strength to grow our business and profits. And Maxwell believed we needed to grow to satisfy our mission obligations. From the Shearson study, we knew we could not meet the objections of our critics and competitors by changing our corporate structure; we would have to achieve our profitability, risk management, and affordable housing objectives with the company as it currently existed and in the face of concerted political opposition. Jim Johnson, Maxwell believed, was the person best equipped to take on that challenge.

Not everyone agreed. Maxwell's plan was to bring Johnson in as vice chairman in January 1990, work with him for a year in a CEO transition process, then have the board elect him chairman in January 1991. Word of the impending hire leaked out. Out of the blue, Maxwell received a call from his old Yale classmate Nicholas Brady, who at the time was Treasury secretary under the first President Bush. "Max," Brady said (nobody else called Maxwell "Max"), "I have it from the highest authority that you're going to hire Mondale's campaign manager. You can't do that." The "highest authority" was the president, who had heard the rumor from his brother, Washington, D.C., banker Johnny Bush. Maxwell explained to Brady why he thought Johnson was the best person for the job, but Brady was not convinced. Johnson had a good relationship with Bush's director of OMB, Dick Darman, who told Johnson he would calm the president down. He did, although a flag had been raised.

Having a high profile Democrat as chairman would put a brighter spotlight on Fannie Mae.

Johnson joined Fannie Mae as we were winding up our work with Volcker. He accompanied Maxwell, Roger Birk, and me on a trip to New York early in 1990 to discuss a draft of the letter Volcker was writing. After our meeting was over, Jim Wolfensohn invited us to lunch in his dining room. (Volcker could not stay; he had a class to teach at Princeton that afternoon.) During the lunch, Wolfensohn told us in confidence that he had just been offered the chairmanship of the John F. Kennedy Center for the Performing Arts. Although taking the job would be a logistical nightmare—he had a business to run in New York, and the Kennedy Center was in Washington— Wolfensohn said he was leaning toward accepting it, and he talked about what he might want to do at the institution. Nobody ever would have guessed that the man who was sitting to his right as he told us this, Jim Johnson, would end up succeeding Wolfensohn when he left the Kennedy Center in 1996.

Johnson's legacy at Fannie Mae was affordable housing. Like Maxwell, he believed that Fannie Mae's charter advantages carried with them a duty to expand the availability of mortgage financing to as many of the country's citizens as possible, consistent with our risk objectives, and he understood that leadership in affordable housing was essential to maintaining our congressional support. The 1992 legislation gave him a further, and purely financial, reason to intensify our affordable housing focus—not the HUD goals but the capital standard. The new risk-based standard offered us the potential to significantly grow our business, and there would be a limit as to how large and profitable Congress would allow Fannie Mae to become if we did not extend the reach of our affordable housing activities by proportionately much more. Maxwell had transformed the management of Fannie Mae's interest rate and credit risk on the business side; Johnson would use Fannie Mae to transform the way the mortgage finance system provided affordable housing access to the people we were chartered to serve on the mission side.

The Trillion Dollar Commitment

Consistent with his political background, Johnson's signature affordable housing initiative began with an opinion survey. To gain a better understanding of the obstacles to owning a home, in 1992 he hired the research firms of Peter Hart and Robert Teeter to conduct the first in what would become an annual series of National Housing Surveys of Americans' attitudes toward housing and home ownership. From that first survey, we learned that for well over half of renters, buying a home was either a high or a very high priority. We were not surprised that the most important factor holding them back was the absence of an adequate down payment. But other reasons did surprise us. A large number of people cited a lack of information about how the mortgage process worked. Many of them—particularly young people, minorities, and those with lower incomes—said they found applying for a mortgage intimidating and did not consider buying a home because they were afraid of being turned down by their lender. And a substantial percentage of minorities said they did not believe the process was fair. "People like me don't get mortgages" was a common refrain.

Armed with these survey results, Johnson tasked his executive team with developing programs and products that would reduce or remove as many of the barriers to home ownership as possible. We obviously would need to address the down payment constraint. Home buyer education—consumer guides, home buying fairs, and mortgage hotlines—would be a critical component. We would need more flexible underwriting. We would have to develop new products to meet the needs of underserved borrower types. Lenders had to be able to deliver these products to the target customer groups, which required a more diverse staff of loan officers. And Fannie Mae would have to take the lead in making all of this happen.

On March 15, 1994, Johnson announced "Showing America a New Way Home." "Between now and the end of the decade," Johnson pledged, "we will provide $1 trillion to finance 10 million homes for the families and communities that have not been well served by the housing finance system in the past." Almost immediately, Johnson's affordable housing program became known as the Trillion Dollar Commitment.

The Trillion Dollar Commitment was made up of 11 specific initiatives, which over time expanded to 16. They included a comprehensive and coordinated national consumer education effort using television, radio, print advertising, and direct mail to provide renters with information about how to buy a home. We said we would open at least 25 regional partnership offices to work with lenders, public officials, housing advocates, and others to expand our outreach at the local level. There was a new product initiative called "innovations for change." We announced new underwriting flexibilities and experiments. We undertook a series of actions aimed at reducing discrimination in mortgage lending. And we set a very ambitious goal of using technology to lower mortgage origination costs by at least $1,000 through simplifying and streamlining the application process "to reduce the largest barrier to home ownership faced by many families: the cost, complexity, paperwork, and time it takes to get a mortgage."

The scope of the Commitment was unprecedented. At the time of the announcement, Johnson said that "significantly more than half of all the business we do in the next seven years" would have to fall within one or more of its categories for us to accomplish it. This dwarfed the recently enacted HUD goals, which required that only 30 percent of our business be with families at or below their area median income and in central cities. That was by design. Johnson believed it was imperative for Fannie Mae to be the one defining our affordable housing role, not Congress. He told everyone in the company, "Meeting the HUD goals should be a byproduct of our work, not the point of it."

The notion that Fannie Mae took excessive amounts of credit risk to meet the goals of the Trillion Dollar Commitment, or our HUD goals, was a fiction invented and propagated by the company's critics. Johnson was emphatic from the outset that our affordable housing objectives had to be accomplished on a basis consistent with our risk management and profitability goals. All of Fannie Mae's senior officers embraced that discipline, and I had a key role to play in helping us adhere to it.

In February 1990, one month after Johnson joined Fannie Mae, I was named the company's chief financial officer. As CFO I had lead responsibility for setting Fannie Mae's profit targets and for working with officers throughout the company to ensure we made our best efforts to hit them. The portfolio's interest rate risk remained my direct responsibility, and the group that assessed, determined the capitalization for, and priced all of Fannie Mae's credit risk—including the risk on our affordable housing loans—reported to me until 1997, when I merged it with our Credit Policy group (and continued to oversee it). The scope of my responsibilities meant that any potential trade-offs between Fannie Mae's profitability, affordable housing, and risk management objectives at some point came to my attention.

With one brief exception in the late 1990s, which we remedied, throughout my tenure at Fannie Mae, our credit risk assessment function was independent of the areas tasked with developing products for or meeting the goals of our internal affordable housing commitments and annual HUD goals. We used the same analytic tools to evaluate, capitalize, and price our affordable housing loans as for the rest of our business. We did set lower return targets on some of our mission-related products, but we tracked the performance of those products closely and sought to make up their profit shortfalls elsewhere. If our affordable housing initiatives ever posed risk to Fannie Mae, it was to our profits, not to our safety and soundness.

We all understood that accomplishing the goals of the Trillion Dollar Commitment would require an easing of our credit standards, specifically for loans with lower down payments (or higher loan-to-value, or LTV, ratios) and loans to borrowers with less than perfect credit. For the increased risks from these actions not to harm us financially, it was necessary that we make compensating moves to either mitigate those risks or transfer some of them to others, which we did.

Our strategy for managing the risk of higher-LTV lending was a combination of loss mitigation initiatives and increased amounts of private mortgage insurance (MI). In 1993 we had set up a dedicated loss mitigation unit in Dallas, Texas, to manage all of our delinquent loans and to dispose of foreclosed property. This group developed tools and pioneered techniques that lowered the percentage of our delinquent loans that went into default, and it found numerous efficiencies in the foreclosed property disposition process that greatly reduced the severity of loss once defaults occurred. Any defaulted loan we owned or guaranteed that had an LTV over 80 percent also had borrower-paid MI—it was a statutory requirement—which meant that the mortgage insurer, not Fannie Mae, bore the brunt of its credit losses. To give us even more credit protection after the Trillion Dollar Commitment, we required a higher level of MI coverage on all high-LTV loans beginning in 1995. Taken together, our loss mitigation efforts (which reduced total credit losses) and increased amounts of MI coverage (which caused a third party to absorb a larger percentage of the losses that did occur) kept Fannie Mae's credit losses on higher-LTV loans at very manageable levels.

The key to doing credit-impaired lending safely was determining which other borrower, product, and property characteristics needed to be present for a loan to a lower-credit-score borrower to be creditworthy. By 1994 we had that capability. Fannie Mae's Credit Policy group and the credit-pricing staff in my area had incorporated credit scores into a consistent set of applications that evaluated the credit characteristics of the borrower, product, property, and market environment simultaneously, for both underwriting and pricing purposes. These new analytical tools gave us confidence that we could selectively extend our affordable housing initiatives into the credit-impaired segment of the market in a manner that met our risk standards.

Fannie Mae completed the Trillion Dollar Commitment in February 2000, and by the end of that year, our credit losses as a percentage of total mortgages owned and guaranteed had fallen from an already low four basis points in 1993 to just a single basis point—one cent for every $100 in mortgages. Some of this improvement was due to the strong housing market, but by no means all of it. The average mortgage credit loss rate at large commercial banks barely budged during this same period and remained much higher than ours, falling only to 14 basis points in 2000 from 15 basis points in 1993. Fannie Mae was financing vastly more affordable housing loans than anyone else and doing so with vastly superior financial results.

Check-Ups from the Government

The two criticisms to which Fannie Mae was most vulnerable in Congress were "too much risk to taxpayers" and "not doing enough for housing." We believed the Trillion Dollar Commitment definitively addressed the second criticism. As to the first, the Financial Housing Enterprises Safety and Soundness Act offered us a way to make the case for our risk management quality directly to the government.

There is a saying on Capitol Hill about hotly contested legislation: "Winners get bills; losers get studies." As a consolation to the interests that had pushed for tighter regulation, stricter business restrictions, or higher capital for Fannie Mae and Freddie Mac but didn't get them, the 1992 legislation included language mandating Treasury, HUD, the GAO, and the CBO each to conduct "a study regarding the desirability and feasibility of repealing the Federal charters of the Federal National Mortgage Association and the Federal Home Loan Mortgage Corporation, eliminating any Federal sponsorship of the enterprises, and allowing the enterprises to continue to operate as fully private entities." The 1992 Act required us to give these agencies access to our books and records and also requested that the agencies solicit our views on the issues they would be addressing.

We considered the studies to be the equivalent of a medical check-up and were confident we would pass with a clean bill of health. We also welcomed the focus on privatization. We were not far removed from our own study of the subject, and we knew that its "feasibility" would be exceptionally hard for any of the groups to demonstrate. As to the "desirability" of privatization, its advocates first would have to identify the problem to which Fannie Mae and Freddie Mac privatization was the solution. When the studies finally got under way in 1995, the U.S. mortgage finance system was functioning more efficiently, serving a broader range of potential home buyers, and operating with less systemic financial risk than at any time in the past 30 years.

It easily could have been otherwise. As recently as 1975, nearly three-quarters of all U.S. home mortgage credit was supplied by depository institutions—either thrifts or commercial banks. Thrifts had by far the largest share, 57 percent, while banks' share was 16 percent. During and after the thrift crisis, however, thrifts' share of home mortgage holdings plunged an astonishing 40 percentage points, down to a mere 17 percent in 1995. Because of Fannie Mae and Freddie Mac—and really only for that reason—the U.S. mortgage finance system was able to replace all of the lost thrift funding with no discernable adverse effect on home buyers. Our ability to tap the international capital markets for massive amounts of fixed-rate funding allowed the mortgage market to undergo a seamless transition from a deposit-based system to a capital markets–based system in a very short period of time.

Virtually all of the financing share lost by thrifts (36 percentage points) was absorbed by capital markets investors who bought Fannie Mae, Freddie Mac, or Ginnie Mae mortgage-backed securities. U.S. commercial banks were among the largest purchasers of mortgage-backed securities. Banks held almost no MBS in 1975; in 1995 their residential MBS holdings accounted for almost 10 percent of outstanding home loans, and banks' total mortgages—MBS plus unsecuritized loans—financed more than 28 percent of the market, close to double their share 20 years earlier.

In contrast, only a tenth of thrifts' lost financing share went to the GSEs' portfolios, which rose from 6 percent of mortgages financed in 1975 to 10 percent in 1995. But Fannie Mae's portfolio always had been a lightning rod for criticism, and it remained so. Banks, which had replaced thrifts as the largest holders of mortgages, also replaced them as the most vocal opponents of our portfolio business. As the government studies got under way, we expected banks to make arguments for changes to our charter that would make it harder for us to grow the portfolio in the future, and we were prepared to counter them.

Our management of interest rate risk had just been put to, and passed, a severe market test. After falling for most of the first three years of the decade, long-term interest rates suddenly reversed course and shot upward, increasing by almost three percentage points between October 1993 and October 1994. *Barron's* magazine noted at the time that it was the worst 12-month period for long-term bonds since 1927. With interest rates rising so sharply, the average durations on our fixed-rate mortgages lengthened considerably, and we had to quickly lengthen our debt durations and add shorter-term assets to keep the portfolio within our risk limits. We did both. Having a theory and a strategy for managing a portfolio of fixed-rate mortgages is important, but there is no substitute for actual experience. We got a big dose of that experience in 1994 and came out of it in excellent shape.

Going into the studies, then, we felt we could demonstrate that our portfolio was performing the important function of channeling funds from the capital markets to mortgage borrowers with far less financial risk than any other type of intermediary, including banks or thrifts. In addition we were managing our credit risk demonstrably better than other financial institutions and had just launched an extraordinarily ambitious set of affordable housing initiatives targeted at previously underserved potential home buyers. To both our critics and the government entities studying us, our position was, "The current U.S. housing financing system works exceptionally well; what ideas do you have for making it work better?"

When the four reports came out between May and July of 1996, none said anything critical about our or Freddie Mac's risk management. That was a highly important validation of our strategies, and with none of the agencies doubting that our secondary market activities lowered mortgage rates, it swung the cost-benefit assessment sharply in our favor. Nor did any of the agencies recommend full privatization. HUD was the only one to make a recommendation at all, and it said, "The Department concludes that there is no compelling reason to fully privatize Fannie Mae and Freddie Mac at this time." The recommendations section of the GAO report was just five words long: "GAO is making no recommendations." But the report itself raised a number of cautions about full privatization—including higher costs and the diminished availability of mortgage credit—while noting only a few general potential benefits, such as "increased competition."

Our biggest concern had been the report by Treasury. Treasury over the years had made no secret of the fact that they favored the elimination of our charter benefits and in 1990 had proposed we be required to obtain a AAA stand-alone credit rating or be forced into full privatization. For the 1996 study, Treasury Secretary Robert Rubin recused himself because of his personal friendship with Jim Johnson, and he delegated responsibility for its preparation to his deputy secretary, Larry Summers. Along with the other agencies, Treasury was required to solicit our views on the issues they were examining. In this case that helped us. Early drafts of Treasury's report contained language endorsing the concept of privatization without clearly defining it or properly addressing the complex transition issues it entailed. Fannie Mae's then general counsel, Bob Zoellick, knew Summers, and Zoellick and I went to see him. After hearing our arguments against the privatization language in the draft report, Summers asked his staff to either change or remove it. In the final report, Treasury pushed the privatization issue into the future, saying, "Firm conclusions regarding the desirability of ending or modifying government sponsorship of Fannie Mae and Freddie Mac are premature," while noting, "Many of the most important issues could benefit from further study."

The great surprise among the GSE studies was the one done by the Congressional Budget Office. Unlike HUD, the GAO, and Treasury—all of which drew on data and facts from the structure and management strategies of our business and the impact we had on the housing market to assess whether we were providing value for the charter benefits we received—the CBO took a theoretical approach to its study. It explained its methodology this way:

> Comparing costs and benefits is essential in evaluating the effectiveness of GSEs as an instrument of policy. A primary consideration, therefore, is to *measure the costs of GSEs to society* [emphasis added] against the gains to intended beneficiaries. If the costs exceed the gains, then current policy is failing the public and alternative policies should be considered.

In the CBO's formulation, Fannie Mae and Freddie Mac's cost to society was the "subsidy" it said we received from our charter. The CBO put this at $6.5 billion in 1995, based on its estimates of the higher interest rates the market would require on our debt and MBS if we did not have GSE status. (Illustrating the subjectivity of these estimates, the GAO was asked by House Majority Leader Dick Armey to make a similar calculation and came up with $2.2 billion.) Our 1995 gains to beneficiaries the CBO pegged at $4.4 billion, based on the dollar amounts of our and Freddie Mac's mortgages in portfolio and outstanding MBS that year and the 35 basis points by which it estimated our activities lowered mortgage rates. The CBO then termed the $2.1 billion difference between its $6.5 billion subsidy estimate and its $4.4 billion benefit estimate the "retained subsidy," which it claimed was kept by Fannie Mae and Freddie Mac's shareholders and executives.

The CBO used uncharacteristically colorful language to summarize the results of its study, calling us "a spongy conduit—soaking up nearly $1 for every $2 delivered." And because its estimates showed us to be receiving more of a subsidy that we were passing on, we were, by its standards, "failing the public." To remedy that failing, it recommended a number of alternative policies, including "imposing a cost-of-capital equalization fee on the debt—not the MBS—of the housing GSEs" and "lowering the maximum-size mortgage that the enterprises are permitted to purchase." The CBO also suggested that the government could "cap and reduce the size of GSE mortgage portfolios."

We did not dispute that our charter had value, but we did dispute the CBO's notion that the theoretical value it put on that charter was an amount we could pass on or retain at our discretion. After attempting unsuccessfully to talk the CBO out of its conceptual framework, we switched to trying to correct what we believed were the evident flaws in its estimates. The two most significant were our credit guaranty subsidy and the effect we had on the mortgage market.

The CBO put a value of 40 basis points on the subsidy to our mortgage backed securities business. In 1995 Fannie Mae charged an average of 22 basis points for our MBS guarantees, before administrative costs of 6 basis points and a loss allowance of about the same amount. Allocating a theoretical subsidy is never easy—there is nothing real to track or reconcile—but we contended that if the 40 basis point mortgage-backed securities subsidy existed at all, most of it was received either by borrowers, who got the benefit of a lower mortgage rate, or by lenders, who might not have been passing all of the lower GSE mortgage-backed securities yields along in their rate quotes. In any event, it could not have been us. How could we in any sense receive a 40 basis point MBS subsidy if all we charged was 22 basis points, before expenses, in the first place?

The second major problem with the CBO's analysis was its insistence that the 35 basis point reduction it found Fannie Mae and Freddie Mac's activities had on conforming mortgage rates applied only to the mortgages we actually owned or guaranteed. That clearly that was incorrect. *All* home owners with mortgages below our loan limit received the benefit of the 35 basis point cost advantage, not just those whose loans we happened to finance. At the time, we owned or guaranteed fewer than half of conforming loans, so properly attributing the 35 basis point cost savings to all conforming loans doubled the CBO's benefit estimate.

Correcting these two obvious conceptual or measurement errors would have caused the CBO's estimate of Fannie Mae and Freddie Mac's benefit to home buyers to have substantially exceeded its estimate of our subsidy, eliminating any notion of there being a residual subsidy retained by our shareholders or executives. The CBO refused to make either correction, insisting on sticking with the assumptions that produced the $2.1 billion retained subsidy—and the "spongy conduit" designation.

We had been prepared to make the case for our value based on an assessment of our actual risks and benefits—and had done so with the three other agencies studying us—but were at a loss as to how to deal with the CBO's approach. It seemed to have set up its analysis to produce a predetermined result. It had defined and calculated our retained subsidy in a way that gave us no control over its amount and no ability to reduce it through any sensible actions we could take. (To the contrary, actions that did make business sense—such as structural or marketing innovations to reduce our debt costs—in the CBO's world actually would have *increased* our retained subsidy.) The CBO could just as well have said, "Fannie Mae and Freddie Mac are inherently bad ideas, and the government must take steps to reduce their roles in the market." This was political, not economic, analysis, and we said as much. In congressional testimony in July 1996, Zoellick called the CBO report "at best an advocacy document and at worst a polemic."

The CBO report heralded a new phase in the battle over Fannie Mae's charter benefits and position in the market. The traditional construct of "are we providing valuable services to the mortgage market and managing our risks well" would not be the only standard against which we were judged. In the future, we also would be judged against carefully selected metrics and custom-tailored standards to which only we and Freddie Mac would be subjected, and which had been concocted precisely because we could be found wanting with respect to them.

An Endorsement from Standard & Poor's

One further study occurred around this time. Although it was only indirectly related to the four government studies conducted in 1996, it served as a fitting bookend for them.

In 1997 the chairman of the Capital Markets Subcommittee of the House Banking and Financial Services Committee, Richard Baker, made a request of OFHEO that it obtain from Standard & Poor's and Moody's stand-alone credit ratings of Fannie Mae and Freddie Mac. S&P and Moody's already gave ratings of AAA and aaa, respectively, to our senior debt and MBS, based on a combination of our financial strength and their expectation that because of our status as government-sponsored enterprises, the government would preserve the value of our securities if either of us got into financial difficulty. Baker and OFHEO were looking for something different, however. They wanted Moody's and S&P to rate us assuming we did *not* have the benefit of GSE status.

Moody's declined to participate in what they called a "hypothetical" exercise, saying they could not assign a rating to an entity—in our case, a non-GSE Fannie Mae—that did not exist. S&P interpreted the assignment differently and accepted it. S&P would do what they called a "risk-to-the-government" rating: it would look at Fannie Mae as we actually were and operated and attempt to assign a rating to the probability of the government's ever having to support us financially. That wasn't what credit ratings normally represented, but at least the concept made sense. I thought of it as a financial strength rating of Fannie Mae done from the perspective of the government as a stakeholder, as opposed to the traditional rating of a bond done from the perspective of the bondholder. To work with S&P on this exercise, we wouldn't have to debate their analytical framework or their definition of our theoretical subsidy; we just would have to explain our risks and risk management to them. Those were things we knew how to do.

As we had done with the GAO, HUD, and Treasury, we took the ratings team from S&P through our growth prospects; the tools, techniques, and strategies we used in our interest rate risk and credit risk management; and our last several years of business and financial results, which had been excellent. The head of the S&P team, Mike DeStefano, told us that our inability to diversify our business beyond mortgages meant that the highest rating we could earn from S&P

was an A+, but after we made our case for a higher rating to S&P's rating committee, we were accorded a risk-to-the-government rating of AA-. In explaining this rating in their write-up, S&P cited our consistently strong profitability and our ability to weather changing market conditions and interest rate environments in support of it.

Very few companies had AA-level ratings. At the time, there were only six bank holding companies rated AA- or higher, and some of the best known, such as Bank of America and Wells Fargo, were rated lower. In 1997 OFHEO still was years away from implementing our regulatory risk-based capital standard, and in its absence the AA- risk-to-the-government rating from S&P served as an important external validation of our financial strength and credit quality.

With the Treasury, HUD, GAO, CBO, and S&P exercises, a clear pattern was established. When anyone focused objectively on our business results, affordable housing initiatives, and risk management capabilities, we looked exceptionally good. The way to get us to look bad was either to invent a standard we couldn't possibly meet or to describe our business as something other than what it was. That was not lost on our adversaries. From this point forward, Fannie Mae would exist in parallel worlds: the financial world of objective reality in which we carried out our business, and the Washington world of funhouse mirrors in which our critics and opponents challenged us politically based on their own distorted depictions of that business. The second of these worlds would prove to be much more treacherous than the first.

CHAPTER 7

Conflicts with Fast-Growing Lenders

D URING JIM JOHNSON'S CHAIRMANSHIP—WHICH RAN FROM THE beginning of 1991 through the end of 1998—Fannie Mae catapulted to a position of prominence in the mortgage finance system while building a broad and bipartisan base of support in Congress that greatly reduced the likelihood that political actions would weaken our business prospects or market role in the immediate future. At the same time, the removal of legal and regulatory barriers to the consolidation of financial services firms led to the rapid concentration of assets at a number of the largest banks and mortgage lenders, who had national rather than regional ambitions and increasingly viewed Fannie Mae as an obstacle to their success. Fannie Mae's market power and political influence, and the business objectives of our now much larger lending partners, were on a collision course, and what previously had been a series of skirmishes between us would escalate dramatically after Johnson left the company.

Fannie Mae Becomes a Powerhouse

Johnson took over a completely different Fannie Mae from the one Maxwell had inherited 10 years earlier. In 1981 Maxwell's overarching priority had been saving a badly flawed company from disaster.

In 1991 the challenge facing Johnson was realizing the potential of the company Maxwell had successfully reinvented. On Johnson's first day as chairman, Fannie Mae was a healthy institution at the center of a huge and fast-growing market whose previous dominant participants, the thrifts, were rapidly disappearing. Our prospects for fulfilling the mission of our charter and the expectations of our shareholders seemed almost limitless.

By background, personal attributes, and temperament, Johnson was ideally suited to lead Fannie Mae at this stage of our history. During the Maxwell years, the company's most pressing priorities had been internal: building a strong leadership team, instilling management disciplines, revamping our business practices, updating our operations and technology, and of course rethinking and modernizing the techniques we used to manage our interest rate and credit risks. Once those issues had been addressed to our satisfaction, however, the bulk of our focus shifted outward—toward our customers, other mortgage industry professionals, and our political constituents. External relations and politics were Johnson's gifts.

In the final year of his chairmanship, the *Washington Post* ran a flattering two-page article on Johnson in its *Style* section. In that article, prominent Washingtonian Harold Ickes called him "the chairman of the universe," humorist and syndicated columnist Mark Shields labeled him "the face of the Washington national establishment," and Washington insider Vernon Jordan said, "If you're chairman of Fannie Mae, the Kennedy Center and Brookings, you're an extraordinarily powerful person in this town." But in 1991, Johnson was chairman only of Fannie Mae (he added Brookings in 1994 and succeeded Jim Wolfensohn at the Kennedy Center in 1996). Johnson's early impact on the company was attributable to his personal qualities and drive, rather than to his reputation or power base; those came later.

What to me made Johnson so effective was his rare combination of a clear sense of purpose, a relentless and sometimes ruthless ambition to achieve his objectives, and an unparalleled ability to persuade or if necessary maneuver others into supporting what he wanted to accomplish. He was engaging and personable. He was exceedingly smart and was smooth without being slick. He could talk to anyone about business or political issues. He was a master at relationship building and worked tirelessly at cultivating people. He rarely dined at home. And he had an extraordinary network of high-level contacts. In an age when people still had Rolodexes, Johnson's assistant kept two giant ones. I had the office next to his and could see the steady stream of visitors being escorted in to see him.

Johnson paid meticulous attention to detail and had little patience with anyone who did not. For me, both of those attributes were epitomized by his advance operation, a discipline he brought to Fannie Mae from his days in politics. Before any trip he took, a team of two or more people would go to the destination in advance. They arranged or confirmed all the details and logistics for his meetings and activities, timed the drives on the routes he would take, and produced a schedule of where he would be and when, down to the minute. When Johnson was met at the airport, he already would have been checked into his hotel and on arrival would be handed his room key. If anything went awry, the team was there to handle it. It was a highly precise operation with no tolerance for error.

On one occasion, Johnson was in Las Vegas to speak to the National Association of Home Builders. His to-the-minute schedule gave the exact time when a person on his advance team, a man named Marc Bien, was to meet him at the elevator to escort him to the speaking area. Bien was there well before he needed to be and while waiting decided to play the slot machines. He hit a jackpot. But he couldn't just take his money and go; he had to fill out tax forms. Rather than leave the money behind, he chose to stay and fill out the forms. It took longer than he expected, and when Johnson emerged from the elevator precisely on schedule, Bien was not there to meet him. Shortly afterwards, Johnson's advance team had a new member.

Like Maxwell, Johnson set extremely high performance standards for the executives who worked for him. In an interview with *Mortgage Banking* magazine in January 1992, outgoing Fannie Mae President Roger Birk, who knew both men well, said, "When you work at

Fannie Mae you can't fake it. You get found out pretty quickly and you get pushed aside one way or another." Maxwell prized competence, integrity, and discipline; Johnson insisted on those attributes, too, but he also had strong preferences about the manner in which people did their jobs. To be a part of the Johnson circle, one needed to meet his expectations for style as well as substance.

Johnson's two earliest recruits to Fannie Mae did both. In the spring of 1991, Johnson called his senior management together to introduce us to the two people he said would be joining him in an "office of the chairman" to lead Fannie Mae during his tenure as chairman. Succeeding Birk as president and chief operating officer would be Larry Small, then a vice chairman at Citicorp, and joining the company in the new role of vice chairman would be Frank Raines, an investment banker from Lazard Frères specializing in municipal finance.

Raines joined first, in July 1991, and Small came two months later. They formed a complementary team. Small was the quintessential banker—a no-nonsense "numbers guy" with a laser-like focus on the bottom line—with the superb people skills necessary to be effective as COO of a company full of talented but headstrong senior executives. Raines's interests and expertise were in business strategy, technology, and public policy. A Harvard-educated Rhodes scholar, he had served in the Carter administration as an associate director of the Office of Management and Budget before going to work at Lazard. Even though I was chief financial officer and responsible for Fannie Mae's largest operating business, Johnson had me report not to the COO Small but to Raines.

The 1992 GSE legislation was passed shortly after Johnson's new leadership team was in place. In that legislation, Congress explicitly reaffirmed its support for Fannie Mae's charter and housing mission, clarified the rules under which we were expected to operate, and gave us a capital standard that allowed us to price our business competitively as long as we adhered to stringent risk controls. To Johnson, Small, and Raines, the message in the legislation could not have been more clear: we were to use the advantages of our charter, and all of the creativity and initiative we could marshal, to bring the benefits of Fannie Mae financing and services to as many potential home buyers as we could and at as low a cost as possible, while not putting the taxpayer at risk. Johnson would say years later in a speech to the Mortgage Bankers Association, "What Congress gave us was a clear mandate to 'just do it'—to do whatever it takes to get the job done, for the benefit of consumers, of lenders, and of the nation as a whole." We believed that if we "just did it," as a shareholder-owned company we would have earned any financial rewards that came our way.

Having a charter that restricted us to the secondary market imposed an obvious constraint that was easy to overlook: while we could purchase mortgages for our portfolio in the open market, we could increase the amount of credit guaranty business we did only if we offered something of value to our lenders. That was a challenge our new office of the chairman eagerly embraced. Johnson made it a priority for our marketing staff to get much closer to our lenders to better understand how we could meet their needs. We developed a number of new products. And perhaps most importantly, we made a major commitment to use technology to make it faster, easier, and cheaper for our lenders to do business with us.

Fannie Mae was not a pioneer in underwriting technology; Freddie Mac had been ahead of us, as had several of our larger lenders. But once we got into it, we caught up quickly, and with the active involvement of and guidance from Raines, we soon became a leader. We began investigating automated underwriting in 1993. By early 1994, we were working on the design of what we called Desktop Underwriter (DU), which we made available to lenders in 1995. (Freddie Mac already was using an automated underwriting system called Loan Prospector.) By 1997 we were able to tell lenders that using DU could reduce the time it took to get a loan approved "from four weeks to four minutes." Lenders' use of our technology expanded rapidly, to both their and our benefit. Lenders who used DU needed to make fewer representations and warranties about the quality of loans they delivered us, while we were able to better evaluate the credit risk of their loans and more accurately monitor the underwriting variances and product permissions we granted them as we attempted to expand our business. We used DU as the delivery mechanism for most of the new products we introduced under the Trillion Dollar Commitment, and of course it was essential to our pledge to use technology to cut the cost of originating a mortgage by at least $1,000 per loan.

All of this innovation and activity produced extremely impressive results for Fannie Mae's business and financial performance. In 1998 our combined book of business—our mortgage portfolio and outstanding mortgage-backed securities—crossed the $1 trillion mark, having grown at an average rate of nearly 13 percent per year since 1990, more than twice the 6.3 percent average growth rate of the mortgage market as a whole. During this time our MBS business grew at a 10 percent rate, and we had been able to use the newly developed callable debt market to grow our mortgage portfolio at a 17 percent rate. By the end of 1998, our portfolio financed nearly one in every 10 mortgages in the country, while our mortgage-backed securities helped finance close to another 14 percent of those loans. And we were highly profitable. From $1.2 billion in 1990, our net income grew by 14 percent per year to $3.4 billion in 1998—more than $800,000 for each of the roughly 4,000 people we employed. We had grown our earnings at a double-digit rate in every year since 1986, and we were one of only seven companies in the Standard & Poor's 500 to have done so. We were a force to be reckoned with.

Visible Results, Clearly Communicated

We had concluded during David Maxwell's chairmanship that as a private company with a public purpose—and to insulate from political criticism the returns we were providing to our shareholders—we could not allow our profitability to get out of balance with the benefits we provided to home buyers. With the Trillion Dollar Commitment, Johnson took that concept one step further. Fannie Mae, he felt, should strive for "indispensability." That is, we should do so much for the housing market through our mainstream business and our affordable housing initiatives that it would become unthinkable for anyone to suggest constraining or eliminating our charter for fear of losing that support.

And here he added a brilliant insight. It would not be enough for us to simply outperform on the mandate of our charter. Our two key constituencies, home buyers and Congress, had to see and understand what we were doing as well. When Johnson took over as chairman, that was far from true. As a secondary market institution, Fannie Mae was invisible to home buyers. They knew their lender but not us. And because we operated behind the scenes, Congress did not have a good understanding of our business or the role we played. We were a complicated company and along with Freddie Mac were unique. I made my share of visits to Capitol Hill, and with both members and staff we had what we called a "retention problem." We would tell them how we worked and what we did, but the next time we saw them, they would have forgotten most of it. Rather than us telling the story, far better for members and staffers to hear from people in their districts how much of a difference we made to their and their neighbors' lives. From that notion flowed the companion to Johnson's idea of indispensability, which he called "tangibility": Fannie Mae's activities had to be visible on the ground, and we had to take an activist role in making sure our key constituents knew about them.

Johnson's premier tangibility initiative was our partnership offices. As part of the Trillion Dollar Commitment, we pledged to open at least 25 regional partnership offices, beginning with 10 in 1994, to "work in a practical way with lenders, public officials, housing advocates, and others, to expand Fannie Mae's outreach and service in those communities." The very first partnership office was in San Antonio, Texas, the home of the chairman of the House Banking Committee, Henry Gonzalez. Critics tended to dismiss these offices as political. They certainly were that, but they were much more. They were a masterful mix of substance, communication, politics, and public relations.

The substance was why they worked. There were no other mechanisms for bringing together at the local level all the groups that had an interest in solving affordable housing problems. We soon hit on a formula for integrating the objectives of the offices. First, working with our partners, we would come up with a specific plan for what we believed we could accomplish out of that office, usually with high-profile initiatives as centerpieces. We would announce our plan at a public event, almost always with a congressman or senator present. We then would work to accomplish what we had set out to do, with events during the year marking the milestones. We would meticulously track everything we did in the region covered by the partnership office—not just our special initiatives but our progress under the Trillion Dollar Commitment and our regular business as well. At the end of the year, we would hold another event, with local, state, and national politicians present, to report on how Fannie Mae helped to provide x billion dollars to enable y million families in their districts achieve their goal of home ownership. These activities and events produced tremendous grassroots awareness of our importance and impact, which we subsequently could (and did) tap for support in Washington.

The partnership offices were an effective way of communicating our results to Congress; to communicate with consumers, we employed several techniques of outreach, most involving advertising. We had learned from our Hart-Teeter surveys that lack of information about buying a home and getting a mortgage was a major impediment to home ownership. We produced home-ownership materials in a dozen different languages and used targeted television advertising to offer these guides and workbooks free to anyone who wished to receive them. (Fannie Mae's name was mentioned prominently in the ads.) We discovered that basketball fans were an ideal mix of opinion leaders and affordable housing constituents, so we formed a partnership with the National Basketball Association we called "Home Team." We advertised on NBA games, and in conjunction with the 12 teams we had Home Team partnerships with, we held events attended by players to showcase local affordable housing initiatives. We also held home buying fairs throughout the country and sponsored home ownership counseling centers.

Johnson took a number of other steps to increase our political support. In 1995 we contributed $350 million in Fannie Mae stock to our charitable foundation. As the stock rose in value, we had a large sum of money to use both for our consumer advertising (which we moved to the foundation with IRS approval) and for greatly expanded grant making to entities important in the affordable housing arena. We formed closer formal ties with groups like the Congressional Black Caucus and the Congressional Hispanic Caucus. Maxwell had established a national advisory council, and Johnson significantly expanded it to between 40 and 50 leaders of the housing and mortgage finance industries. We held three meetings a year at which attendees were briefed on our activities and treated to candid presentations by prominent members of Congress. Advisory council members frequently became influential ambassadors for Fannie Mae.

Johnson also substantially beefed up Fannie Mae's political capabilities. He was personally acquainted with most of the top political operatives in town, and he put many of them on retainer (in some cases just to keep our adversaries from using them). Johnson also strengthened our internal staff, bringing in a number of well-connected and experienced people to work in our legal, government affairs, regulatory policy, and public relations areas—among them Jamie Gorelick, Tom Donilon, Arne Christenson, and John Buckley.

Critics at the time and subsequently viewed our political activities as inappropriate for a government-sponsored enterprise. But put yourself in Johnson's shoes. Our business and ideological opponents knew that the best way to restrain or hobble us was to go to Congress and seek changes to our charter. Johnson knew that too, and he wanted as large and sophisticated an arsenal of tools as possible with which to defend his company.

In his final speech to the New York Society of Security Analysts in 1998, Johnson commented on a commitment he had made to them earlier to create a stable and predictable regulatory environment for Fannie Mae. He said:

I believe we have done very well in this area. There is strong bipartisan consensus in favor of Fannie Mae's pivotal role at the center of the nation's mortgage finance business. It is increasingly clear that the benefits that we bring to this country are indispensable, and the value of Fannie Mae's unique contribution to America is greater than at any time in our history.

Few could disagree.

Much Larger Lenders with Much Larger Ambitions

Fannie Mae's rapid growth, increasing market influence, and political success did not escape the notice of our largest competitors and business partners.

While we had grown rapidly during Johnson's chairmanship, our largest lenders had grown even faster. In fact, the 1990s saw the greatest concentration of lending and assets among the 10 largest U.S. banks and mortgage lenders of any decade in the country's history. Between December 1990 and December 1998—the time Johnson ran Fannie Mae—our combined mortgage-backed securities and portfolio businesses grew from 14 percent of outstanding mortgages (4 percent portfolio, 10 percent MBS) to 23 percent (9 percent portfolio, 14 percent MBS). By comparison, the share of mortgage originations of Fannie Mae's top 10 customers—who in 1998 included Wells Fargo, Countrywide, Bank of America, and Chase Mortgage—more than doubled over that same period, rising from 17 percent to 37 percent. The banking industry saw similar concentration. In December 1990, the top 10 U.S. banks held 26 percent of banking assets; in December 1998, that share was 42 percent.

The sudden emergence of very large banks and mortgage lenders had a ready explanation: the progressive easing of restrictions on within-state and interstate banking during the 1980s and 1990s, coupled with rapid advances in technology in the 1990s, provided both the ability and the motivation to grow extremely rapidly through merger and acquisition. Historically Congress had expressed great concern about banks becoming too big or too powerful. It had passed a number of laws to prevent that, and as a consequence, the nation had more than 14,000 commercial banks at the beginning of the 1980s. In 1982, however, the Reagan administration Justice Department began liberalizing the rules governing banking mergers within states. Then, in 1994, Congress passed the Riegle-Neal Banking and Branching Efficiency Act, eliminating previous prohibitions on interstate banking. The results were predictable. Between 1980 and 1998, the number of banks in the United States fell by nearly 40 percent, to fewer than 9,000. While some failed, most merged or were acquired. At first the acquisitions occurred within state boundaries, but following Riegle-Neal, they were nationwide. Cost cutting was a motivating force behind many of the mergers, but technology—which could give banks an edge over their competitors and was most cost-effective when spread among a large number of customers—played a larger role.

Bank consolidation and concentration transformed the mortgage industry. The independent mortgage banking company virtually disappeared during the 1990s. Most were acquired by commercial bank holding companies or by banks themselves. By 1998, six of Fannie Mae's 10 largest lenders were commercial banks or bank subsidiaries. Two more (Washington Mutual and Dime/NAMCO) were mutual savings banks that reached their size through acquisition, while another, Cendant, was part of a short-lived conglomerate also created through merger or acquisition. Only one, Countrywide, was still an independent mortgage bank.

The very largest banks and bank-owned mortgage lenders viewed Fannie Mae much differently from our other customers. Small and middle-sized mortgage bankers saw us as a helpful partner: whether through our portfolio purchases or credit guarantees, we made it possible for them to be in the business of originating (and servicing) mortgages, and our interests rarely if ever conflicted. Small and middle-sized banks and thrifts did not like our portfolio business because it competed with theirs, but that abstract objection was outweighed by the fact that our portfolio purchases and mortgage-backed securities guarantees were cost-effective ways for them to originate and profit from a greater volume of mortgages than they were able to own or felt comfortable owning. The newly emergent group of very large banks, on the other hand, had a much more serious problem with us. Our dominant position in the secondary market was a major impediment to their growing ambitions in the primary market.

The large national banks saw residential mortgages as key to their success with the consumer. Mortgages were by far the largest consumer loan market, and the biggest banks also had learned that a mortgage relationship with a customer led to greatly increased sales of their other retail products. The challenge they faced was distinguishing the mortgages they offered from everyone else's. The majority of their mortgage customers wanted 30-year fixed-rate conventional conforming loans, and any lender making these loans wanted them to be eligible for sale in the secondary market, whether they intended to sell them immediately or not. In the 1990s, Fannie Mae and Freddie Mac had the best prices in that market, so lenders wishing to sell to us had to originate to our standards. That greatly limited their flexibility in customizing their products. Making matters more difficult was the fact that even as lenders looked to put their own brand on mortgages, actions initiated by Johnson with our automated underwriting, new products, and consumer advertising were expanding the visibility and footprint of the Fannie Mae brand.

It was a legitimate conflict. Fannie Mae and our largest lenders had different objectives as well as different business models. Our objectives were expanding the universe of borrowers who could qualify for and afford a "Fannie Mae mortgage," reducing borrower costs, ensuring that our credit standards were prudent and consistently applied, and making money for our shareholders. Our largest lenders shared none of these. In addition, we were a wholesale institution in the secondary market; they were retail institutions in the primary market. We made our money primarily on volume, not margin or fee rates. We did not originate, so reducing the cost of origination did not lower our revenues as it did lenders'. Because we and not the lender took the credit risk on the loans we purchased or guaranteed, we believed it was our responsibility to set reasonable credit standards and to be able to enforce those standards. We also believed that the growing concentration of primary mortgage lending among very large institutions worked to both our and borrowers' disadvantage, and we sought to use our technology and position in the market to try to keep as many lenders in the game as we could.

In the battle for control over what types of mortgages were made and how they were originated, our and Freddie Mac's position as gatekeepers of the secondary market gave us the upper hand. Our largest lenders found that highly frustrating, and their response was to accuse us of overstepping the bounds of our charter by "blurring the line between the primary and secondary market." But in reality, there was no bright line, other than our not being permitted to originate. Lenders' two biggest complaints involved our consumer advertising and our technology. Our advertising was aggressive (Freddie Mac did not advertise), but we justified it as a means of promoting home buyer education and improving our image with consumers. Technology was a different matter. While we had made ourselves visible with our pledge to lower origination costs by $1,000 per loan, the application of technology to the mortgage business eventually would have wrung out excessive costs no matter what we did, just as technology had advanced bank consolidation through the economies of scale it brought. We did not cause the technology revolution; we merely sought to use it to our and consumers' best advantage.

In congressional testimony in March 1998, mortgage industry consultant Tom LaMalfa summed up large lenders' objections to us by saying, "They are siphoning most of the economic value from the mortgage business." That was hyperbole, but the underlying sentiment was accurate: our presence made it harder for large primary market lenders to make the amount of money they wanted to in the mortgage business. And their fear was that unless they could stop us in some way, we would continue to achieve our objectives at their expense.

A Gambit Backfires

Our drive to meet our affordable housing, risk management, and profit goals caused similar conflicts with private mortgage insurers and resulted in similar friction. Private mortgage insurance was an industry that owed its size and influence to the lobbying prowess of the founder of the Mortgage Guaranty Insurance Corporation (MGIC), Max Karl. Karl had set up MGIC in the late 1950s, with thrift institutions as its primary client. In the 1970 Emergency Home Finance Act that created Freddie Mac, Karl convinced Congress to require both Freddie Mac and Fannie Mae to obtain mortgage insurance or its equivalent on any high LTV conventional loan we acquired. The legislation was an unabashed gift to the mortgage insurers because it ensured them a steady flow of business. I used to tease MI executives about that. While Fannie Mae and Freddie Mac may have been government sponsored enterprises, or GSEs, I said, private mortgage insurers were government *mandated* enterprises, or GMEs. The acronym GME, of course, was pronounced "Gimme."

The mortgage insurers did not see it that way. GE and AIG each had mortgage insurance company subsidiaries—GEMICO and United Guaranty, respectively—and the heads of the parent companies, Jack Welch and Hank Greenberg, resolutely viewed them as private and Fannie Mae as the government. Their objections to us—which were grounded in ideology, politics, and competition—were ardent but ill informed. We would get frequent reports of Greenberg railing against Fannie Mae in private meetings, saying, "Why are they even *in* the business of guaranteeing mortgages?" (That was how we structured our mortgage-backed securities.) And at one meeting of the Business Roundtable attended by both men, Frank Raines asked Welch, "Who are GEMICO's customers, other than us and Freddie Mac?" Welch had no response to that question, nor did he seem to grasp its import.

We did not begrudge the MIs their position in the market, but we did want them to add value with the insurance they provided (which was paid for by the borrower, not us). And with the consolidation of mortgage lending, they were doing less of that. Traditionally MIs added discipline to the system by pulling back from overheated regional markets or by changing their pricing in those markets. The MIs stopped carrying out those practices as lenders got larger, however, for fear of losing their business. Under the Trillion Dollar Commitment, we were making a greater number of higher-risk loans, and we needed the MIs to be true risk-sharing partners. If they were not going to add value on the front end of the lending process—by screening out loans they deemed to be too risky—we wanted them to help us manage the risks of those loans after we acquired them.

In May 1998 we introduced a product called Flex 97, which required only a 3 percent down payment that could come in the form of a gift or a loan. This was a higher-risk mortgage (available only through DU), and for it we dropped our per-loan MI coverage from 30 percent of the loan amount to the statutory minimum of 18 percent but charged the lender a 1½-point fee. Once we assessed the riskiness of the Flex 97 loans we were delivered, we used some or all of the upfront fee to buy supplemental MI coverage on a group of these loans together. This arrangement gave MIs less revenue automatically from the borrower—since we dropped to minimum front-end coverage—and to get revenue from us, they had to quote competitive prices for coverage on the back end. We told them that over time, our intention was to move more of our standard high LTV business to this combination of low front-end MI and supplemental back-end coverage, both to save borrowers money and to give us more effective risk protection. This was a change in the insurance relationship the MIs did not like. To get our business, we were requiring the individual companies to compete with one other and to add value with the insurance they provided. They had not been accustomed to having to do either.

While we were working with the MIs to try to get more value out of the insurance we were required by statute to use them to provide, Freddie Mac took a different approach: they attempted to do away with their MI requirement entirely. In October 1998, Senate Banking Committee Chairman Alphonse D'Amato of New York put what he and Freddie Mac claimed was a "technical amendment" into the conference report of a HUD/VA appropriations bill, allowing Freddie Mac to use any method they chose to insure their high loan-to-value ratio mortgages as long as it was "financially equal or superior" to private mortgage insurance. No other lawmaker was aware that the language was added to the bill, which already had passed the House and Senate. The language was not technical at all. The mortgage insurers found out about it the next day and immediately went to Senator Phil Gramm of Texas, who inserted his own language into an already-passed omnibus budget bill repealing D'Amato's appropriations bill provision.

Freddie Mac had informed us beforehand about their self-insurance plan and had asked us if we wanted to be included in the amendment. We said no but did not attempt to talk them out of trying it for themselves. That was a mistake. Reaction in the industry and on the Hill to the incident was swift and severe. Freddie Mac's stealth initiative hit all our critics' hot buttons. It was an attempt to aggressively expand their business powers. It leveraged our congressional support to (almost) achieve an objective contrary to our opponents' interests, without public discussion or debate. It would have resulted in more risk going on Freddie Mac's books. It reinforced critics' views of the ineffectiveness of our regulator (OFHEO had sent a letter to D'Amato supporting the move, saying it would have no adverse effect on Freddie Mac's safety and soundness). And perhaps worst of all, it was a frontal assault on the economics of an entire industry; stocks of publicly traded mortgage insurers plunged 30 percent when news of the Freddie Mac amendment got out.

Freddie Mac's self-insurance gambit was the spark that lit the fire. For our critics and competitors, it cemented their views that we and Freddie Mac had become too big and too powerful, with nothing in sight that would change that. Nobody had singlehandedly been able to slow our expansion or to weaken us in Congress. Studies by government agencies had not produced the results our critics wanted, nor had academic conferences (such as the one sponsored by Ralph Nader earlier that year).

At some point following the Freddie Mac MI episode, several of our largest lenders and insurers began to talk about banding together to form and fund an anti–Fannie Mae and Freddie Mac lobbying group to try to accomplish collectively what had eluded them individually. In April 1999, the *American Banker* reported on the creation of a Competitive Consumer Lending Coalition, whose mission was to contain the business expansion of Fannie Mae and Freddie Mac. When this group formally was announced two months later, it had been given the name FM Watch. Its initial sponsors were three large bank-owned mortgage lenders—Chase Mortgage, Wells Fargo, and PNC Mortgage; one subprime lender, Household Financial; and GE and AIG, the parent companies of two mortgage insurers. Revealingly, the first head of FM Watch, Gerry Friedman, was the founder of another mortgage insurance company, Amerin Guaranty.

PART THREE

The Fight for the Mortgage Market

CHAPTER 8

A Surprise from the Treasury Department

I n April 1998, Jim Johnson announced that he would be retiring as Fannie Mae's chairman at the end of the year and that Frank Raines would succeed him.

A Rough Greeting for Raines

In a sense, Raines had been preparing for the Fannie Mae job his entire life. Growing up poor in Seattle as one of six children, he had early experience with the importance working-class families put on the goal of home ownership and the role played by capital in attaining it. His father, Delno, was a custodian for the city park service, and his mother, Ida, worked as a cleaning woman for Boeing (on whose board Raines later would serve). Raines's parents could not qualify for a mortgage from a traditional lender—their only access to credit was through finance companies charging ruinously high interest rates—but unlike most people, they did not let that deter them from becoming home owners. Delno Raines purchased a condemned property from the state for $1,000. He salvaged lumber from the ramshackle house, dug by hand the foundation for the new home he wanted to build, and over the next five years put in the drywall and plumbing for it himself. Delno Raines's commitment to and persistence in achieving his dream of home ownership—and his lack of access to credit that would have helped him do so more easily—made lasting impressions on his son.

In high school, Raines was a star debater and captain and quarter-back of his football team. He became interested in politics and served as junior class president and as student body president. With the help of a scholarship, Raines was able to go to Harvard. While there he worked during the summers in Washington, D.C., as an intern in the Nixon administration with Daniel Patrick Moynihan, then Nixon's urban affairs advisor. After attending Magdalen College in Oxford as a Rhodes scholar and Harvard Law School, also on scholarship, Raines returned to Seattle to practice law. Seven months later, President Carter asked him to come to work in the White House on welfare reform—the subject of his senior thesis and a topic on which he had continued to do work at Oxford and Harvard Law. Carter appointed Raines associate director of the Office of Management and Budget (OMB) in 1978, where he worked until becoming an invest-ment banker at Lazard Frères in 1979.

Raines had several meetings with Johnson before he joined Fannie Mae as vice chairman. I recall having seen him either in the executive office waiting area or going into Johnson's office on at least three occasions in early 1991, and wondering to myself, "Who is this person?" I soon found out. When he came to Fannie Mae in July of that year, he became my boss. Virtually from his first day at the company, his primary area of interest was technology. He liked to tell the story that shortly after joining us, he asked where in the building he could go to cash a check, only to learn that a company that at the time financed more than $400 billion in mortgages did not have any cash on the premises. Everything was on computers. Raines quickly realized the potential of technology as a competitive tool. Under his leadership, we expanded the focus of our technology efforts from improving the efficiency and reducing the costs of our back-office functions to developing cutting-edge tools that lowered costs on the front end of the business—for consumers, lenders, and ourselves—and improved our risk assessment capabilities.

Raines was a relentless force for innovation. He set up a group called Corporate Development to do research on market, industry, and competitive trends and to develop ideas for new initiatives, and he continually challenged Fannie Mae's business leaders to think broadly and strategically about their responsibilities and opportunities. He also was a tremendous asset to our political efforts. He shared Johnson's commitment to and passion for the company's mission, understood our business and finances as well as anyone, and was an articulate and persuasive advocate for Fannie Mae's issues and interests on Capitol Hill and elsewhere.

All of Raines's colleagues thought extremely highly of him, and we were not the only ones who did. In the summer of 1996, Vice President Al Gore approached him about joining the Clinton cabinet as director of the OMB. As much as Raines liked his job at Fannie Mae, it was a request he felt he could not turn down. Clinton was serious about balancing the federal budget, and the OMB director would play a central role in that effort. Raines went to the OMB in September 1996. The cooperative and pragmatic approach he took to budget issues that in the past had been highly contentious helped the administration reach a balanced-budget agreement with House Republicans in 1997. During the 1998 fiscal year—which ran from October 1997 through September 1998—the budget moved into the black for the first time in almost 30 years, and it remained in surplus for the rest of Clinton's second term.

Raines's intention had been to remain at the OMB at least through 1998 to participate in deliberations on Social Security reform, but in early March of that year he received a surprise phone call from Johnson. Johnson had a question for him: would he be interested in returning to Fannie Mae and succeeding Johnson as chairman and CEO the following January? Although the timing was not ideal from Raines's standpoint, it was a once-in-a-lifetime opportunity, and he did not hesitate to accept it. He returned to Fannie Mae in May 1998 as chairman and CEO designate, and when Johnson stepped down in January 1999, Raines became the first African-American CEO of a Fortune 500 company.

Raines did not get much of a grace period. Less than six months after he became chairman, on June 17, 1999, FM Watch held a splashy coming-out event at The Washington Press Club. As a symbol of the group's intent to "shine a spotlight on the activities of Fannie Mae and Freddie Mac," it passed out flashlights. FM Watch Chairman Gerry Friedman introduced as its executive director a man named Mike House, an attorney with the Washington, D.C.–based law firm of Hogan and Hartson and the head of their lobbying practice. Friedman and House each spoke at the event, and the two revealed the FM Watch mission statement:

> Recognizing the critical importance of Fannie Mae and Freddie Mac's unique charters, FM Watch will monitor the activities of these government-subsidized enterprises and: Alert the public to Fannie Mae and Freddie Mac actions which benefit the interests of investors at the expense of homebuyers and taxpayers, support market competition that results in affordable housing for consumers, promote Federal policies that do not allow the GSEs to move beyond their unique charters into markets and services already provided by the private sector, and support federal policies that prevent exposure to unnecessary risks that could require a massive bailout by the American taxpayer.

Initially we underestimated the FM Watch threat. Our public response was to label it "The Coalition for Higher Mortgage Costs," as a way of emphasizing that the policies it advocated made its members better off at the expense of consumers. During its early years, FM Watch had no legislative agenda; its efforts were directed at cultivating relationships with influential journalists, members of Congress, and administration officials and at disseminating its opinions about Fannie Mae and Freddie Mac along with critiques of what we were doing. The visible activities of FM Watch—a website it maintained and the statements it made about us in newspaper and magazine articles—struck us as amateurish and unlikely to do much harm. Yet the surface ineffectiveness of FM Watch masked the real danger it posed: it brought together Fannie Mae's critics and opponents and emboldened them to be more aggressive in their opposition to us. House emphasized this point in comments he made to the *Legal Times* a year after FM Watch was formed: "I said when we first started out on this thing that Fannie Mae was a lot like the school bully in grammar school, and that if somebody finally stood up and gave him a bloody nose, then everybody on the school ground would get a lot more courage."

One individual who "got a lot more courage" about confronting us was Republican Congressman Richard Baker of Louisiana. The son of a Baptist minister and a graduate of Louisiana State University, Baker had been a realtor and a state legislator before being elected to Congress, representing Baton Rouge, in 1987. When Republicans gained control of both houses of Congress following the 1994 midterm elections, Baker was appointed chairman of the Subcommittee on Capital Markets, Securities, and Government-Sponsored Enterprises (the "Capital Markets Subcommittee") of the House Banking and Financial Services Committee, with jurisdiction over Fannie Mae and Freddie Mac.

We knew him well. Shortly after Baker became subcommittee chairman, Fannie Mae's head of government relations Bill Maloni hired Duane Duncan, Baker's chief of staff, to come work for us. Given the change in Congress, Maloni wanted to beef up his team on the Republican side, and as he spoke with people on Capitol Hill, Duncan's name kept coming up as one of the top Republican staffers there. It is quite common for congressional staff to take higher paying jobs on the business side. Maloni talked to Baker before he offered Duncan a job, and Baker said he had no objection to it. (Johnson, on the other hand, advised Maloni against making the hire, for fear Baker might hold it against us.) When Duncan joined Fannie Mae in 1995, we considered Baker a friend.

Baker had spent relatively little time on GSE-related issues during his first four years as subcommittee chairman. That changed abruptly in 1999. On August 8 of that year, the *Washington Post* ran an extensive article on the front page of its business section headlined

"Fear of What Fannie May Do." The article focused on FM Watch and reported that Fannie Mae now was facing criticism from mortgage lenders, mortgage insurers, and government officials in a wide range of areas: our excessive profitability, unchecked business ambitions, charter benefits, poor risk management practices, and the need to do more to support affordable housing. Prominently featured in the article was Richard Baker. "The mood has changed," Baker was quoted as saying. "Members of Congress are now hearing publicly for the first time from other participants in the housing market about concerns over encroachment into free markets by government-sponsored enterprises such as Fannie Mae." Baker had found his issue—or rather the issue had found him. With the support, assistance, and political contributions of FM Watch and its organizers and allies, the primary objectives of Baker and his subcommittee would now be putting tighter controls on Fannie Mae and Freddie Mac and limiting our roles in the market.

Summers and Greenspan Enter the Fray

Baker's embrace of his new cause came at a perfect time for him. Only a few months earlier, Robert Rubin had announced his decision to step down as Treasury secretary after more than four years in the position, and his deputy secretary, Larry Summers, had been nominated to take his place. When Summers was confirmed on July 2, 1999, he needed no convincing from anyone to make Fannie Mae and Freddie Mac a higher policy priority for Treasury than we had been under his predecessor.

Summers was a brilliant economist who had spent the bulk of his career in academia and government. The son of two PhD economists—and with two uncles who were Nobel Prize winners in economics—he had been one of the youngest tenured professors at Harvard. He served on the staff of the Council of Economic Advisors during the Reagan administration in 1982 and 1983 and was chief economist of the World Bank between 1991 and 1993. In 1993 Summers joined the Clinton Treasury Department as undersecretary of international affairs and became deputy secretary when Rubin succeeded Lloyd Bentsen as Treasury secretary in 1995. Summers remained in that role until he was named as Rubin's replacement.

Rubin had shown no interest in government-sponsored enterprise-related issues at Treasury. In his memoir, *In an Uncertain World*, Rubin mentions Fannie Mae only once, and that is to describe Jim Johnson in 1984 as someone "who later became the CEO of Fannie Mae." Fannie Mae–related topics almost certainly were brought to Rubin's attention, whether by career staffers at Treasury or during the breakfasts and lunches he, Federal Reserve Chairman Alan Greenspan, and Summers (collectively dubbed the "Committee to Save the World" by *Time Magazine* in February 1999) had each week. Rubin's reluctance to engage on any of them may have been because of his friendship with Johnson, but it also may have stemmed from his years at Goldman Sachs, where he came to know Fannie Mae as a complex and sophisticated financial institution that defied the simplistic portrayal of the company shared widely within Treasury and at the Fed.

When Summers was given responsibility for Treasury's 1996 GSE study in the wake of Rubin's recusal, the report he produced avoided recommendations or even firm conclusions about the issues Treasury had been asked to review. But that did not mean he agreed with us on Fannie Mae's role and value in the mortgage market. He most decidedly did not. Like Greenspan, Summers fervently believed that compared with government involvement, intervention, or regulation, unfettered markets produced superior results for the economy and the financial system. Greenspan and Summers both viewed the GSEs' federal charters as the antithesis of the free-market principles they cherished. Their shared ideology led them to advocate tighter restrictions on the government-sponsored enterprises while simultaneously seeking to relax regulations on banks—which they considered to be free market entities in spite of the fact that they benefited from federal deposit insurance and a regulator, the Fed, willing to lower their cost of funds by dropping market interest rates whenever they got into difficulty (as banks periodically did).

Greenspan had pushed for banking deregulation from the time he succeeded Paul Volcker as Fed chairman in August of 1987. That November he testified at a House Banking Subcommittee hearing in favor of repealing the 1933 Glass-Steagall Act separating the powers of investment banks and commercial banks. Banking industry executives strongly favored Glass-Steagall repeal, as did Treasury; the Fed had been the holdout. Volcker was skeptical of the benefits of bank deregulation, and he had concerns about its risks. When the Fed's board of governors relaxed regulations on banks' activities in commercial paper, municipal bonds, and private-label mortgage-backed securities during Volcker's chairmanship, it did so over his objections. Greenspan's replacement of Volcker gave banks, the Treasury, and members of the Federal Reserve Board a committed ally in their quest for broader bank powers and fewer restrictions on what could be done with them.

Greenspan's 1987 endorsement of Glass-Steagall repeal was insufficient to convince a majority of the members of the House to introduce legislation, and when Reagan left office, congressional interest in bank deregulation waned. Greenspan's interest did not, and as Fed chairman, he had ample opportunity to further it. With Greenspan's approval, the Fed in December 1996 issued a very aggressive ruling that allowed bank holding companies to own investment-banking operations that could contribute up to 25 percent of their revenues. For the largest bank holding companies, this effectively did away with Glass-Steagall; their explosive growth in commercial banking in the wake of the Riegle-Neal Act made a 25 percent ceiling for investment banking revenues an almost meaningless constraint.

The next step in Glass-Steagall repeal involved both the Fed and the Treasury. In 1998 the nation's second largest bank was Citicorp (soon-to-be FM Watch member Chase Manhattan Bank was the largest). John Reed, the chairman of Citicorp, and Sandy Weill, the chairman of Travelers Insurance Group, worked with Greenspan and Rubin to structure a proposed merger between their two firms in a manner that technically was illegal but conformed to the Fed's interpretation of Glass-Steagall. When the merger was announced in April 1998, the new merged entity, called Citigroup, would have to divest itself of Travelers' insurance operations unless Congress changed the banking laws within two years.

The Travelers-Citicorp merger "called the question" on Glass-Steagall, and at that point it was a foregone conclusion. Investment banks had opposed repeal, but they changed their stance after the Fed's 1996 holding company ruling when they realized that the barriers between commercial and investment banking were being eliminated but only in one direction. Banks and bank regulators had lobbied for Glass-Steagall repeal for over a decade, investment banks finally were in favor of it, and the clock was ticking on a potential unwind of the Citicorp-Travelers merger. Congress passed the Gramm-Leach-Bliley Act repealing Glass-Steagall in November 1999. On the day the act was passed, Summers said, "Today Congress voted to update the rules that have governed financial services since the Great Depression and replace them with a system for the twenty-first century. This historic legislation will better enable American companies to compete in the new economy." A milestone in banking deregulation had been achieved. Now it was time for Summers and Greenspan to turn their attention to putting more restrictions on the government-sponsored enterprises.

There is considerable irony in the fact that Frank Raines's move to the OMB in 1996 indirectly led to the decision by Summers in 2000 to seize an opportunity offered by Baker to publicly oppose Fannie Mae, which by then was being run by Raines. Raines's main goal as OMB director had been to engineer an agreement in Congress on an approach to a balanced budget. He did, and in fiscal year 1998, the federal budget was in surplus by $69 billion. The surplus rose to $126 billion in fiscal 1999 and to $236 billion in fiscal 2000. The Treasury, the Fed, and Fannie Mae all were affected by the shift in the budget from deficit to surplus, and the different ways we each reacted to it set the stage for what was to follow.

Debt market investors were discussing the implications of persistent budget surpluses as early as 1997. If the government did run surpluses, some maturing Treasury issues would run off without replacement, leaving investors with the need to find other securities to buy.

At Fannie Mae we sensed an opportunity to make our debt the security of choice for those investors. In December 1997, we announced that in 1998 we would begin issuing what we called Benchmark Notes. The core idea behind Benchmarks was to appeal to the buyers of Treasuries by replicating key features of Treasury's debt sales. Benchmark Notes would be issued in large dollar amounts—between $2 and $5 billion—to enhance their liquidity and would be sold on a predictable schedule announced well in advance. We said we would issue at least one 5- and 10-year Benchmark Note each quarter and other maturities on an as-needed basis.

We sold $42 billion in Benchmark Notes in 1998, and in 1999 we added Benchmark Bonds (with maturities longer than 10 years), Benchmark Bills (with maturities under a year), and Callable Benchmark Notes. The Benchmark program was a huge success. In 1999 we sold $114 billion in Benchmark securities, with more than one-third going to foreign investors. (Politically, we could and did point to the fact that Benchmarks were recycling trade deficit dollars back to the United States to support housing.) The success of our Benchmark program combined with the continued shrinkage in Treasury debt led many to speculate that at some point, corporate and other types of debt might be priced with respect to Fannie Mae Benchmark securities rather than Treasuries. The name we had given the program did not discourage such speculation.

Just as the shrinking supply of Treasuries provided an opportunity for Fannie Mae, it presented challenges to the Fed and the Treasury. The Fed purchased Treasury securities to add reserves to the banking system, and its holdings of Treasuries had grown along with the economy. With the amount of Treasury debt declining, the Fed had to decide on other types of securities to buy. Corporate bonds were problematic. The relatively small sizes of these bonds, coupled with the Fed's large appetite, easily could distort their market prices. The obvious alternative was GSE debt, but that was anathema to Greenspan; the last thing he wanted to do was institutionalize GSE debt in the workings of the U.S. monetary system. The Fed had begun to use GSE mortgage-backed securities as a vehicle for providing temporary reserves to the banking system (in the form of what were called repurchase agreements, or repos) in 1999, and it seemed only a matter of time before the Fed would have to start buying them on a permanent basis. That was not a prospect Greenspan relished.

Budget surpluses also complicated Treasury's debt management. With more debt maturing than Treasury needed to sell, they had to decide where along the yield curve to allow their debt to run off. Their decisions had implications for the liquidity of the various maturity sectors as well as for the nation's interest costs. In an attempt to balance competing debt management objectives, early in 2000 Treasury would begin buying back outstanding debt issues for the first time in 70 years.

As Treasury debt was shrinking, Fannie Mae debt was soaring. In 1998 and 1999, we had our fastest portfolio growth ever. At the end of 1997, our portfolio stood at $317 billion; by the end of 1999, it had reached $524 billion—an increase of over $200 billion and an average growth rate of 29 percent per year. This growth was entirely market driven. During and after the Russian debt crisis and the near-failure of Long-Term Capital Management, investors around the world bid more aggressively for Fannie Mae Benchmark securities than they did for GSE mortgage-backed securities, and we responded by issuing more of the debt those investors wanted and using the proceeds to buy the mortgage-backed securities they had less interest in. Politically, however, the portfolio growth that resulted from these actions could not have come at a worse time. Treasury debt was contracting, Fannie Mae debt was growing furiously, and investors openly were discussing when our Benchmark securities might replace Treasuries as the basis on which all fixed-income issues were evaluated and priced. For Summers, Greenspan, and our other opponents and critics, this was their worst GSE nightmare.

Treasury's Bombshell

It did not take long for Treasury to respond. Baker introduced H.R. 3703, the Housing Finance Regulatory Improvement Act, on

February 29, 2000. Among its components were the creation of a new regulator for Fannie Mae, Freddie Mac, and the Federal Home Loan Banks; tight new restrictions on what were termed "new activities" by the government-sponsored enterprises; and repeal of Treasury's discretionary (and by now symbolic) authority to purchase up to $2.25 billion in GSE debt. There was little support for this bill even in Baker's own subcommittee, but he insisted on holding hearings on it. He scheduled the first for March 22, and he asked Treasury to testify. This gave Summers an opening he could not pass up. After consultation with both the White House and Greenspan, Summers asked his undersecretary for domestic finance, Gary Gensler, to appear at Baker's hearing, and Summers armed him with testimony he knew would command attention.

Gensler began that testimony by noting the rapid growth of the government-sponsored enterprises. He cited the fact that "our government's fiscal discipline is leading to less Treasury debt," adding, "These factors have caused the GSEs to occupy a more central role in capital markets than ever before." He stated that "the GSEs' growing role in the capital markets is aided by the numerous benefits derived from their federal charters," which he went on to describe in detail. After a discussion of systemic risk, Gensler then addressed the specific provisions of H.R. 3703. Referring to what he called the Treasury's $2.25 billion "line of credit," Gensler dropped his bombshell: "Repeal of the line of credit," he said, "would be consistent with the congressional requirement that all GSE securities carry a disclaimer that they are not obligations of the U.S. government. Thus, as part of a package of reforms, we would support repeal of the line of credit." He went on to make a further recommendation on an issue *not* in the Baker bill: "GSE debt obligations are exempt from banks' investment securities limits," Gensler said. "We believe that Congress should seriously consider the best way to repeal such exceptions, including a sufficient transition period to prevent any market disruption."

This was the first time a senior Treasury official—or any top official in the government—had publicly endorsed or suggested a change in Fannie Mae's charter. The market reacted immediately and violently: prices of Fannie Mae debt plummeted, sending our borrowing costs soaring. Raines and our top public relations officials were out of the office when news of the Gensler testimony hit the wire, and a member of our communications staff asked me if I wished to respond. My practice was to make comments to the media only on Fannie Mae business issues, not on political ones, but in this case I made an exception. I put out a statement condemning Gensler's remarks, calling them "either inept or irresponsible."

The Gensler testimony, in my mind, embraced what I called the "onion theory" of our agency status. We had about a dozen charter attributes that collectively led our investors—particularly those overseas—to put our securities in a special credit category. Many of our opponents thought you could peel those attributes off one at a time, like layers of an onion, and that as you did so, our agency status would shrink proportionally. I believed our agency status wasn't an onion; it was a balloon. Either we had it or we didn't. If an agency attribute investors didn't care about was eliminated, nothing would happen, but if we lost an attribute they valued, the effects could be uncontrollable.

I thought there was a reasonable chance we could do away with the $2.25 billion Treasury borrowing authority, although I wasn't eager to test the proposition. I was considerably more troubled by a limit on banks' ability to buy our debt. From a systemic risk standpoint, it made little sense: most of the banks with large holdings of GSE debt were small community institutions, which if forced to sell it almost certainly would replace it with something riskier. My much larger issue, however, was that in March 2000, banks in the aggregate held over $200 billion in GSE debt. Were they to have to sell a large amount of that debt, who would buy it, and at what price? And wouldn't investors begin to anticipate another round of reductions in our agency attributes? I believed that Gensler, or Summers, had badly underestimated the possibility of destabilizing selling of our debt in response to the Gensler testimony, and my choice of words in criticizing it reflected that concern.

Treasury took exception to my comments, but their greater worry was the severity of the market's reaction. We made several calls the next day to both Treasury and the White House to reiterate our strong objections to the testimony and to urge a clarification. Later that afternoon, Gensler put out a statement saying that his testimony "was consistent with longstanding principles in this area" and that "it does not represent a change in the government's relationship with the GSEs." The latter was what the market had been waiting to hear, and with it things finally calmed down.

The Voluntary Initiatives

The matter did not end there, however. Shortly afterwards Summers called Raines and requested him to come to Treasury. He did, and when he was escorted into Summers's conference room, he was surprised to see Greenspan there as well. Raines recognized it as the sort of show of force the Fed and Treasury were used to putting on for the banks they regulated, in which they would call a banker in, inform them how they had transgressed, and tell them to go and sin no more. (The regulatory term for this was "moral suasion.") In their meeting with Raines, however, neither Summers nor Greenspan—both of whom Raines knew well from his days in the Clinton administration—ever asked him to do anything. Raines was expecting them to request that we stop growing our portfolio, but they never did. They merely emphasized that "something must be done," leaving it up to Raines to divine what that might be. Hoping to find a path to peace, Raines proposed a series of meetings between senior Fannie Mae and Treasury and Fed officials to determine their real concerns about us, so we could try to address them. Summers agreed to these meetings and to be their host.

We settled on an agenda of discussion topics at our initial session, which Summers and Raines attended but Greenspan did not (nor did he attend any future sessions). It was apparent at this first meeting that none of the top Treasury officials, including Summers and Gensler, had a particularly good understanding of Fannie Mae or our business. We proposed a set of briefings on the mortgage finance system and how we (and Freddie Mac) fit into it, along with presentations on the risks we took and how our management of those risks compared with other holders or guarantors of mortgages. Treasury in turn asked us to address the concentrations of interest rate and credit risk on our books and what they called the "implicit subsidy" they believed we received from our federal charter.

We held seven sessions over a two-month period to discuss these topics. Fannie Mae's team consisted of myself; Tom Donilon, our executive vice president for law and policy and a good friend of Summers; Peter Niculescu, senior vice president for portfolio strategy; and Arne Christensen, senior vice president for regulatory policy. Treasury's team was headed by Gensler and included half a dozen under- and assistant secretaries. Greenspan sent only one junior staffer, a long-time Fannie Mae critic, to represent the Fed. I prepared the materials for and led the discussions on the market, risk, and business concentration issues. We decided that the best way to deal with the subsidy question—which unlike the other topics was more a matter of theory and opinion than fact—was for us to prepare a paper for Summers containing our views and send a copy of it to Greenspan.

During the course of our meetings, we learned that Treasury's two major concerns about our business were that our agency status insulated us from market discipline—which Summers and Greenspan valued as superior to regulation in controlling the risks of banks and other financial institutions—and that a misstep in our risk management might make it impossible for us to roll over our maturing debt, triggering destabilizing effects for the rest of the financial system. We believed we could allay both concerns by agreeing to a set of initiatives responsive to them.

The centerpiece of these initiatives deliberately included two elements we knew Summers favored: more capital, and subordinated debt ("sub debt"). As the name indicates, the claims of holders of sub debt are junior to those of senior debt holders—and, for banks, depositors—giving sub debt holders strong incentives to closely monitor the risks of the companies that issue it. At the time of our meetings at Treasury, the Fed and Treasury were putting the finishing touches on a joint study required by the Gramm-Leach-Bliley Act of "the feasibility and desirability of a mandatory subordinated debt requirement for systemically important depository institutions"— that is, large banks. The recommendation of their study would be to do further research, but we knew that Summers personally was a strong advocate of mandatory sub debt issuance. We proposed to impose upon ourselves a discipline the Fed and Treasury had shied away from imposing on the large banks they regulated: we would issue subordinated debt at least twice a year, in an amount sufficient to bring our combined equity and sub debt to 4 percent of our assets within three years and keep it at that level.

To deal with Treasury's concern about loss of debt market access, we offered to maintain enough liquidity to sustain our activities for three months with no new debt issuance. Our remaining proposed initiatives were aimed at giving investors more information on our risks: we would make monthly disclosures of measures of our interest rate risk and quarterly disclosures on our credit risk, publish the results of our internal version of the 1992 risk-based capital stress test until OFHEO could complete theirs (which they still had not done), and obtain and publish a "risk to the government" rating from Standard & Poor's and a "bank financial strength" rating from Moody's. Because Treasury's concerns about GSEs were not limited to Fannie Mae, we sought and obtained Freddie Mac's agreement to undertake what we were calling the "six voluntary initiatives" if we did.

But we wanted something from Treasury in return. In exchange for the voluntary initiatives, we asked Treasury to work with us on a memorandum of understanding (MOU) that contained a set of statements we would make jointly about our business and risk management. We negotiated a document with Gensler's team that we were comfortable with, complete with signature lines. Raines signed the MOU on behalf of Fannie Mae, and we gave it to Treasury for Summers's signature.

Summers did not sign it. He did not tell us that he wouldn't sign it or that he wanted any changes made to it; he just didn't sign it. We were not going to agree to the voluntary initiatives without getting some acknowledgment from Treasury of the effectiveness of our risk management, so we waited. While we were waiting, Freddie Mac decided, on their own and without informing us, to offer the voluntary initiatives to Baker for nothing in exchange. We were furious when we found out what they had done, but it was a fait accompli. The media reported that Freddie Mac had negotiated the initiatives with Baker and that Fannie Mae had agreed only reluctantly and at the last minute to be included.

Baker called a press conference to announce the initiatives on October 19. He called them "a meaningful first step toward a major victory for American taxpayers" and said that they addressed his concerns about our safety and soundness, although he added that he still intended to pursue "reforms" of our business powers and regulation the following year. Summers said nothing at all. Treasury's official response was a low-key statement attributed to an assistant secretary who called the initiatives "useful ones that have the potential to promote market discipline and increase transparency," before noting that "there remains a range of issues with respect to the GSEs that warrant continuing attention from financial authorities, the Congress, and their regulators."

There was no substantive disagreement between Fannie Mae and Treasury on the facts relating to our business, and just as with the government studies four years earlier, Treasury made no recommendations for change in either our interest rate or credit risk management. Where we had run aground was over what we called our charter benefits and Summers called our subsidy. We summarized our position in a letter we sent to Greenspan, transmitting the paper we did for Summers on the subject:

> Our earnings are produced in competitive markets. They reflect both the efficiencies of our operations and the returns required competitively for the risks we manage. For that reason,

it is our view that the benefits stemming from our charter and our activities are not retained by Fannie Mae as excess earnings, but are passed through in a competitive, market-driven pricing process.

Summers, however, simply didn't agree with us, and that seemed to have been enough to keep him from signing the memorandum of understanding.

If so, we were back to ideology. If Summers and Greenspan thought Fannie Mae retained the benefit of a subsidy, that commercial banks did not, and that retained subsidies produced bad results irrespective of how well the risks of a "subsidized" company were managed, we were not going to get their support no matter what we did.

With the voluntary initiatives episode, Treasury formally took sides in the mortgage wars. In contrast to what Paul Volcker had done 10 years earlier, Treasury was not going to sign on to a deal that could make Fannie Mae stronger, even if it involved a reduction in taxpayer risk. Treasury's opposition was absolute. They, along with the Federal Reserve, were committed to constraining us and over time to replacing us as the foundation of the U.S. mortgage finance system with the free market alternatives they favored.

CHAPTER 9

Private-Label Mortgage-Backed Securities

T HERE WAS NO AMBIGUITY IN THE ATTITUDE OF TREASURY, THE Fed, and commercial banks and thrifts toward Fannie Mae's portfolio business. They opposed it—whether for ideological, competitive, or other reasons—and consistently sought to convince Congress to remove some or all of our charter benefits in order to raise our debt costs if not eliminate the portfolio altogether. These same groups took a different approach to our mortgage-backed securities guaranty business: rather than try to constrain it, they focused on developing a private-market alternative that could compete with it.

MBS, CMOs, and REMICs

Following its creation in 1968, Ginnie Mae was the first entity to issue mortgage-backed securities. Freddie Mac began issuing them shortly after that time (they called theirs participation certificates, or PCs). Both issued what were called "pass-through" securities, in which all interest and principal payments from the individual loans composing the securities were passed through directly to investors in proportion to their ownership. Ginnie Mae mortgage-backed securities were backed by the full faith and credit of the U.S. government and also contained loans insured by the FHA or the VA. Freddie Mac

PCs contained conventional, or nongovernment insured, loans and were backed only by the company, although investors took note of Freddie Mac's status as a government-sponsored enterprise in assessing the value of their guarantee.

In 1983, Freddie Mac and the First Boston Corporation issued the first collateralized mortgage obligation, or CMO. A CMO was a clever innovation aimed at dividing the universe of mortgage investors into segments. Unlike a traditional pass-through mortgage security, a CMO created different classes of security, called "tranches" (after the French word for "slice"). The first and simplest form of CMO was known as "fast pay, slow pay." It had three tranches. The first tranche received pro rata interest payments but also got *all* the principal payments—both regular amortization and prepayments—until it was paid off. As a consequence, the first, or fast-pay, tranche had a relatively short expected life. After the first tranche was retired, scheduled and unscheduled principal payments began going to the investors in the second tranche, who would continue to receive them until *they* were paid off. Only then would investors in the third, or slow-pay, tranche start to get principal payments. That gave the last tranche the longest expected life of the three.

The collateralized mortgage obligation did not change the prepayment uncertainty associated with the mortgages that backed it, but by creating different payment priorities, it produced more payment certainty for one tranche at the expense of another. That small difference was enough to bring new investors into the mortgage sector. Many different types of cash flow transformation could be made in a CMO, and Wall Street quickly developed a number of popular variations on the tranching scheme.

There was, however, a problem that held back both the volume of collateralized mortgage obligations and the amount of complexity Wall Street firms felt comfortable putting into them. The tax laws that applied to the transformation of cash flows within a trust structure—which was the vehicle a CMO used—were ambiguous. Under existing law, it was possible that some types of CMO cash flows could be subject to taxation at the pool level as well as at the investor level.

Wall Street firms and others interested in achieving the full potential of tranched mortgage-backed securities wanted more certainty about their tax treatment.

In 1985, serious discussions began about legislation to change the tax law governing structured mortgage transactions. The Reagan administration Treasury Department favored creating a new legal vehicle for issuing structured mortgage transactions that would resolve the tax issues, but it was firmly opposed to allowing Fannie Mae and Freddie Mac to utilize it. That potentially put us at odds with our Wall Street partners. They underwrote and traded the debt we issued to finance our portfolio purchases, and they issued and made markets in our mortgage-backed securities, but here our interests diverged. If they could align with Treasury and successfully exclude us as issuers of the new type of CMO, they would have this market to themselves.

Wall Street, the administration, and Congress had collaborated during the previous year on legislation to improve the competitiveness of what were known as "private-label" mortgage-backed securities. Salomon Brothers issued the first private-label mortgage-backed security, backed by mortgages originated by Bank of America, in 1977. The earliest types of private-label mortgage-backed securities were neither easy nor profitable to sell because they had cumbersome registration requirements and were not legal investments for most types of regulated financial institutions. To eliminate those impediments—and with the ultimate goal of putting private-label securities on an equal footing with GSE securities—the pioneer of Salomon Brothers' mortgage department, Lew Ranieri, had worked with the administration to draft the Secondary Mortgage Market Enhancement Act (SMMEA), which Congress passed in 1984.

To make private-label securities easier and less costly to issue, the drafters of SMMEA exempted them from state antifraud (or "blue sky") laws and registration requirements. To expand the securities' investor base, however, the drafters elected to follow a precedent set by the Securities and Exchange Commission in 1975, when it linked broker-dealer capital requirements to credit ratings received from one or more of the three national credit rating agencies (Standard & Poor's, Moody's, and Fitch). SMMEA similarly made private-label security tranches legal investments for federally and state-chartered banks and thrifts—as well for as insurance companies, pension funds, and other regulated entities—provided they carried investment-grade ratings from at least one of the three credit agencies. The rating agencies had no regulator themselves, but in SMMEA they nonetheless were made the de facto regulators of credit standards in the private-label securities market.

Yet even SMMEA could not make private-label mortgage-backed securities a competitive alternative for mortgages eligible for a Fannie Mae or a Freddie Mac guaranty, because of the value investors attached to our GSE status. That was why it was an easy call for Wall Street to use the cover provided by Treasury and do its best to keep Fannie Mae and Freddie Mac from being allowed to issue CMOs in the hoped-for new legal structure.

Salomon Brothers took the lead for Wall Street on the CMO initiative, with Ranieri driving the legislative strategy. The legislation he targeted was a comprehensive tax reform bill. Ranieri positioned the proposed CMO fix as a technical cleanup to the tax code, which succeeded with the House Ways and Means Committee but got no traction in the Senate Finance Committee. Wall Street could get a CMO bill through the House, but getting it through the Senate required Main Street. For that, Ranieri was forced to turn to Maxwell and Fannie Mae. By emphasizing how the CMO taxation fix would benefit home buyers—as opposed to just financial firms, which had been the essence of Ranieri's pitch—we were able to convince key members of the Senate Finance Committee to agree to a provision both we and Wall Street could support. The Tax Reform Act of 1986 that finally passed in December contained a section authorizing real estate mortgage investment conduits, or REMICs, as a new form of special purpose vehicle for issuing structured mortgage-backed securities.

In joining forces to get the REMIC provision in the Tax Reform Act, Ranieri and Maxwell had not agreed on the role of Fannie Mae and Freddie Mac as issuers; they agreed only to move the fight to a different forum. The act gave Fannie Mae and Freddie Mac temporary authority to issue REMICs but left to our regulators (HUD and the Federal Home Loan Bank Board, respectively) the task of determining whether we should be given this authority on a permanent basis. Wall Street did not pull any punches in making their case against it. Their argument was that keeping us out of the REMIC business was a rare opportunity for the government to arrest the growing "federalization" of the mortgage market. On our side, we emphasized that preventing us from issuing REMICs would result in fewer market efficiencies and higher REMIC issuance costs, with those costs ultimately being borne by home buyers.

As with most issues involving Fannie Mae, the question of our REMIC authority was settled politically. HUD Secretary Sam Pierce, a Reagan appointee, was sympathetic to the free-market argument made by Wall Street. We believed REMIC authority was critical to our future, and fearing we would not be able to convince Pierce to give it to us on the merits, we went back to Capitol Hill. We had good friends on the staff of the House Banking Committee, and they were able to convince the leaders of that committee to put a provision in a piece of pending legislation that stripped HUD of its authority to approve our new mortgage programs. That got Pierce's attention. Pierce wanted to retain program authority over Fannie Mae more than he wanted to prevent us from issuing REMICs. One Saturday morning during a meeting he was having with his leadership team, Maxwell got a call from Pierce's assistant offering a trade: HUD would give us $15 billion worth of REMIC issuance authority if we would ask the Banking Committee to pull the program authority provision. The trade was agreed to and made. Shortly afterwards, HUD lifted the cap on our REMIC authority entirely.

Resolution of the REMIC battle made it official. Fannie Mae and Freddie Mac would be the dominant secondary market entities in the conventional conforming loan market—consisting of mortgages below our loan limit that met our underwriting standards—and we would set the standards and determine the rules for business transacted in this market. In the so-called "nonconforming" loan market—consisting of mortgages Fannie Mae and Freddie Mac either could not buy (because of their loan balance) or would not buy (because of their risk features)—Wall Street firms as issuers of private-label mortgage-backed securities would be the dominant secondary market entities, and they, along with the credit rating agencies, would set the standards and determine the rules governing *that* market.

The Very Different Risks of GSE and Private-Label Mortgage-Backed Securities

SMMEA had been passed to spur the development of a private-market alternative to Fannie Mae and Freddie Mac mortgage-backed securities. Private-label mortgage-backed securities indeed are alternatives to GSE mortgage-backed securities, but because of their structural differences, they are by no means substitutes for them.

The most critically important difference between a Fannie Mae MBS (or a Freddie Mac PC) and a private-label MBS is the nature of the credit protection provided to the investor. Investors in a Fannie Mae MBS are protected by the company's corporate guaranty of the timely payment of interest and principal, irrespective of how the loans backing the MBS perform. If Fannie Mae misjudges the quality of the loans in a Fannie Mae MBS, it's the company's problem; Fannie Mae bears the credit losses, and the investor still gets paid in full as long as Fannie Mae remains able to satisfy its obligations. In contrast, credit protection for investors in a private-label MBS is provided by structural credit enhancements built into the security by its issuer. If those credit enhancements turn out to be inadequate, it's the investor's problem; there is no independent guarantor to absorb the excess losses.

As the private-label market evolved, Wall Street firms and issuers developed a number of mechanisms and techniques for providing credit enhancement. These included overcollateralization (putting enough loans in a structure that investors still could get all their money back even after a certain percentage of the loans went bad), third-party insurance (a form of corporate guaranty, made by an entity other than the issuer), and letters of credit. But what became by far the most commonly used technique for private-label mortgage-backed securities was what is called the "senior-subordinated" structure.

Senior-subordinated structures work similarly to simple CMOs, except instead of prepayments being allocated to tranches in priority order, it is credit losses that are allocated that way. Senior-subordinated securities include an equity piece, typically retained by the issuer, that takes the initial amount of credit losses (anywhere between 1 and 4 percent, depending on the riskiness of the underlying loans). Losses over that amount are absorbed by the holder of the most junior tranche; when that tranche has no principal left, losses then are borne by the holder of the next most junior tranche, and so on throughout the structure.

Pursuant to SMMEA, credit rating agencies played a crucial role in the structuring of a senior-subordinated private-label mortgage-backed security. Using their own statistical models of loan performance, together with the product and risk characteristics for a particular group of loans provided by the issuer, rating agency personnel determined how many loss-absorbing junior tranches a senior-subordinated private-label MBS containing those loans needed to have—and what percentage of the total security size those junior tranches needed to make up—in order for the rest of the tranches in the structure to merit AA or AAA ratings.

The theory is a sound one. If a senior-subordinated MBS has enough loss-absorbing junior tranches, even in a highly adverse credit environment, the most senior tranches should have a vanishingly small chance of not being repaid in full and thus could safely be accorded AA or AAA ratings. But there is one glaring weakness in the design of a senior-subordinated private-label MBS compared with a Fannie Mae MBS: in a Fannie Mae MBS, the interests of the issuer are aligned with those of the investor; in a senior-subordinated private-label MBS, they are not.

Transactions in the secondary mortgage market always have had issues of risk alignment. In the primary mortgage market— where a local lender makes a loan to a borrower and retains it in portfolio—the lender has a strong financial incentive to underwrite that loan properly because it will bear the consequence of the borrower not being able to repay it. That incentive changes when a lender makes a loan for sale to or guaranty by Fannie Mae (or Freddie Mac) and transfers the risk of credit loss to the company. With Fannie Mae as a purchaser or guarantor, loans with higher amounts of credit risk actually may be more profitable for the lender, because it can charge higher fees to borrowers of riskier loans and also do a greater volume of business if it makes higher-risk loans as well as less risky ones. It was precisely because of these conflicting financial incentives that Fannie Mae devoted so many resources to mortgage credit analysis and the refinement of the underwriting standards we required our lenders to follow.

The holder of a Fannie Mae mortgage-backed security benefits from the due diligence the company has an incentive to do on its own behalf as a shareholder-owned company. If Fannie Mae properly assesses the risks it assumes in its credit guaranty business—and charges a fee that covers those risks and allows for a competitive return on its invested capital—it will be stronger financially, and its guaranty of the investor's MBS will be worth more, even before consideration of any potential support that may be forthcoming from the U.S. government as a result of Fannie Mae's GSE status.

In contrast, due diligence done on behalf of the investor in a senior-subordinated private-label mortgage-backed security is conducted by the credit rating agencies, whose incentives to accurately identify credit risk can conflict with their goals as profit-making enterprises. Rating agencies are paid for their ratings of private-label mortgage-backed securites by the securities' issuers. If a rating agency is too conservative in the amount of subordination it requires in a proposed private-label transaction and the issuer does not go ahead with it, the rating agency does not get paid at all. On the reverse side, if the rating agency requires too little subordination in a proposed transaction and investors in the more highly rated tranches experience losses, the rating agency itself suffers no adverse financial consequences. Irrespective of the capability or the intent of the professionals working for them, the role the rating agencies are asked to play in the private-label MBS credit enhancement process, along with the manner in which they are compensated, creates a built-in bias toward underestimating credit risk that runs counter to the interests of the private-label security investor.

The ratings bias inherent in private-label securitization is made worse by the fact that the originators of loans financed by these securities have an unambiguous incentive to put higher-risk mortgages into them. Because Fannie Mae is a corporate guarantor, it sets limits on the types of credit risk it will accept in the loans that go into a Fannie Mae MBS. Similar limits do not exist for private-label securities; riskier loans simply mean more or larger junior tranches will be required to provide protection for the AA- and AAA-rated tranches. For a mortgage originator using private-label mortgage-backed securities as a financing outlet, the riskiest loans present the greatest opportunity for profit. If an originator can convince a group of borrowers that their loans are very risky, it can charge them large origination fees as well as very high interest rates. And if the originator then can convince the rating agencies that these same loans are *not* that risky, the ratings put on the tranches in the private-label security will result in interest payments to investors that are less than what the originator receives from the borrowers. The originator will pocket the difference.

Strong incentives for the originators of loans financed by private-label securities to make high-risk mortgages and understate their riskiness, weak or conflicting incentives on the part of rating agencies to detect excessive credit risk in a proposed private-label transaction, a senior-subordinated structure that once agreed to by an issuer and a rating agency has no flexibility to accommodate credit losses that are worse than envisioned at the outset, and the lack of a corporate guarantor whose role is to absorb excess losses all make a private-label mortgage-backed security a markedly more risky instrument than a Fannie Mae MBS.

Promoters of the private-label market as a competitor to GSE securitization—which included Wall Street firms, the Federal

Reserve, and the Treasury—ignored these critical structural differences when they depicted the AAA-rated private-label MBS as simply the private market version of AAA-rated GSE mortgage-backed securities. They most assuredly were not, and any investors who believed them to be did so at their peril.

Subprime One

The two sectors that benefited the most from the structuring technology of private-label securities and the absence of significant restrictions on or regulation of the types of loans that could go into them were subprime mortgages and mortgages to finance manufactured housing, or mobile homes.

Subprime mortgage lending had its roots in the consumer finance industry, made up of companies like Household Finance, Beneficial, and The Associates. Customers of these companies traditionally had poor credit, could not qualify for bank loans, and were willing to pay high interest rates for either debt consolidation loans or loans to purchase consumer hard goods. Prior to the 1980s, consumer finance companies did not offer mortgages to their customers because state usury laws prevented them from charging high enough interest rates to compensate them for the credit risk they believed they were taking. In 1980, however, the Depository Institutions Deregulation and Monetary Control Act removed state usury ceilings on mortgages, and not long afterwards the Tax Reform Act of 1986 eliminated the tax deductibility of interest on consumer loans but retained it for residential mortgages.

The loss of tax-deductibility on consumer loans coupled with the legality of charging higher interest rates made mortgage lending—particularly second mortgage and cash-out refinance lending—much more attractive to finance companies. And Fannie Mae and Freddie Mac effectively ceded these lenders a very large customer base. Although this would change in the mid-1990s, at the time neither of us purchased or guaranteed mortgages made to individuals with bad credit, no matter how high their incomes or how much equity they put or had in their homes. In fact, a subprime loan then was defined with respect to Fannie Mae and Freddie Mac underwriting standards: the loans we would buy or guarantee were deemed to be prime, and any loans below those standards were "subprime."

Subprime mortgage loans were ideal material for private-label securitization. Wall Street firms could provide subprime lenders with one-stop shopping for their financing needs—first extending short-term credit, called warehouse lines, that enabled lenders to keep newly made mortgages on their balance sheets until they could be packaged for sale, then working with the rating agencies to create private-label security structures for virtually any type or quality of loan a lender originated, and finally finding investors for the various tranches of securities that resulted from this process.

The first subprime mortgage boom was triggered by a collapse in the market for exotic types of REMIC and derivative securities. The variety and complexity of REMIC structures increased greatly following the Tax Reform Act of 1986. Sharp and persistent increases in interest rates in 1994 caused many investors, and a few Wall Street firms, to suffer large and in some cases fatal losses from complex REMICs and derivatives. These securities quickly fell out of favor, and for many investors, AAA-rated subprime mortgage securities seemed like the best alternative way to get additional yield for what appeared to be little additional risk. Between 1994 and 1998, the volume of subprime loan securitizations more than quadrupled. Spurred by readily available credit and national advertising campaigns by companies like The Money Store, subprime lending caught on with the public. And it became extremely profitable for lenders. Existing subprime lenders did so well that many new ones were formed. Wall Street firms eagerly underwrote a number of high-profile initial public offerings for subprime companies during this time.

The first subprime lending and securitization boom was short-lived. Just as sharply rising interest rates in 1994 had sparked it, an abrupt reversal in interest rates extinguished it even more quickly. In the fall of 1998, the one-two punch of the Russian debt crisis and the liquidity squeeze and subsequent failure of the hedge fund

Long-Term Capital Management caused interest rates to plummet. Investors fled risky financial assets for safer investments like Treasury securities and Fannie Mae debt. Interest spreads between Treasuries and subprime securities widened dramatically, and the market for new subprime issues dried up almost overnight. Wall Street firms stopped lending to subprime originators, who then were unable to obtain financing from any source. Interest rates at their lowest levels since the 1950s led large numbers of borrowers with subprime loans to refinance them. Many subprime lenders had assumed their securitized loans would have long average lives, and they had booked income on those loans in advance. That income had to be reversed when the loans were refinanced. Coming on top of everything else, earnings restatements proved too much for many subprime lenders to survive. Large numbers of them failed.

Nobody, including the Federal Reserve and the Treasury, connected the boom and bust in subprime mortgages with the way in which they had been financed. The subprime collapse occurred in the context of a broader financial crisis that devastated other high-risk markets and instruments, and because most subprime lenders were smaller specialty firms that did home-equity rather than purchase money lending, their demise had only an indirect effect on home sales and housing starts and therefore little impact on the overall economy.

The subprime meltdown was easy for investors and regulators to dismiss as a freak event of relatively little consequence. Much less understandable is how anyone possibly could have missed the significance of what happened when Wall Street and the rating agencies met the manufactured housing industry.

A Dress Rehearsal for the Crisis

Loans for manufactured housing, or mobile homes, looked on the surface like residential mortgages. They were anything but. Most manufactured housing loans were made by manufactured home builders' captive finance subsidiaries, whose dual objectives of facilitating sales and maintaining underwriting discipline conflicted. The pricing on manufactured housing was opaque, with added fees and charges that raised the prices of the homes but not their resale values. High sales commissions increased the chance of improper valuation. Finally, many if not most buyers of manufactured homes had below-average incomes, weak credit histories, and few financial reserves, making them relatively poor credit risks. A manufactured housing loan was an amalgam of a consumer finance loan and a sub-prime mortgage, collateralized by an asset that was notoriously difficult to value.

Manufactured housing was definitely outside the reach of financing by Fannie Mae or Freddie Mac, so it was fair game for Wall Street and the rating agencies. Still, their decision to get into the sector when they did was curious. Manufactured housing historically had been financed with 12- to 15-year fully amortizing loans. That made sense, because shorter-term loans repaid principal more quickly and built a cushion of protection for the lender or investor. But in a move to increase mobile home affordability in the early 1990s, the industry had moved to 20- to 30-year loans, often with very low down payments. Virtually no data existed on the performance of these loans in the financing of manufactured housing because they were so new.

Notwithstanding this fact—made more problematic by the complex relationship between manufactured home builders and their financing subsidiaries and the idiosyncrasies of the asset class—Wall Street and the rating agencies determined that manufactured housing was ripe for private-label securitization.

Mobile home lenders suddenly finding themselves with easy access to a deep source of low-cost financing took full advantage of it. Once the rating agencies specified the requirements for AA and AAA ratings, manufactured home loan originators met those requirements, then added new types of risk the rating agencies either did not recognize, understand, or know about. Many involved costs that could be rolled into the purchase price and financed, such as built-in accessories or even the cost of travel to the dealership. Securitized mobile home loans with stated loan-to-value ratios of 90 percent often had actual loan-to-value ratios of well over 100 percent, putting borrowers under water before their homes left the dealer's lot.

Under the impetus of cheap, readily available financing and liberalized underwriting practices, sales of manufactured housing skyrocketed. Between 1992 and 1998, shipments of manufactured homes increased by 74 percent, while over the same period starts of "site-built" single-family homes rose by only 20 percent.

Fannie Mae did not escape the lure of the mobile home frenzy. We were very much aware that mobile homes had risen from less than 20 percent of single-family housing construction in 1992 to nearly a quarter of it in 1998. We felt we should not ignore this market, but at the same time we knew that manufactured housing loans had credit risks that were fundamentally different from loans on site-built homes. Several of our senior executives made visits to manufactured home builders to learn more about that industry, and we generally were impressed by what we found. On one of those visits, our president, Larry Small, asked about construction quality. The builder's response was, "All our homes are tested by being towed down the highway at seventy miles per hour; how many site builders can say that?"

We decided to enter the market cautiously. Not everyone was enthusiastic about the idea—some disparagingly referred to manufactured housing loans as "deals on wheels"—but collectively we agreed that modest purchases of AAA-rated tranches of private-label manufactured housing securities would enable us to gain experience on the performance of these loans without taking on their credit risk directly. We purchased about $10 billion in manufactured housing securities in the late 1990s. The experience we got from these securities was not what we had in mind when we bought them.

The financing-driven surge in manufactured home sales was not sustainable. Sales began to fall in 1999, and by 2001 they were below where they had been when the lending and building booms began. Unsold inventories of mobile homes drove prices lower, triggering waves of delinquencies and defaults on poorly underwritten loans made previously. With falling sales of new units, servicers of manufactured housing loans found it hard to sell foreclosed mobile homes at any price. Rising defaults and astronomical loss severities led the rating agencies to belatedly begin downgrading private-label manufactured housing securities, causing their prices to plunge. Many investors, including Fannie Mae, took significant write-downs on their holdings of supposedly riskless AAA-rated tranches beginning in 2002 and 2003.

The boom and subsequent collapse of the manufactured housing industry was as clear a demonstration of the weaknesses in the private-label mortgage securitization model as it was possible to have. All of the elements were there: an absence of third-party credit standards, mortgage lenders introducing risky new products or loan features into a market, rating agencies attempting to make risk assessments on these products and features despite a lack of adequate or applicable historical experience, and a combination of relaxed underwriting and ample credit availability bringing in previously unqualified borrowers who pushed demand and prices well above sustainable levels, from which they subsequently plummeted.

The Federal Reserve and Treasury, incredibly, drew no lessons whatsoever from this experience. Their unwavering commitment to a free-market alternative to the mortgage securitizations of Fannie Mae and Freddie Mac seemingly made it impossible for them to acknowledge the obvious and irremediable flaws in the private-label securitization mechanism they championed.

Regulators' blindness to what they did not wish to see was a failure of monumental consequence. At the very time investors were assessing their losses on the AA- and AAA-rated private-label manufactured housing securities they owned, the market for private-label subprime mortgage securities was reconstituting itself and gathering steam, ready to trigger exactly the same sequence of events all over again. Only this time the victims would not be the borrowers of and investors in home-equity and manufactured housing loans; they would be the home buyers and investors in the entire U.S. single-family housing market.

CHAPTER 10

A Gathering Storm
of Opposition

WHEN GEORGE W. BUSH TOOK OFFICE ON JANUARY 20, 2001, Larry Summers left Treasury and was replaced as secretary by Paul O'Neill. O'Neill combined Washington policy experience with a highly successful career in business. In the early 1960s, O'Neill had been a systems analyst at the Veterans Administration before moving to the OMB in 1967, where he rose to become deputy director in 1974 under President Ford. O'Neill joined International Paper when Ford left office in 1977. In 1987 he was named chairman and CEO of Alcoa, the world's largest producer of aluminum. He remained at Alcoa until his retirement in 2000.

Frank Raines and O'Neill knew each other from their service together on the board of a nonprofit called Manpower Demonstration Research Corp in the 1990s, and they had their OMB experience in common. Two days after O'Neill was sworn in as secretary, Raines went to see him. The timing of Raines's visit was deliberate. He wanted to brief O'Neill on Fannie Mae and our business before Greenspan could get to him with *his* version of the Fannie Mae story. O'Neill's business perspective and OMB background made it easy for him to grasp the most important message Raines wished to convey: that the real Fannie Mae was a very different and much more sophisticated company than the one portrayed by our Washington adversaries.

Raines's briefing paid an immediate dividend. A reporter from Bloomberg News interviewed O'Neill five days into his job. The reporter prefaced a question with a reference to "the subsidies Fannie Mae and Freddie Mac receive," and O'Neill interjected, "No, that is not right . . . They don't receive a subsidy." When the reporter demurred ("Okay, we can debate that point later . . .") and persisted with a line of questioning premised on false assumptions, O'Neill did not allow himself to be led. Instead, he went to a broader point, saying:

> One of the things that I am working on very hard is to raise the level of debate in our society about things like this so that we get the real facts on the table . . . I really find it not helpful at all to the making of intelligent policy to use selective facts to try to achieve a purpose because I don't think it's in the interest of the American people.

O'Neill's insistence on substance over spin was refreshing, and on the Fannie Mae issue it worked to our advantage. But it was not as well received elsewhere. Before his first two years were over, O'Neill's persistent criticisms of the Bush tax cuts and the war in Iraq had cost him his job.

The Regulators: Greenspan and Falcon

The change from Summers to O'Neill at Treasury deprived Baker of an ally in his quest to address the remaining two items on his GSE agenda—regulation and business powers. It also defused Greenspan. Greenspan did not want to be seen as taking on the government-sponsored enterprises himself. He liked to work through Treasury to expand his sphere of influence in areas in which he had an interest but were beyond the authority of the Fed to accomplish directly, and Baker's taking up the FM Watch cause had given him a perfect opportunity to do that on the GSE issue. Summers was a sympathetic and willing collaborator. Treasury took the lead in proposing changes to the GSEs' charters, and Treasury's high profile on the Baker bill allowed Greenspan to lend his stature to it through public comments that were supportive of the legislation but vague enough to keep him outside the debate personally. O'Neill's lack of interest in what Baker called "GSE reform" closed off that avenue of influence for Greenspan for the duration of O'Neill's tenure.

Greenspan's opposition to Fannie Mae was ideological and almost entirely based on our mortgage portfolio. I had been running the portfolio business for 15 years. The first few times I either read or heard about Greenspan saying something about the portfolio that I knew was incorrect, I was puzzled. He was a world-class economist who almost certainly knew better. After one of these instances, I suggested to Raines that we go and see Greenspan to give him the right information. Raines told me it wasn't necessary. "He knows that," Raines said. I saw Greenspan once a year—at Raines's annual Christmas party—but otherwise had no personal or business relationship with him. Raines met with Greenspan at the Fed three or four times a year. He was able to explain the portfolio business to Greenspan as well as I could, and he did. Greenspan simply dismissed his explanations and went on saying whatever suited his beliefs and objectives.

One such statement of Greenspan's was that Fannie Mae's portfolio had no effect on either the supply or the cost of funds to housing and served only to boost our profits. Another was that we had a lower funding cost than banks. To reinforce both assertions, Greenspan pejoratively referred to the portfolio as "the big fat gap"—a reference to the fact that the portfolio's 100 basis point, or 1 percentage point, net interest margin (its interest income less interest expense, expressed as a percentage of the mortgage balance) was five times the roughly 20 basis point average fee we charged for guaranteeing a loan as a mortgage-backed security.

Fannie Mae's portfolio linked the bond and mortgage markets. Whenever mortgage rates rose relative to our debt costs—whether because of market events or because, as during refinance periods, large volumes of new fixed-rate mortgages required higher interest rates for investors to absorb them—we would issue debt (both bullet and callable) in the bond market and use the proceeds to buy loans in the mortgage market. We would continue to do this until mortgage rates fell back closer to our debt costs, at which point portfolio purchases became less attractive to us. We stood to profit from these purchases, but home buyers benefited as well. Our portfolio was an added source of mortgage demand, and the portfolio's purchases kept mortgage yields closely tied to our debt costs. Far from having no value, Fannie Mae's portfolio was a critical complement to our credit guaranty business, ensuring that home buyers always had access to the cheapest source of capital.

To understand why it was false to say that the government-sponsored enterprises had a lower funding cost than banks, all one had to do was look at bank balance sheets: in 2001, banks held over $200 billion in GSE debt as assets, which they financed with their own borrowings. Had the rates on GSE debt truly been less than what banks paid for their funding, all those investments would have lost money, and there would have been no reason for banks to make them. Banks' own actions in holding all the GSE debt they did proved indisputably that they had the lower borrowing costs. There really was no mystery here. Fannie Mae and Freddie Mac had no source of funding cheaper than the debt we issued in the capital markets. Nearly half of commercial banks' funding came from federally insured deposits, which paid much lower rates than any debt we could issue. In making their funding cost comparisons, however, our critics simply ignored insured bank deposits; they compared our capital market debt only with banks' capital market debt. And, yes, if you elected not to count the half of banks' funding that carried an explicit government guarantee and was their cheapest, then Fannie Mae debt, with its implicit guarantee, *did* have a lower cost than the rest of bank funding.

The "big fat gap" label was almost as disingenuous. The average net interest margin for the commercial banks Greenspan regulated was over 300 basis points—more than three times the 100 basis point margin of Fannie Mae's portfolio. (The 300 basis point bank net interest margin was true for all sizes of institutions—small, medium, and large.) Ours was so much lower partly because we did not have low-cost government-insured consumer deposits, but mainly because we did a lot more hedging than banks did. We could have had a 300 basis point net interest margin had we financed the portfolio with short-term debt. Instead, to reduce our risk, we issued more expensive intermediate- and long-term debt and spent still more on callable debt and derivatives to protect against interest rate swings. Those hedges added about 200 basis points to our interest costs and reduced our net interest margin by a like amount. But they brought us no credit from our ideological critics, including Greenspan, who would have continued to claim that our portfolio business was risky and unnecessary no matter how well we managed it.

Greenspan's opposition to and mischaracterizations of Fannie Mae's business were illustrative of the regulatory disadvantages we faced as our battle for market supremacy with large bank and non-bank lenders intensified. The vast majority of these lenders were regulated primarily if not exclusively by the Federal Reserve and Treasury. The Fed and Treasury did not believe in close federal regulation for any of the institutions they supervised; to the contrary, they actively sought to deregulate them further and on top of that to increase their business powers and assist their competitive position however and whenever they could. Yet the Fed and Treasury *did* believe in, and advocated forcefully for, tighter regulation of and restrictions on the GSEs. And then there was Fannie Mae's own safety and soundness regulator—the Office of Federal Housing Enterprise Oversight, or OFHEO. OFHEO was unlike any other financial regulator anywhere.

OFHEO was created in 1992 after intense debate about what type of safety and soundness regulation, and what regulator, would best achieve the government's complex mix of objectives of minimizing the risk Fannie Mae and Freddie Mac's operations posed to taxpayers, placing as few impediments as possible in the way of the fulfillment of our charter mission, and allowing us to earn competitive returns on the capital provided by our shareholders. Congress ultimately determined that a special-purpose institution placed within but independent of our program regulator, HUD, and with specifically defined and limited regulatory powers and duties, was the right choice.

Not everyone agreed with that choice, including many who joined OFHEO after they became operational. OFHEO's first director was a low-key individual named Aida Alvarez. Alvarez was a municipal bond specialist with First Boston who earlier in her career had been a journalist and then a television news anchor in New York. The secretary of HUD, Henry Cisneros, had introduced her to President Clinton, and he appointed her to head OFHEO in June 1993. Alvarez's first task was to get her new agency staffed and running. Not surprisingly, most of the people interested in and qualified for the senior positions at OFHEO came either from Capitol Hill or a government agency, such as Treasury or the CBO. The deputy director hired by Alvarez was Mark Kinsey, who had been at Treasury and worked on the GSE legislation, and as OFHEO's chief economist she hired Pat Lawler, formerly a senior staffer on the Senate Banking Committee.

At the beginning of his second term, Clinton nominated Alvarez to be administrator of the U.S. Small Business Administration. Alvarez accepted the nomination, and upon her departure from OFHEO in February 1997, Kinsey became that agency's acting director. He remained in this position for two and a half years, until in September 1999 the Senate confirmed the appointment of a young Texas lawyer named Armando Falcon to be the next director of OFHEO.

Falcon was the son of an aircraft technician, one of six children, raised outside San Antonio. He attended the University of Texas Law School and Harvard's Kennedy School of Government and went into private practice before being hired in 1990 by House Banking Committee Chairman Henry Gonzalez to serve as the committee's general counsel. Falcon left that job in 1997 to return to San Antonio to run in a Democratic primary race for Congress, which he lost. He came back to Washington, D.C., and was working as a consultant to OFHEO when Clinton nominated him to a five-year term as OFHEO's next director.

Two developments just prior to Falcon's appointment gave impetus to the contentious relationship he and Fannie Mae would have throughout his tenure as director. In April 1999, OFHEO issued their long-awaited notice of proposed rulemaking (NPR) to implement the risk-based capital standard mandated by the 1992 legislation, and Fannie Mae's response to it was highly critical. Then, two months later, FM Watch was formed.

As Fannie Mae's regulator, OFHEO was a primary target for FM Watch. Next to Congress, OFHEO had a greater ability to influence our business than any other entity, and it was no secret that there were many senior people at OFHEO, including Kinsey and Lawler, who were sympathetic to the objectives of the group's members and organizers. It is highly likely that while consulting at OFHEO, Falcon was exposed to both the supporters and the messaging of FM Watch. Whether he was or not, an early hire he made as director left little doubt about his awareness of and attitude toward the group. In March 2000, Falcon brought on as his general counsel a man named Alfred Pollard, who previously had been chief lobbyist for the Financial Services Roundtable (FSR). Formerly the Bankers Roundtable, the FSR was a lobbying organization that represented the 100 largest commercial banks, insurance, and investment banking companies, and it was a charter member of FM Watch.

OFHEO's notice of proposed rulemaking (NPR) for their risk-based capital standard, when finally published after five years of development, took up 217 triple-column pages in the Federal Register. The NPR confirmed our worst fears about the approach OFHEO had insisted on taking to implement the standard, and our comments on the rule, both public and private, reflected that opinion. As we learned when he became director, Falcon took great exception to our reaction. He viewed it as a challenge to OFHEO as an institution and as unwillingness on our part to submit to tough regulation. It was neither. We legitimately believed that the NPR was a bad rule, one that by not accurately capturing the risks we were taking would create a conflict between our regulatory and business risk management incentives and at the same time would place unwarranted and arbitrary penalties on many different aspects of the business we did, particularly in affordable housing.

We filed a comment letter on the NPR, spoke with OFHEO about it, and also made our objections known to the administration and to the OMB, which had to approve the rule. Our preference was to have OFHEO scrap the NPR entirely and redo it following an approach that determined Fannie Mae and Freddie Mac's required risk-based capital using the companies' internal risk models, run with OFHEO's stress assumptions. Failing that, we identified about a dozen key fixes to the NPR that if implemented would make it more workable and less distortive. As had been the case from the beginning, OFHEO would not change their approach to the standard, and they also were resistant to our suggested fixes. A last-ditch appeal to the OMB was our only alternative and, over Falcon's objections, we pursued it.

The final risk-based capital regulation had to be cleared by the White House's Office of Information and Regulatory Affairs (OIRA), a part of the OMB. In November 2000, Tom Donilon and I went to see them. The OIRA meeting was held in the Old Executive Office Building, and the driver of the car we took there had been allowed to enter West Executive Avenue, which runs between the Old EOB and the White House, and to park and wait close by. Our meeting was not successful. As we got back into the car to leave, our driver was told by security to stay where he was. The president was walking out of the White House, and all traffic on the grounds of the complex had to cease. While we were waiting, Donilon saw White House Chief of Staff John Podesta coming from the West Wing to the Old EOB. Donilon knew Podesta, and he called out to him because he wanted to introduce me. Podesta came up to the car, reached through the open back window to shake my hand, and said in his best Michael Corleone imitation, "I just want you to know this isn't personal, it's strictly business." I badly wanted to ask him whose business it was to allow the OFHEO capital rule to go through essentially as proposed, but I knew he wouldn't tell me, so I didn't. My guess was Treasury.

One further incident added to Falcon's mistrust of us. When Baker announced the voluntary initiatives, it was painfully apparent that OFHEO had known nothing about them beforehand. Falcon professed to be unperturbed by that, but in fact he was deeply resentful; he felt we had diminished the stature of his agency by not having involved them. What he did not know, and we could not tell him, was that when we began our discussions with Treasury that led to the initiatives, Treasury specifically instructed us not to tell OFHEO what we were doing. Fannie Mae was not alone in our assessment of OFHEO as a poor regulator.

Political Quiet from Washington

The first two years of the Bush administration turned out to be unexpectedly hospitable to Fannie Mae politically. Treasury did not engage on the GSE reform issue while O'Neill was secretary. Greenspan as a consequence remained on the sidelines. After elections to the Senate produced an even number of Republicans and Democrats, control of that body switched to the Democrats in June when Jim Jeffords of Vermont announced he would leave the Republican party, register as an independent, and caucus with the Democrats. At that point, Maryland Senator Paul Sarbanes became chairman of the Banking Committee. He was unlikely to consider, let alone pass, any legislation adverse to Fannie Mae's interests. In the House, Baker had a new full committee chairman—Mike Oxley of Ohio—who was less tolerant of Baker's showcase GSE hearings with no chance of legislation than his predecessor, Jim Leach of Iowa, had been. The biggest surprise, however, was that President Bush embraced minority home ownership as a national objective and in 2002 was publicly praising Frank Raines and Fannie Mae for the leadership we were showing in this area.

Minority home ownership had been a top priority for Raines from the time he became Fannie Mae's chairman in 1999. The home ownership rate for minorities was more than 20 percentage points below the average for the country as a whole, and Raines did not know why. From his seats on the boards of PepsiCo and AOL, he saw that each company did extensive research on segments of their customer base in a way Fannie Mae did not. Raines hired a seasoned marketing executive named Vada Hill—who most recently had been chief marketing officer at Taco Bell and had developed their famous "talking Chihuahua" campaign—to help us determine how to better connect the various segments of the consumer market with our products. Hill studied all segments of the home-buying market, but his focus was on African-Americans and Hispanics.

From Hill's work we learned that the circumstances, beliefs, motivations, and behaviors of minority borrowers were fundamentally different from those of what Hill called the "financially confident" consumers whose loans we traditionally financed. Only about 10 percent of minority borrowers got their mortgages from banks (the vast majority got them from mortgage brokers), and in spite of the fact that over half of the people Hill surveyed described themselves as "living from paycheck to paycheck," they were notoriously price-insensitive: they were so fearful of being rejected, they would pay almost any amount to "get a yes." This made them extremely susceptible to predatory lenders in the subprime market, and the brokers and "trusted advisors" they relied upon for guidance when applying for a mortgage steered them to that market even when they could have qualified for a traditional loan at a much lower interest rate.

Research conducted by Fannie Mae and others showed that nearly half the borrowers being offered subprime loans were very close to being eligible for a Fannie Mae loan. To tap this segment, Raines created two new products, Expanded Approval (EA) and Timely Payment Rewards (TPR). EA was aimed at a wider range of borrowers, including those with impaired credit, while TPR rewarded qualified borrowers with a rate reduction after a specified number of on-time payments. By introducing what we called "risk-based pricing"—through which we charged somewhat higher guaranty fees than on our standard products, but much less than what was charged by subprime lenders—we were able to offer EA and TPR (often combined as EA/TPR) on terms consistent with our risk standards. We also created a Minority Lending Initiative that used African-American brokers to reach inner city borrowers not served by our traditional lenders.

Subprime lenders complained bitterly that EA/TPR and our Minority Lending Initiative went beyond the bounds of our charter and subjected us to excessive credit risk. They were wrong on both counts. The business wasn't outside our charter, and it wasn't that risky. Subprime lenders' true complaint, which of course they couldn't voice, was that by taking their best loans—and ones that never should have been in their market in the first place—we were hurting the economics of their business without hurting ours.

But the criticism we took over our minority lending activities highlighted a much bigger problem we were having: Fannie Mae's ambitions for growth and market leadership were becoming a greater and greater irritant to the large lenders and mortgage insurers who were the dominant members and supporters of FM Watch.

The month before FM Watch unveiled itself, in May 1999, Fannie Mae held its tenth Biennial Investor/Analyst Conference. It was Raines's first major shareholder presentation, and he wanted to set out his long-term expectations for the company. We had been able to add record amounts of mortgages to our portfolio at very high spreads to our debt costs during the previous seven months, and we knew these investments would benefit us for years to come. Reflecting this, Raines told his audience, "I expect that Fannie Mae's EPS [earnings per share] growth over the next five years will match or exceed the average 13.6 percent EPS growth of our last five years." He then went on to add, "In fact, the future's so bright that I'm willing to set as a goal that our EPS growth will double over the next five years." (Doubling EPS would require average growth of 14.9 percent per year.) Raines explained that with growth in the primary market expected to average 6 to 8 percent per year and Fannie Mae's net interest margin and guaranty fees remaining relatively stable, about half of the EPS growth he envisioned would come from faster portfolio growth and gains in our MBS market share.

It is interesting to speculate whether we would have made the prediction of doubling our EPS in five years had our biennial conference come one month *after* the debut of FM Watch, rather than one month before. Possibly we still would have. Since the Johnson years, we had been unapologetic about aggressively pursuing both our mission goal of increasing the availability and lowering the cost of mortgages and our private goal of producing superior returns to shareholders. Raines believed that technology would fundamentally change the mortgage business and that we had a responsibility to Congress and our shareholders to exploit these changes in ways that benefitted consumers and Fannie Mae alike. His pledge to double our EPS in five years was intended as a message of confidence to our investors that we would be in the forefront of the mortgage market transformation he envisioned and also as a message of motivation to our employees to find the new sources of revenue he believed this transformation would produce.

Fannie Mae's larger lenders, however, took a very different message from the EPS goal: that our meeting it would come at their expense. This was the issue that had led to the formation of FM Watch in the first place. Lenders called it "mission creep." They feared that unless some legislative or regulatory restraints were put in our path, we would enter areas of the mortgage business that were outside the bounds of our charter and either earn profits from or drive down costs in those areas to their disadvantage.

From its inception, FM Watch consistently emphasized three themes in its criticisms of us: that our activities posed excessive risk to taxpayers, that we were not doing enough for housing, and that we were engaging in mission creep. Of the three, the sponsors and members of FM Watch cared most about mission creep, but that issue did not resonate either with Congress or the public. It was hard to define, and to the extent there were gray areas in our charter, having Fannie Mae active in them benefitted home owners and for that reason did not stir people up. To get support for their goal of restraining Fannie Mae, FM Watch and its supporters found they had to make sensational allegations with their first two themes—our risks and the support of our mission. So that is what they did.

In fact, both of Fannie Mae's two main groups of adversaries—free-market ideologues, which included the Fed and the Treasury, and our major competitors, the large mortgage lenders and insurers—had their own versions of the same problem. The reason they each had for opposing us was not one they could come right out and say directly. For the free-market ideologues it was, "The government should not be involved in housing," and for our large competitors it was, "We could make a lot more money if Fannie Mae were more tightly constrained." To get broad-based support for their ideological or competitive objectives, both instead had to say, "Things are terribly *wrong* at Fannie Mae, and something must be done about it!" The fact that most of what they claimed to be wrong was not, or was misstated or greatly exaggerated, was not considered to be a drawback in a Washington policy fight, where "defining your opponent" and "going negative" were accepted practices with few if any rules.

Media Noise from the Critics

The *Wall Street Journal* did not need any prodding from FM Watch to engage in these practices or to throw its weight behind the anti–Fannie Mae cause. The *Journal*'s editorial board was well known for its free-market ideology, and in service of that ideology, it was more than willing to use a few of the barrels of the ink it bought to help create an image of Fannie Mae that had little to do with the reality of our business or the way in which we managed it.

The editorial and news pages of the *Journal* were said to be independent—and we did not dispute that—but what we found occurred was that the editorial writers would create their own distorted version of Fannie Mae on the opinion pages, and when the *Journal*'s reporters did news stories on us, they would use the editorial board's descriptions of our company and its operations as factual reference points. We knew we couldn't affect the *Journal*'s editorials, but we did try to get more balanced coverage from their reporters. Early in 2001, Raines met with the *Journal*'s managing editor, Paul Steiger, national news editor Marcus Brauchli, and others to discuss a series of instances in 2000 in which we believed the *Journal*'s coverage of Fannie Mae had not met their professed standard of fairness. The meeting was cordial, but it had little effect on the *Journal*'s treatment of us in their news pages going forward.

And their editorials were over the top—replete with misrepresentations, inaccuracies, and inventions. An early example was a July 2000 editorial ("Fannie Mae's Problems") in the guise of a Dear Abby letter from Fannie Mae, which claimed, "Right now, we [Fannie Mae and Freddie Mac] own or guarantee almost 80 percent of all middle-class home mortgages." At the time, the two companies owned 17 percent of all residential mortgages and guaranteed another 24 percent. These actual shares were not high enough for the writers of the editorial, so they concocted their own undefined concept of a "middle-class" mortgage to nearly double them. A later editorial, "Fannie Mae Enron?" in February 2002, bordered on the irresponsible. It used wildly inaccurate figures, gross mischaracterizations, and alarmist language—"poorly run hedge funds," "snarkily hedged risk," "even scarier," "disclosure is terrible," and "Shaking in your boots yet?"—in a glib and contorted attempt to exploit investor jitteriness over the Enron debacle at our expense.

We fell into a pattern. The *Journal* would do an editorial about us. We would compile a list of the factual inaccuracies it contained, produce a document with the correct information, and send it to our investors and security analysts that day. Next we would write a letter to the *Journal*'s editor, taking exception to the editorial and giving our most important corrections to it to try to balance the record. The *Journal* would print our response—and we would wait for the next editorial to appear. When it did, we would go through the same process again.

From the first Baker hearing through the middle of 2002, the *Journal* wrote 10 editorials about Fannie Mae. No other company—and possibly no other single topic—was the subject of as many. The first several pieces had the objective of painting a picture of Fannie Mae as the *Journal*'s editors wanted their readers to perceive us, so their topics were our size, capital, debt costs, profitability, risk management, business practices, and competitive position (as the editors chose to depict them). The message of these editorials was always the same: "privatize," which to the *Journal* meant renouncing our charter and leaving the mortgage market to the fully private lenders and securities issuers they championed. In the spring of 2002, the *Journal*'s editorial focus switched to critiques of specific aspects of our business. In the space of six months, they wrote four editorials about our corporate governance, derivatives exposure, disclosures on mortgage-backed securities and insider trading, and exemption from SEC registration requirements.

There was no constructive response we could have made to the editorials that distorted and then criticized our business—other than to write letters back to them—but in the areas raised in *Journal* editorials where we believed we could improve, we attempted to. We undertook a major initiative for best-in-class corporate governance and then asked Standard & Poor's to rate our governance practices. S&P gave us an exceptional score of 9.0 on a 10-point scale and said, "Fannie Mae's corporate governance practices are judged . . . to be at a very strong level on a global basis of comparison." We were one of the first companies to begin disclosing insider stock trades in real time and to announce we would begin expensing stock options. We voluntarily added to our MBS disclosures (even though the *Journal*'s criticism of our previous disclosures had been misplaced), and we added seven pages of information on derivatives to our 2003 annual report. We also volunteered to register our common stock with the Securities and Exchange Commission and come under the SEC's disclosure regime permanently. We filed our first 10K with the SEC in March of 2003 (and in so doing put ourselves in a position less than two years later to receive a surprising and unwelcome ruling from the chief accountant of that agency).

None of these initiatives, however, had the slightest effect on the tone, tenor, or frequency of the criticism we continued to receive. We were playing the political equivalent of whack-a-mole. As soon as we responded to one criticism, another one popped up.

The objectives of the disinformation campaign launched by FM Watch and supported by the *Wall Street Journal* were twofold: to attempt to make the public's opinion about Fannie Mae more negative in the hope of weakening our support in Congress and, by raising concerns in investors' minds that we were in danger of losing our political support, to put pressure on our stock price in the hope we would be tempted to "sue for peace" to get it back up. To date we had been able to counter the FM Watch strategy in Congress by going directly to members and their staffs, pointing out the inaccuracies of the FM Watch claims and explaining how their recommendations would benefit the large banks and mortgage insurers that backed it at the expense of home buyers. But we had no good way of countering the effect the negative publicity had on our investors, mortgage finance professionals, or the general public.

The impact of the FM Watch campaign on Fannie Mae's investors could be measured by the divergent performances of our earnings and our stock price. In 2002 Fannie Mae's earnings per share were more than 40 percent higher than they had been in 2000, yet between December 31, 2000, and December 31, 2002, the price of Fannie Mae stock fell by over 25 percent. Most of our investors and security analysts attributed this divergence to what they called our "political risk."

Not at all measurable but more broadly significant was the effect the FM Watch campaign had on the general perception of risk in the mortgage market. Constant repetition of the assertion that the GSEs' operations posed great risk to the financial system led a large majority of mortgage industry professionals and opinion leaders to believe that this was true. Few knew that it was not, and even fewer understood that the disinformation about the GSEs was being disseminated for political purposes by advocates of private-market financing mechanisms that really *did* pose great risk to the system. With so many seemingly credible sources, including the *Wall Street Journal*, saying with such frequency and fervor that the risky GSEs must be replaced by far safer private-market alternatives, what possible reason would anyone have for thinking otherwise?

CHAPTER 11

Fannie Mae Tightens
Its Disciplines

T
HE CONSTANT OUTSIDE SCRUTINY TO WHICH FANNIE MAE WAS
subject made us extremely sensitive to any potential vulnerabili-
ties we might have with respect to our business operations, mission-
related activities, or risk management. In this environment, three
issues that arose during Raines's chairmanship led us to reexamine
our risk profile and risk management strategies in 2003. These were
the adoption of a new accounting standard for derivatives, a negative market reaction to a portfolio imbalance we developed in the
fall of 2002, and unexpected losses from our holdings of AAA-rated
private-label manufactured housing securities.

An Accounting Rule Adds Confusion

Normally, accounting standards do not affect a company's risk or risk
management. The new rule for accounting for derivatives that took
effect in 2001, called Financial Accounting Statement 133 (FAS 133),
was an exception.

A derivative is a contract whose terms are based upon, or "derived"
from, a financial asset. Fannie Mae used derivatives in our portfolio
to help manage our interest rate risk and to hold down our debt costs.
The very large majority of our derivatives fell into two categories:

interest rate swaps and what were called "swaptions," which were options to enter into interest rate swaps at some point in the future. We used interest rate swaps as substitutes for the noncallable long-term debt we issued in the bond market and swaptions as substitutes for callable debt. Since the mid-1990s, we had used both types of derivative to keep our debt costs down as we grew the portfolio rapidly, and as a result, over 40 percent of our debt had either a swap or a swaption attached to it at the end of 2000.

Prior to the implementation of FAS 133, we had been able to account for our swaps and swaptions the same way we accounted for our noncallable and callable debt, on a historical cost basis. That made sense, both to us and to our investors, because the economic effects of our debt and derivatives were identical. But in 1994 a series of high-profile investor losses in derivatives—most notably in Orange County, California, but also elsewhere—caused the Financial Accounting Standards Board (FASB) to commit to develop a new derivatives accounting rule that would require all derivatives to be measured at their current market, or "fair," values. The only way historical costs could be used under this new standard, FAS 133, would be if the derivative in question met the definition of a "qualifying transaction," in which case hedge accounting, on a historical cost basis, could be elected.

There was a lively debate among accounting professionals over whether historical cost or fair value was the better accounting treatment. Most preferred one to the other, but no one advocated mixing the two. Yet under FAS 133, we ran the risk of having to do precisely that—with our mortgages and the debt financing those mortgages accounted for at historical cost, but with some or all of our derivatives accounted for at fair value. That would make our financial statements difficult if not impossible for investors to understand and interpret.

As the head of the business that used derivatives—the mortgage portfolio—as well as Fannie Mae's CFO, I took the lead in devising our FAS 133 implementation strategy. I determined that the most promising way to accomplish our objectives of complying with the standard as written, accurately reflecting the economics of the derivatives we used and maintaining clarity in our financial statements, was to try to convince FASB to write FAS 133 in a manner that achieved their goals but minimized the distortive effects on companies' financial statements, including ours. Fannie Mae's accounting policy staff worked tirelessly toward this end, and I made three trips to FASB's Connecticut headquarters myself to meet with its chairman and board members. Our efforts succeeded in obtaining changes to early FAS 133 drafts that in the final rule made interest rate swaps eligible for hedge accounting. But try though we might— and I thought we had excellent arguments—we could not get hedge accounting for swaptions.

When FAS 133 went into effect on January 1, 2001, therefore, all of Fannie Mae's income statement on a generally accepted accounting principles (GAAP) basis was recorded at historical cost except for one new line item reflecting our swaptions called "purchased options expense." Purchased options expense was recorded at fair value, and because of that, it rose and fell with interest rates, adding tremendous volatility to our GAAP earnings that was unrelated to any change in our business risk. In 2000, the average change in Fannie Mae's GAAP net income from one quarter to the next had been about $30 million. In 2001, with FAS 133 in effect, that average quarterly change soared to nearly *$600* million, some 20 times as great. Virtually all of the increased volatility was an accounting artifact of marking to market only a portion of our hedges—our swaptions—while keeping all of our mortgages and the rest of our debt and derivatives at their historical costs.

In response to this artificial volatility in our GAAP earnings, we introduced a new non-GAAP measure we called "operating earnings" (renamed "core business earnings" after we became an SEC registrant in 2003) as soon as FAS 133 took effect. In operating earnings, we replaced the fair value treatment of purchased options expense with the historical cost accounting we employed prior to FAS 133. Our investors and security analysts welcomed the new measure, because it used consistent accounting throughout and was comparable to what we had published previously. The randomness of our purchased options expense made it impossible for them to project our post-FAS 133 GAAP earnings. They could, and did, project our non-GAAP operating earnings, and they tracked and evaluated our financial performance using that measure.

We had developed operating earnings as an alternative measure, but we still had to publish our GAAP earnings. And there was nothing we could do about the fact that most newspapers and wire services, when they reported our quarterly and annual financial results, gave the GAAP numbers first and wrote their headlines based on them. Our operating earnings were covered later in the stories, but rather than providing clarity, they often just created more confusion about what our true financial performance was.

Prior to FAS 133, we had been able to tell both our supporters and our critics that we had a simple business with manageable risks, and we had a history of predictable and steadily growing earnings to buttress that contention. FAS 133 changed that. From the first quarter of 2001 on, our GAAP financial results made our business look risky. And of course FM Watch and our critics did not hesitate to point to the volatility of our GAAP financials as evidence that we were indeed as risky as they claimed we were. Against that backdrop, two episodes in 2002 that truly did indicate a greater degree of business risk at Fannie Mae triggered a quick and decisive response on our part.

Mind the Gap

One of our voluntary initiatives was monthly disclosure of measures of the portfolio's interest rate risk. These included the duration gap—the difference in months between the durations of the portfolio's mortgages and debt. We had provided duration gap information previously in our annual report but only as of the end of each year.

We fully expected our monthly duration gap disclosures to be subject to outside scrutiny and analysis when we began them in March 2001. In our 1999 annual report, we had revealed that our "preferred target range" for the duration gap was between plus and minus six months. Prior to releasing the new monthly data, we told our investors and security analysts that since 1990, the duration gap had been outside its target range about one-third of the time, and that when it was, we took rebalancing actions—lengthening or shortening the durations of our debt and derivatives and adding shorter- or longer-duration mortgages—to bring it back. We told them that to minimize our cost of rebalancing, we did not have a fixed timetable for accomplishing it unless the duration gap exceeded certain "established reference points," which we did not identify externally. Internally, they were set at plus or minus 12 months.

During 2001 our duration gap was inside its target range in every month but three, with the largest outlier a 10-month negative gap in October. It remained within target for the first six months of 2002, but as mortgage rates moved lower during the summer, we reported a negative nine-month duration gap for July. Then, on September 16, we disclosed that the August duration gap had fallen to a negative 14 months. The gap had been at that level once before, in October 1998, under conditions very similar to what we were experiencing in 2002. In 1998 we had been able to get comfortably back to within our target range by the end of the year, primarily by adding large amounts of newly refinanced (and longer duration) mortgages and financing them with shorter-term debt. Our plan for reducing the negative 14-month duration gap in 2002 was substantially the same.

In 1998, however, we were not making monthly duration gap disclosures. Public reaction to our August 2002 number was extremely negative, and it caught us by surprise. In retrospect it probably should not have. We were in the post–FM Watch era, and our opponents and critics were poised to pounce on any piece of information that could be interpreted as evidence we were taking excessive risk. We also had a highly politicized regulator.

We had informed OFHEO of the August duration gap before we made it public, and Director Falcon saw it as an opportunity for some favorable publicity at our expense. On the day of our duration gap disclosure, he released to the media a letter he had sent to Richard Baker and ranking subcommittee member Paul Kanjorski saying that he had met with senior Fannie Mae officials about the duration gap and that he was requiring us to make weekly reports to him on our progress in reducing it. Falcon's letter also said, "In the event there are adverse developments with management's effectiveness in reducing the level of interest rate sensitivity, OFHEO may take additional action." (OFHEO had yet to take any "action" at all, other than requesting us to tell them how we intended to bring the duration gap back down.) Baker responded in a letter back to Falcon, also released to the public, decrying our August duration gap and criticizing OFHEO for "allowing unacceptable levels of risk to continue for far too long."

Freddie Mac deliberately worsened our situation by publishing, for the first time, their own version of a duration gap two days after we reported our August figure. Freddie Mac said that their duration gap for August was zero, and that for the past 13 months, it had never been wider than plus or minus one month. The stability of Freddie Mac's new duration gap measure contrasted starkly with the volatility in ours. The two measures, however, were not comparable. Ours was the simple arithmetic difference between the cash flow durations of the mortgages in our portfolio and the debt financing those mortgages. Freddie Mac's calculation used a different (although completely legitimate) definition of duration, called "modified duration," which measured the sensitivity of the prices of their mortgages and debt to changes in interest rates. Freddie Mac's version also included their nonmortgage assets and what they called the "interest-rate sensitive" portion of their mortgage-backed security guarantees, whereas ours did not. We believed we did take somewhat more interest rate risk in our mortgage portfolio than Freddie Mac, but the difference was not remotely as great as suggested by the contrasting volatilities of our existing duration gap measure and Freddie Mac's new one.

But now we had a problem. OFHEO's high-profile reaction to our August duration gap figure, Freddie Mac's release of their own version of a duration gap, and negative commentary from many of our critics raised considerable alarm among our debt and equity investors. The price of our stock fell 10 percent in a week. In an attempt to allay investor concerns, I put out a written statement saying that we had seen similar volatility in our duration numbers in prior refinancing periods and had managed it without difficulty, and I mentioned some of the tools and techniques we had available to bring us back within our target range promptly. I addressed these issues again in a conference call with debt investors and in a previously scheduled presentation to equity investors.

Our cost of rebalancing became a serious issue. Falcon's letter to Baker raised speculation in the bond market that we would be forced by OFHEO to reduce our duration gap more quickly than we otherwise might have. One rumor that became widespread was that we would have to buy large amounts of long-term Treasuries to lengthen our asset durations. Enough bond traders acted on that rumor—buying in anticipation of purchases by Fannie Mae—that yields on 10-year Treasuries fell by a quarter of a percentage point between the day we announced our August duration gap and the end of September. We had not purchased Treasuries in the past to rebalance and did not do so this time, but the rebalancing we did do was made much more expensive by actions of dealers and bond traders who knew what we needed to accomplish. Previously when we had a large negative duration gap but had not disclosed it publicly, we had been able to take rebalancing actions quietly and efficiently. This time was radically different.

It was neither easy nor inexpensive, but with transactions in the derivatives markets (primarily the termination of interest rate swaps) and purchases of fixed-rate mortgages funded with short-term debt, we were able to reduce our duration gap to a negative 10 months on September 30. We decided to make that figure public immediately after we had calculated it, two weeks in advance of the normal release date of our monthly financial information. The markets reacted as we expected they would. Treasury security yields rose sharply, and Fannie Mae stock gained almost $5, recouping nearly half its losses over the prior two weeks.

Early release of the September duration gap took the intense focus off the issue. The fact that we had reported a negative 10-month gap the previous October—with neither OFHEO nor anyone else expressing great concern about it—seemed to have been taken as an indication that the immediate crisis had passed. We continued to take actions to bring the duration gap back toward our target range in October and did not encounter any unusual resistance to what we were seeking to accomplish. When we disclosed our October duration gap on our normal mid-November release date, it had fallen to negative six months, and it remained within target for the remaining two months of the year.

The Corporate Financial Disciplines

The duration gap crisis had passed, but it was a wake-up call. We had not changed the risk posture of the portfolio business since we began using callable debt as a primary financing vehicle back in 1990. Our portfolio strategy had been to hedge with callable debt and derivatives about half the prepayment risk of the mortgages we owned, and on our unhedged risk not to begin rebalancing until our duration gap moved outside the plus or minus six-month range. For a dozen years, this strategy had been extremely successful; we believed it permitted us to make billions of dollars more in net income relative to what we would have earned with a more aggressive hedging approach. But in the fall of 2002, we had given a fair amount of this additional net income back, through deferred losses on swap terminations that would be brought into our earnings over time. Rebalancing had been much more expensive than previously, and with our increased size and our monthly duration gap disclosures, there was no reason to think it would be any less expensive in the future. It was time to rethink our approach to interest rate risk.

The timing of the reevaluation of our interest rate risk strategy influenced the way we went about it. In November 2002, Raines moved Fannie Mae's Credit Policy group, which previously had reported to Chief Operating Officer Dan Mudd, over to me in the finance division. As Raines said in announcing the change, his goal was to have both of Fannie Mae's major risk management functions report to a single executive, to ensure "consistency in risk management analytics, metrics, and strategies across the company." To free up time for me to devote to Credit Policy, we asked Peter Niculescu, who ran Portfolio Strategy and was one of my three senior portfolio executives, to become head of the portfolio business and assume day-to-day responsibility for managing it. Niculescu continued to report to me in his new role, and I retained both the title and duties of chief financial officer.

Given my new and broader risk management responsibilities, I very likely would have sought to review Fannie Mae's credit risk management strategies at the same time as we reviewed our approach to interest rate risk management. Emerging problems with our manufactured housing security investments removed any doubt I might have had about the wisdom of doing that.

Beginning in the mid-1990s, we had purchased about $10 billion in private-label manufactured housing securities as a way to support that then-fast-growing segment of the housing market without exposing ourselves directly to the credit risk of an asset class in which we did not have expertise. The vast majority of our purchases carried AAA ratings, although we bought a small number of AA-rated securities as well. After the manufactured housing market collapsed in 2002, sharply falling prices of manufactured homes and soaring delinquencies, defaults, and loss severities on manufactured housing loans led the rating agencies to belatedly downgrade very large numbers of private-label manufactured housing mortgage-backed securities, including many of the ones we owned.

I soon discovered that we had no idea what our private-label securities were worth. No one at Fannie Mae felt it was his or her responsibility to assess or monitor the credit quality of the rated securities the portfolio had bought. The portfolio looked only at the interest rate risk of the securities, and Credit Policy did not look beyond or behind the AAA or AA ratings bestowed upon them by the credit rating agencies. As a consequence, no one realized that on 70 percent of the manufactured housing securities we owned, all serviced by Conseco Finance, there was a flaw in their structure that left

Conseco with no money to service delinquent loans once delinquencies rose above a certain percentage. No servicing meant very high defaults and exceptionally high loss severities on defaulted loans. Our AAA- and AA-rated manufactured housing securities, supposedly risk-free, were in danger of causing us large and unexpected losses, and we didn't understand what we owned or what actions we could take to preserve the economic value of our investments.

Coming on the heels of the duration gap episode, the realization that we did not have adequate business processes in place for assessing the quality of third-party credit enhancements left me with no doubt at all that we needed to take the broadest possible approach to our risk review.

We did exactly that, starting with its scope. Since I had been at Fannie Mae, we had never looked at all aspects of our risk and risk management simultaneously. In the Maxwell era, we had addressed interest rate risk and credit risk sequentially: we had matched the mortgage portfolio's asset and liability durations in the mid-1980s, put in place our integrated underwriting and credit pricing capabilities shortly afterwards, and then added callable debt and new funding and rebalancing strategies to the portfolio business in the late 1980s. In the review we were about to undertake, we would assess both interest rate and credit risks together to ensure we were treating them consistently. We also would reconsider how we were communicating our risk tolerance and risk management strategies to our external constituencies.

Communicating the effectiveness of Fannie Mae's risk management strategies had been an integral part of our corporate objectives since early in Maxwell's chairmanship. And it had been key to maintaining our support in Congress. But in the ensuing two decades, several things had changed. Our business risks had become more complex: we were using more derivatives to manage our interest rate risk, and we had expanded the range of products and credit features we would guarantee as MBS, including loans to borrowers with impaired credit. Our accounting had become more complex with the adoption of FAS 133 and newly volatile GAAP financial results. We had FM Watch and a host of committed critics dedicated to making our business seem more complicated and risky than it actually was. And we had a safety and soundness regulator whose primary focus was political and who could not be counted upon to provide any credible assurances to our investors of our financial health. OFHEO's version of our risk-based capital "Volcker standard" finally had become binding less than a week before we released our August duration gap, and nobody paid the slightest attention to it.

It was with both internal and external objectives in mind that late in 2002, Raines approved a comprehensive review of Fannie Mae's risk tolerances. I put together a high-level team of risk managers headed by Peter Niculescu for the portfolio business and Chief Credit Officer Adolfo Marzol for the credit guaranty business. Raines was an active participant in the project, which took us six months to complete. It culminated in a presentation to Fannie Mae's senior management in June 2003 and in a set of recommendations to the Fannie Mae board in July.

We began with a review of our corporate appetite for risk taking. In the 1980s, we had defined the risk appetites for both our portfolio and credit guaranty businesses as the ability to survive 99 percent of the future environments we projected each could potentially face. When we addressed our corporate risk appetite again in early 2003, we decided to constrain it even further: each business would have to be able to survive 99.5 percent of all projected future environments. This may seem like a minor change, but it was not. It was the equivalent of building a seawall to withstand a 200-year rather than a 100-year storm surge.

We made the change for two reasons. First, we wanted to be able to say publicly that our risk constraints were set at a level consistent with the historical default rates of AA and AAA corporate bonds, which since the Depression had averaged a little over half of one percent. (Even in 2003, there was a huge difference between the default rates for AAA-rated corporate bonds and AAA-rated structured transactions, with the latter being considerably higher.) Second, we concluded from our shareholders' reaction to our August duration gap that they had become more risk averse, and we believed that even though a tighter risk constraint would cost us a significant amount of earnings each year, investors would pay a higher multiple for those earnings if we took less risk to achieve them.

Having set our new risk tolerances, we then moved to the business level. Differences in the structure of our two businesses made for differences in what we would have to do to produce similar returns and risk profiles in each. For the mortgage portfolio, we could achieve our goals of net income stability and minimal insolvency risk by hedging more of the prepayment risk in our mortgages at the time we did their initial funding and by moving more quickly to rebalance the portfolio as interest rates changed. For the credit guaranty business, we would have to limit the credit risks we agreed to accept, use more third-party credit enhancements to share our credit risk (and revenue) with others, and have the discipline to add capital when delinquencies and defaults rose above the average levels assumed in our pricing models.

We received approval from our board for what we called our Corporate Financial Disciplines at our annual strategic retreat on July 14 and disclosed them to our investors the next day in a press release announcing our second quarter 2003 earnings. We published the disciplines again in the spring of 2004 in our 2003 annual report to shareholders. They were:

- To maintain a stand-alone "risk-to-the-government" credit rating from Standard & Poor's (S&P) of at least AA– and to maintain a stand-alone "bank financial strength" credit rating from Moody's Investors Service (Moody's) of at least A–.
- To sufficiently capitalize and hedge our portfolio investment and credit guaranty businesses so that each is able to withstand internal and external "stress tests" set to at least a AA/Aa standard.
- To keep our mortgage interest rate and credit risks low enough [so] that over time our core business earnings are less variable than the median of all AA/Aa and AAA/Aaa S&P 500 companies.

The first discipline, to maintain high stand-alone credit ratings, was intended to signal to investors our willingness to subject our risk management practices to objective, third party review. OFHEO had neither the capability nor the credibility to perform this function, and Treasury was unwilling to do so (for fear, I believed, that their endorsement would enhance our stature in the market). The second discipline was how we chose to express our decision to tighten our risk tolerances to a one-half-of-one-percent chance of insolvency. The final discipline committed us to earnings stability. At its most basic level, risk is uncertainty of return. The only sure way for Fannie Mae to produce a stable pattern of earnings would be through precise measurement and management of our business risks.

In a conference call I held with investors to discuss the disciplines on the day we disclosed them, I explained what they meant for each of our businesses. For the portfolio, I said we would be increasing the hedged portion of our prepayment risk from half to "between 50 and 60 percent" by using more option-based debt, and that "we expect that more frequent portfolio rebalancing will result in our duration gap remaining within a range of plus-or-minus six months substantially all of the time," in contrast to only two-thirds of the time under our previous discipline. For the credit guaranty business, I introduced a measure called credit loss variability and said:

> The concept behind this measure is that some types of loans inherently have default rates or loss severities that are more sensitive to home price and interest rate changes than others. The more of these higher-risk loans we own or guarantee, the more we will need to use some form of credit enhancement or other technique to keep the earnings variability of the credit portfolio as a whole within our defined corporate risk tolerance as we seek to expand our presence in underserved markets.

I concluded by saying:

> Our goal in setting and communicating to the public our corporate financial disciplines, and in detailing the risk

management strategies we will follow to adhere to them, is to leave no doubt at all among investors, policy makers, and others that our commitment to an extremely high level of financial strength is absolute.

In retrospect, the timing of the adoption of our corporate financial disciplines was nearly perfect. After falling for three and a half years, 10-year Treasury rates hit their low point of 3.1 percent on June 13, 2003. They closed at 3.9 percent on the day we announced the disciplines, on their way to over 4 percent a week later. The sudden reversal in Treasury rates was mirrored by sharply rising mortgage yields, which soon would trigger the most extreme reductions in mortgage credit standards in the country's history. Fannie Mae would be squarely focused on the unprecedented types and volumes of credit risks that were about to flood the market—and be uniquely prepared in our response—precisely because of the new financial disciplines to which we had just committed ourselves. No other financial institution in the world had anything remotely comparable to them.

CHAPTER 12

Private Label
Takes Center Stage

Fannie Mae's studied tightening of risk disciplines in the summer of 2003 stood in marked contrast to what had been happening in the subprime mortgage market and with private-label securitization in the years leading up to that point. There, lending practices, capital disciplines, and government oversight all had been noticeably relaxed.

Subprime Resurrected

Subprime lending barely paused following the 1999 collapse. Large lenders and their regulators concluded that the subprime implosion was not the result of the characteristics of the loans in that market, its lack of regulation, or any flaws in the securitization mechanism it used, but rather was the result of the financing dependencies and poor management practices of the specialty lenders active in the market at the time. That diagnosis led to a convenient prescription for change: subprime lenders needed to be larger, more sophisticated, and have diversified funding sources, preferably including consumer deposits.

The consolidation that had occurred in the prime mortgage market was replicated in the subprime market, with banks and other large independent lenders either purchasing troubled subprime specialty lenders or starting up their own subprime subsidiaries. By 2002 only one company that had been among the top 10 subprime lenders in 1995 remained in that category, and that was Household Finance. Joining them in the top 10 in 2002 were units of Citigroup, Wells Fargo, and Washington Mutual, along with independent mortgage lenders Countrywide Financial, New Century, and Ameriquest. Small and mid-sized subprime lenders had all but disappeared. In 1995 the 25 largest subprime lenders accounted for less than 40 percent of subprime lending; in 2002 the same number of lenders made almost 90 percent of subprime loans.

By the early 2000s, the clear line between the prime and subprime mortgage markets that existed prior to the first subprime-lending boom had blurred. During the mid-1990s, Fannie Mae and Freddie Mac both incorporated credit scores into our underwriting and credit pricing models, and each of us began accepting loans to borrowers with previous credit problems provided their loans had other attributes that at least partially offset the poor credit histories.

But the defining attribute of a subprime loan had not changed: subprime loans were made to borrowers with bad credit. And the riskiest types of subprime loans had features that readily distinguished them from prime loans. They had much higher interest rates. They carried substantially higher origination fees. Many had prepayment penalties. Most had adjustable rates. Most did not have full documentation. Relatively few were for home purchases; the large majority were refinance or debt consolidation loans. Subprime borrowers generally had low incomes. And unfortunately, subprime borrowers frequently were subjected to deceptive or abusive lending practices.

The subprime mortgage market had been unregulated from its inception in the early 1980s. In theory subprime lenders were subject to the 1968 Truth in Lending Act, but enforcement of its provisions for nonbank lenders fell between the cracks of the existing patchwork of state and federal financial regulators. Predatory practices were prevalent in subprime mortgage lending throughout its early history.

Problems in this market were brought to the attention of Congress, and in 1994 it responded by passing the Home Ownership and Equity Protection Act (HOEPA). HOEPA specifically cited "second mortgage lenders, home improvement contractors, and finance companies who peddle high-rate, high-fee home equity loans to cash-poor homeowners" as targets of the legislation, which prohibited lenders from making high-cost refinance loans "without regard to consumers' repayment ability."

A key provision of HOEPA directed the Federal Reserve to "prohibit acts or practices in connection with [mortgages] that [the Federal Reserve] finds to be unfair, deceptive or designed to evade the provisions of this [act]." The Fed had been given authority to set mortgage standards for all types of lenders in the Truth in Lending Act, so it was the obvious choice to enforce the provisions of HOEPA. At the time HOEPA was passed, however, the chairman of the Fed was Greenspan. In Greenspan's view, federal regulation did more harm than good by overriding market discipline and impeding the free flow of credit. In a 1997 speech, he framed the issue this way: "The real question is not whether a market should be regulated. Rather, the real question is whether government intervention strengthens or weakens private regulation." He left no doubt where he stood on this issue, and under his leadership, the Federal Reserve declined to use its HOEPA authority to regulate subprime or other mortgage lending practices in any meaningful way.

In the absence of federal action, some states passed their own laws to combat predatory lending. Those laws, however, ran afoul of the Office of the Comptroller of the Currency (OCC). The OCC had the authority to preempt state laws that applied to any national bank it regulated or to national banks' state-chartered subsidiaries. Fearing that national banks could not easily manage predatory lending laws that differed from state to state, the OCC insisted on preempting them all. That doomed the efforts. State antipredatory lending laws from which any OCC-regulated lender was exempt would have been unworkable. The OCC may have had a different reason from the Fed for opposing subprime regulation, but the practical result was the same: subprime lending, even when conducted by subsidiaries of bank holding companies, remained unregulated.

None of this was lost on the executives whose companies were in the process of resurrecting the subprime mortgage industry. Irrespective of the form in which they operated, they and their competitors knew they would be free to originate any type of mortgage they could devise and that a borrower would agree to. The only practical constraints they might face would come from the issuers, rating agencies, or investors in the private-label securities market they relied upon for permanent financing. Here, too, however, subprime lenders would benefit from the actions of financial regulators, who were committed to helping private-label securitization supplant GSE mortgage-backed securities as the preferred financing vehicle for subprime and prime mortgages alike.

Private-Label Securitization Gets a Regulatory Endorsement

The share of U.S. single-family mortgages financed by private-label securities had grown from virtually nothing in the mid-1980s to about 8 percent in 2000, but that still was less than a third of the combined amount of Fannie Mae and Freddie Mac mortgage securities outstanding. Proponents of private-label securitization believed that the reasons for the market share discrepancy were the legal and regulatory advantages GSE mortgage-backed securities had over private-label MBS. One of these was the more favorable capital treatment accorded GSE securities by international bank regulators.

In 1988, the Basel Committee on Banking Supervision had recommended that all international banks hold capital equal to at least 8 percent of their risk-weighted assets. Under the Basel scheme, different asset types were given different percentage risk weights. Residential mortgages, which from a credit perspective were considered safer than most other loan types, received a 50 percent risk weight, lowering their minimum required capital to 4 percent. Most private-label mortgage-backed securities also had a 50 percent risk weight (the risk weight for some was 100 percent). The Basel risk weight on Fannie Mae and Freddie Mac debt and mortgage-backed securities, however, was only 20 percent. With the risk weights, a bank owning $1 billion in most private-label MBS needed to hold $40 million in capital; a bank with the same amount of Fannie Mae MBS needed only $16 million in capital.

This impediment to parity between GSE and private-label mortgage-backed securities became a high priority of U.S. banks and their regulators to eliminate, for two reasons: it was significant, and it was within their power to do so. The Federal Reserve, OCC, OTS, and the Federal Deposit Insurance Corporation (FDIC) first proposed a 20 percent risk weight on AAA-rated private-label mortgage securities as part of a broader rule-making proposal issued for comment in November 1997. The complexities of this proposal caused regulators not to be able to agree on its details, and it stalled. Seeking to advance the issue, in May 1999 six financial services trade groups sent a joint letter to the Fed urging it and other regulators to give private-label MBS parity with GSE mortgage-backed securities by lowering the risk weights on AA as well AAA private-label securities to 20 percent. Not long afterward, in March 2000, depository institution regulators issued a revised and simplified version of their 1997 proposal.

In the new proposal, AAA- and AA-rated private-label MBS were each given 20 percent risk weights. The risk weight for A-rated tranches remained at 50 percent, while BBB-tranche risk weights were raised to 100 percent, and risk weights on BB tranches (typically the lowest rated) were set at 200 percent. What were called the equity or residual pieces, which took the first losses, had to be capitalized dollar for dollar. Comments on the rule were due in June.

Fannie Mae's objections began with the rule's premise. Our opponents and critics' assertions notwithstanding, AAA- and AA-rated private-label securities were *not* the economic equivalents of GSE securities. GSE mortgage-backed securities had an additional layer of credit protection from our corporate guaranty, limits on the riskiness of the loans that could go into them, and the implicit support of the U.S. government. (This last, of course, was what bank regulators so fervently wished to offset.) Private-label mortgage-backed securities had none of these. Second, because most of the dollar amount of a private-label security was given a 20 percent risk weight, the proposal allowed a bank holding all but the most risky mortgage types to reduce its 4 percent capital requirement for unsecuritized mortgages to about 3 percent simply by putting them into a private-label MBS and keeping all the tranches. That was nonsensical.

The third flaw in the proposal was that the capital requirements on the junior tranches of private-label securities were not set high enough. The 16 percent capital requirement on BB-rated security tranches (8 percent capital with a 200 percent risk weight) seemed like a lot, but in a $1 billion structured transaction, the BB tranche might be only $20 million in size. After the equity or residual piece, the BB tranche stood to take losses from the entire $1 billion in mortgages in the structure, and in just a moderately severe loss scenario, it could be wiped out entirely. This part of the proposal was the opposite of risk-based capital: it allowed a bank to bear the risk on $1 billion worth of loans but imposed a capital requirement only on the $20 million tranche the bank owned.

We and Freddie Mac made these and other points in our comment letter. The proposal was an ideological and competitive initiative dressed up as regulation. Our substantive arguments against it were irrefutable, but we were alone in making them. Virtually all the other comments came from financial institutions or trade groups with a stake in expanding the private-label market. These groups lauded the regulators for "aligning risk ratings more closely with actual risk" (which they had not done), and they uniformly praised the rule for creating a "level playing field" between private-label and GSE securities (which it attempted to do but shouldn't have). Our objections were labeled as self-serving and dismissed, and the rule was adopted as proposed.

It took until the fall of 2001 for the Fed, the FDIC, the OCC, and the OTS all to approve the final rule. The rule went into effect on January 1, 2002, and when it did, it signaled to investors around the world that U.S. financial regulators considered AAA- and AA-rated private-label MBS to be the credit equivalents of GSE securities. The fact that this was far from true would not become apparent until much too late.

The Private-Label Market Rises, and Credit Standards Fall

In January of 2001, the Federal Reserve responded to a weakening economy by embarking upon a series of cuts in short-term interest rates. Rapidly falling rates sparked a lending surge in both the prime and subprime mortgage markets. Originations of subprime loans—which in 2000 had accounted for about 10 percent of total mortgages—rose by 25 percent in 2001, surpassing their previous high in the late 1990s, then nearly doubled between 2001 and 2003. Private-label securitization of subprime loans rose at an even faster pace, more than tripling between 2000 and 2003.

The credit quality of the subprime loans made during this period was even worse than it was during the first subprime lending wave in the mid-1990s. No significant regulatory restrictions had been imposed in the interim, and the larger lenders who now dominated the market relied heavily on independent mortgage brokers for business volume. Brokers were compensated by what was called a "yield spread premium": the higher the interest rate on the loans they delivered to their primary lender, the more money they made for themselves. The highest interest rates were on the riskiest loan types and the loans with the most risky credit features. Subprime brokers had a powerful financial incentive to produce more of these loans, and they did.

Prime mortgage lending took off even faster than subprime lending. In contrast to the subprime market—where a fairly consistent majority of the loans were for refinances—in the prime market a lender's mix of purchase and refinance loans was highly sensitive to interest rate changes. Only about 20 percent of prime mortgage originations had been refinances in 2000, but as 30-year fixed mortgage rates declined irregularly but persistently over the next two and a half years, the percentage that were refinances soared to over 70 by the end of 2002, and then stayed at that level for another six months. This refinance percentage was all the more impressive given that the purchase loan market was growing rapidly as well. After modest gains in 2001, existing and new home sales increased by 6 and 7 percent, respectively, in 2002, and then by 10 and 12 percent in 2003, while home prices rose at an 8 percent clip throughout the period. Purchase mortgage originations kept pace with the growth in home sales and prices. Strength in both the purchase and refinance markets pushed total prime mortgage originations in 2003 to almost three and a half times their level of 2000. Prime origination volumes in the first six months of 2003 were higher than in any other six-month period in history.

It was an exceedingly profitable time for everyone. Fannie Mae's traditional lenders were able to resist the temptations of the reviving subprime market because they had all the business they could handle in the prime market. We did as well. Between the end of 2000 and the second quarter of 2003, our combined book of business—our mortgage portfolio and outstanding mortgage-backed security guarantees—soared from $1.3 trillion to $2.1 trillion, an average growth rate of almost 20 percent per year.

But then suddenly the music stopped. The Federal Reserve had cut the overnight federal funds rate from 7 percent in December 2000 to only one-quarter of 1 percent in September 2002, and vastly lower short rates had their intended effect: the economy was growing strongly, and housing was booming. Bond market investors had seen the yields on 10-year Treasury notes fall from more than 6.5 percent in 2000 to just over 3 percent in mid-June of 2003 when their collective psychology abruptly changed. They began to worry about future inflation. Ten-year Treasury yields stopped falling and reversed course, shooting up to nearly 4.5 percent by the end of July.

The sharp reversal in Treasury yields flowed through to mortgage rates, quickly putting the brakes on the refinancing boom. The suddenness and severity of the change took Fannie Mae's lenders by surprise. They had become accustomed to the high business volumes and record profitability of the last few years, and they did not want to see them end. To keep their volumes and profits as high as possible, they turned to the purchase market to try to replace as much of their dwindling volumes of refinances as they could.

It was precisely at this point that a decade's worth of unchecked subprime lending excesses burst the bounds of that market and became the inspirations for prime mortgage lenders looking to keep their origination pipelines full. The key to increasing the volume of purchase money mortgages was to expand the pool of borrowers qualified to finance a home. And as subprime lenders had shown conclusively, the fastest and easiest way to do *that* was by relaxing underwriting standards and introducing new "affordable" mortgage products so that people who had not been able to qualify using the old standards and products could by using the new ones.

In August 2003, I had been responsible for Fannie Mae's Credit Policy group for 10 months. We had just announced our corporate financial disciplines, and I was working to ensure that Credit Policy had the proper tools and business processes in place to do the detailed credit risk assessment and tracking required by these disciplines for the new loans that would be coming on our books. From this front-line vantage point, the changes in the types and characteristics of the loans our lenders were offering us were immediately apparent to me as they unfolded.

The most obvious change was a rapid shift from fixed-rate to adjustable-rate mortgages. Short-term interest rates had stayed low (the Fed would not increase the federal funds rate for nearly another year), and because lenders' practice was to qualify borrowers at the ARM start rate rather than at the fully indexed rate, ARMs quickly increased in popularity. In the second quarter of 2003, only 14 percent of conventional conforming mortgage originations had been ARMs; by the second quarter of 2004, the ARM share had reached 38 percent.

Shifts from fixed rates to ARMs were typical of periods of rising interest rates. When they had occurred in the past, we had been able to maintain a reasonable volume of ARM guaranty business because the credit risk features of the ARMs stayed roughly the same. But this time there was a new product in the market: the interest-only ARM. As the name indicates, borrowers using an interest-only ARM make only interest payments on their loan for a set number of years. They are qualified at the interest-only payment. In future years, their monthly payment will rise as they begin to pay off principal, and it can rise substantially further if short-term rates move higher. Interest-only ARMs are a very risky product and become even more problematic if other high-risk features are added.

And that in fact was happening. The second unequivocal change we saw beginning in the second half of 2003 was considerably more of what was termed "risk layering." In risk layering, a lender allows a combination of high-risk features—such as high loan-to-value ratios, low credit scores, high debt-to-income ratios, or reduced documentation—to be present in the same loan. Initially the most prevalent type of risk layering was reduced documentation in conjunction with a second high-risk feature, but other high-risk combinations, including multiple risks, appeared as well. We had found in the past that as the amount of risk layering in a loan rose, our experience with traditionally underwritten mortgages became progressively less reliable as a basis for evaluating and pricing it.

Fannie Mae's combined MBS issues and commitments to purchase loans for portfolio had averaged $160 billion per month during the first nine months of 2003. In the last three months of the year, they fell by almost 60 percent to just $65 billion per month. Mortgage originations were down because of falling refinances, but only by about 40 percent. Our purchase loan volumes were dropping even as purchase originations were rising. At this point, only a small percentage of the new purchase loans being made fell short of our credit standards, so that was not the problem. What was happening instead was that a large percentage of the new higher-risk loans were being financed in the private-label market.

The reduction in bank risk-based capital requirements had added some additional demand for private-label mortgage-backed securities, but not enough to explain the suddenness and extent of our loss of competitiveness to that market. When we investigated it, the trail led to the rating agencies. The price a lender received for selling mortgages through a private-label MBS was heavily influenced by the number and relative sizes of the junior tranches that were required to get AAA and AA ratings on the rest of the tranches. The fewer and smaller the junior tranches in a private-label deal, the better the price to the lender. The reason we were losing business to the private-label market was that the rating agencies were assessing the new loan types and risk combinations as being less risky than we thought they were.

It was understandable. We were a credit guarantor and had just made a public commitment to stability in our financial results. Were we to underestimate the credit risk of the new business—and not grade and price it in a way that covered our capital costs and allowed for the increased risk we believed these loans had—we would suffer the consequences by falling short of our income goals and having to add capital to stay in compliance with our financial disciplines. The rating agencies were in an opposite position. They provided a service for a fee. If they did not attempt to grade the new business using whatever data existed, together with rough rules of thumb—or if they were too conservative in their risk assessments—they would not earn any income at all. The inescapable explanation for our competitive disadvantage against the private-label market in financing higher-risk mortgages was that we stood to lose financially from underpricing their credit risk, while the rating agencies and private-label issuers stood to gain from it.

There had been prior instances when for a short period of time the private-label market had better pricing on certain credit guaranty transactions than Fannie Mae was able or willing to provide. What always had ended these spurts before was limited investor demand for the higher-risk tranches on which the senior tranches depended for credit protection. As more and more junior tranches came on the market in new private-label issues, their small buyer base would demand higher and higher yields to continue to purchase them. Ultimately—and typically fairly quickly—this would eliminate the private-label MBS pricing advantage.

The private-label MBS market was Wall Street's version of GSE mortgage-backed securities, and Wall Street was the source of the innovation that all but eliminated the bottleneck that had constrained the capacity of the private-label market in the past. In the early 2000s, Wall Street financial engineers seized on a technique previously used to finance consumer and commercial loans, known as the collateralized debt obligation, or CDO, and in conjunction with the rating agencies adapted it to the mortgage market. The mortgage CDO was born.

A mortgage CDO used a senior-subordinated structure, but rather than being collateralized by individual mortgages, it was composed of lower-rated tranches of previously issued private-label securities. An issuer would take a group of these tranches and cut them into junior and senior tranches. The rating agencies made the assumption that even in a stress scenario, only a small percentage of these lower-rated tranches would default at the same time (in statistical terms, their performance would be independent, rather than "correlated"), so that when they were put into a new structure and "retranched" as a CDO, a large percentage of that CDO's tranches could safely be rated AAA. It seemed like alchemy, but few questioned it. Securities that the rating agencies themselves had given A, BBB, or BB ratings could be purchased, pooled together, and retranched into a CDO, and three-quarters of the resulting security tranches would get AAA ratings. The CDO became the buyer of the risky private-label tranches, magically turning them into more AAA-rated securities eagerly purchased by other investors based on their top-tier credit rating.

The CDO transformed the mortgage market. From the time Fannie Mae became a shareholder-owned company in 1968, it and Freddie Mac had set the credit quality standards for prime conventional mortgages sold in the secondary market. The mortgage CDO changed that by dramatically expanding the scope and scale of the private-label market. If traditional mortgage lenders did not like the GSEs' underwriting standards or the guaranty fees we charged, they now had a ready financing alternative in private-label securities, whose AA- and AAA-rated tranches, endorsed by U.S. financial regulators, could be sold to a seemingly limitless universe of buyers across the globe.

In the second quarter of 2003, private-label securities made up less than 20 percent of all residential mortgage-backed securities issues—including Fannie Mae, Freddie Mac, Ginnie Mae, and private label. Barely a year later, so much new business had shifted to this market that in the third quarter of 2004, fully half of all MBS issues were private-label securities.

The replacement of Fannie Mae and Freddie Mac by private-label security issuers as the main source of financing for prime mortgage originators had an immediate and negative impact on mortgage credit quality. In private-label securitization, everyone in the mortgage lending chain except the investor—from the mortgage broker originating a loan to the primary lender acquiring it to the credit agency rating the tranches of the security that financed it to the Wall Street firm issuing the security—could make money from originating, packaging, and selling loans that might never be repaid. Neither private-label security issuers nor the rating agencies put any practical limit on the riskiness of the loans they would finance, and financial regulators refused to. Under those circumstances, the credit quality of a typical prime conventional home mortgage eroded dramatically in a remarkably short period of time.

Fannie Mae Eclipsed

The weakening in credit standards and use of higher-risk loan products that began in the second half of 2003 continued and accelerated in 2004. In January 2004, the Fannie Mae board approved the formation of a management-level Risk Policy Committee, which I chaired. All issues related to the company's interest rate or credit risk management were brought to this committee for review and decisions. I used Risk Policy to keep senior Fannie Mae management apprised of the changes in the profile of the loans we were seeing from our lenders and for discussing possible actions we might take in response to them.

One emerging trend was the increasing prevalence of "stated income" loans, where for a somewhat higher interest rate, a borrower would simply tell a lender what his or her income was but provide no documents to verify it (these later would come to be called "liar loans"). We also saw more loans on investment properties and more interest-only ARMs offered to weaker borrowers in high-cost areas where home prices had been rising rapidly. Then there was the pay-option ARM. In this new loan type, borrowers could choose whether to make a higher monthly payment if their interest rate rose or to have the amount of the payment increase added to the balance of their loan. We did not purchase or guarantee pay-option ARMs.

There was little we could do about the changing mix of products in the market other than try to assess and price them accurately or decline to accept them when pricing was too uncertain. We attempted to protect ourselves where we could. For several years, we had been purchasing AAA-rated private-label securities for our portfolio. We continued to buy them in 2004 but did our own independent stress analyses to verify their credit quality, and for over half our private-label portfolio holdings, we required some form of third-party credit enhancement, such as bond insurance, on top of the AAA security rating.

In the fall of 2004, we discussed using our stature in the market to develop and promulgate what we called "suitability standards" for interest-only mortgages. Ironically, what stopped us from going ahead with the idea was the fact that there were so little data on these loans' performance that we did not feel we had adequate justification for attempting to override our lenders' judgment as to which of their customers should be offered these loans and which should not. We let the matter drop.

Since 1990 Fannie Mae had increased its share of single-family mortgages financed in each successive year through 2003. During that time, the percentage of U.S. home mortgages we either purchased for portfolio or guaranteed as mortgage-backed securities more than doubled, rising from under 14 percent in December 1989 to over 28 percent in December 2003. This sustained growth, and our market dominance, had spurred increasingly concerted efforts by our opponents and critics to find a way to slow or reverse it. Legislative attempts to do so had been unsuccessful, but now, in 2004, the alternative private-market financing mechanism whose construction had begun 20 years earlier with the Secondary Mortgage Market Enhancement Act of 1984 was poised to accomplish what decades of political opposition could not.

Fueled by the relaxation of underwriting standards and the new types of high-risk loan products being introduced, growth in outstanding residential mortgages—which had been in double digits since 2001—accelerated to 14 percent in 2004. That same year, Fannie Mae's combined portfolio and mortgage-backed securities grew by less than 5 percent. The credit guaranty business we were losing to the private-label market had a related effect on our portfolio. Diminished issuance of Fannie Mae mortgage-backed securities led investors with a preference for these securities to bid up their prices, and this caused spreads between the yields on Fannie Mae debt and MBS to fall to a level where many fewer mortgages met our risk and return criteria for purchase. The portfolio, having grown at an average rate of 14 percent between 2000 and 2003, barely grew at all in 2004. With faster market growth and much slower growth in each of our two businesses, Fannie Mae's 28 percent share of outstanding mortgages financed in December 2003 plunged to 26 percent just 12 months later.

Beginning in 1986, Fannie Mae had reported double-digit growth in earnings for 17 consecutive years. We already had told investors we would be ending that string in 2004. Internally we were projecting 8 percent earnings growth for the year, and our outlook for the following year was much worse. As 2004 drew to a close, our very low credit guaranty and portfolio volumes—which we had no reason to believe would improve anytime soon—were leading us to anticipate no growth at all in earnings in 2005. I was working on how best to deliver that unwelcome message to the company's investors and security analysts in the conference call I was scheduled to have with them in the coming January.

The Fannie Mae board was keenly aware of, and concerned about, our loss of business to the private-label market. In what would be my penultimate financial report in October 2004, I told them:

> We think that both the rating agencies that determine the structuring requirements for these securities and the purchasers of subordinated private-label securities are underestimating their potential credit risk, particularly for IO [interest-only] ARMs. We are looking very hard at our own credit risk assessment and pricing for these products, but we suspect that there is a large percentage of ARM product being originated today for which we just aren't going to be the best bid, if we assess and price it using our best estimate of its riskiness.

Having lost to the private-label market the ability to influence the types of loans being made to borrowers, our job now had become to maintain our credit discipline and protect ourselves as best we could so that when the private-label market finally succumbed to its excesses (as it inevitably would), we would be in a position to step back in and help the recovery process. How long that might take—and how much damage would be done to borrowers, the mortgage market, and the housing market in the interim—was anybody's guess.

CHAPTER 13

A Compromise Attempt Turns into Full-Scale War

FANNIE MAE'S RELATIONSHIP WITH OFHEO, WHICH HAD BEEN difficult since Armando Falcon became director in the fall of 1999, worsened noticeably after Falcon hired Steve Blumenthal as counsel to the director in July 2002. Blumenthal came to OFHEO from Schwab Washington Research Group, where he followed Fannie Mae and Freddie Mac as an analyst specializing in financial services. Prior to moving to Schwab, Blumenthal had served as counsel to the House Energy and Commerce Committee and then been vice president and director of regulatory relations for the Securities Industry Association (SIA, now SIFMA), a trade group representing securities firms, banks, and asset managers.

Tensions with OFHEO Escalate

My first experience with Blumenthal came soon after he joined OFHEO. In September 2002, I had been called to OFHEO to brief Falcon on how Fannie Mae planned to reduce the 14-month August duration gap we were about to report publicly.. Blumenthal was at that session. Shortly afterwards I flew out West for a series of investor meetings. In one of them, a senior portfolio manager at a mutual fund told me he had received a phone call from "an assistant to Mr. Falcon" (subsequently confirmed to have been Blumenthal), informing him that Falcon had directed us to bring the duration gap to 12 months or less by the end of September or face regulatory consequences. That was not true, and even if it had been, it was highly improper for an OFHEO official to make a selective disclosure of nonpublic information about a company his agency regulated.

We learned of other instances in which Blumenthal made what we believed were inappropriate disclosures of regulatory information, and in January 2003, Fannie Mae General Counsel Ann Kappler sent a letter to OFHEO General Counsel Pollard citing several of these instances and asking OFHEO to put a stop to the disclosures. Kappler told Pollard that she was making this request out of a fiduciary duty to Fannie Mae's shareholders and in spite of the danger of regulatory reprisal. The response to Kappler's letter came not from Pollard but from Falcon. Falcon denied that any of the information Blumenthal had disclosed was nonpublic. He also said that OFHEO had begun a program of outreach to Fannie Mae and Freddie Mac's institutional investors at his direction, for what he claimed were safety and soundness reasons, and that the outreach would continue.

We were battling OFHEO over another issue at around the same time. Since 2001 Falcon had been saying that his economists and researchers were working on a report about Fannie Mae and Freddie Mac's systemic risk. This was one more example of the profound difference in the way Fannie Mae and banks were regulated. Just as no bank regulator would have had their senior officials call the investors or security analysts of any of the companies they regulated, neither would the Federal Reserve or Treasury ever have considered putting out a report titled "Large Commercial Banks and Systemic Risk." We thought the Fannie Mae systemic risk study was a very bad idea, and we said so to Falcon.

Throughout 2001 and 2002, FM Watch and its allies had been conducting a relentless campaign to convince the public that Fannie Mae posed unacceptable risk to the financial system. We knew that was not the case, but we were virtually alone in saying so. I often thought how valuable it would have been to have a safety and soundness regulator with the objectivity and expertise to examine our risk management practices and the credibility to vouch for them (or critique them) publicly. In OFHEO we had just the opposite. During my time at Fannie Mae, no senior OFHEO official—outside of the examination staff—expressed any interest in learning about how we viewed and managed our financial risks. From what we had been able to gather, the proposed OFHEO systemic risk study was not going to be about our risks and how we managed them. Instead it would be an exercise focused on the role of OFHEO in mitigating the systemic effects triggered by a hypothetical failure of either Fannie Mae or Freddie Mac. Far from helping to counteract the FM Watch propaganda, the OFHEO systemic risk study would reinforce and build on it.

Early in 2003, it was apparent that Falcon was going to publish his study in spite of our opposition, so we went to Treasury and the White House and asked them to intervene to stop it. Falcon picked February 4 as the day for the systemic risk study to be released. He arranged for copies to be sent to key politicians and scheduled a speech before the Bond Market Association in New York to publicize it. Before he could give that speech, however, he received a call from the White House personnel office requesting his resignation so that President Bush could appoint his own director, a man named Mark Brickell, to run OFHEO. Falcon resigned that day, although he said he would remain in office until the Senate confirmed his successor. Stories the following day in the major newspapers covered the Brickell appointment but made little mention of the systemic risk study.

The timing of the White House call convinced Falcon that Fannie Mae had arranged it in retaliation for his having gone ahead with the study. That gave us too much credit. The White House had given us a heads-up before the announcement, but we were not consulted in advance. Falcon was a Democrat, a protégé of Henry Gonzalez, and a Clinton appointee. The White House had been looking for a replacement for him and finally had found one in Brickell. Brickell was CEO of a derivatives trading company called

Blackbird Holdings, who had spent 25 years with JP Morgan and was one of the country's leading experts in derivatives. He founded the International Swaps and Derivatives Association—the trade group for participants in the over-the-counter (OTC) derivatives market—and while at JP Morgan had spent countless hours in Washington lobbying members and their staffs on OTC derivatives-related issues. The administration believed that Brickell's combination of derivatives knowledge and Washington experience made him an ideal candidate to head OFHEO.

But Brickell could not get confirmed, ironically because of questions raised by Senate Democrats, led by Sarbanes. At a hearing in July, Sarbanes cited Brickell's lobbying against the regulation of derivatives and his support for Fannie Mae's proposed "supervisory" approach to OFHEO's risk-based capital standard while at JP Morgan as reasons for concern that he might not be tough enough on us. Those reservations could not be overcome, and almost a year after Brickell's nomination, in January 2004, the White House withdrew it. Falcon remained at OFHEO, believing Fannie Mae had tried but failed to have him removed. Had there been any doubt before, from that point on he was a committed enemy.

Ten Years of Peace

The political landscape shifted again in 2003. After the 2002 midterm elections, Republicans regained control of the Senate, and Alabama Senator Richard Shelby replaced Sarbanes as chairman of the Senate Banking Committee. Treasury Secretary O'Neill was forced to resign by President Bush in December 2002 and was replaced by John Snow. Like O'Neill, Snow had a mix of government and private industry experience. He held a PhD in economics and a JD in law. After a short stint as a practicing attorney, Snow took a series of jobs in the Department of Transportation under President Ford in the 1970s, ultimately being named administrator of the National Highway Safety Commission in 1976. His experience in the Ford administration led him to a career in the railroad industry, where he rose to become chairman of a railroad conglomerate called CSX in 1991. He held that position until sworn in as Treasury secretary in February 2003.

As he had done with O'Neill, Raines went to see Snow very shortly after he assumed office. The two men knew each other from the Business Roundtable—a group of business CEOs who sought to have an impact on public policy issues—and they were able to draw on that familiarity to establish an open and candid dialogue. Raines quickly found that unlike Larry Summers, Snow did not have predetermined views on the issues that gave rise to the conflict between the GSEs and our competitors and critics, and more so than Paul O'Neill, Snow felt he might be able to play a useful role in helping to resolve those issues. Snow's willingness to engage on what Treasury called "the GSE problem," together with his lack of any personal or ideological agenda on its key components, suggested to Raines a possible way of addressing the intense political opposition to Fannie Mae that had been building since the beginning of his chairmanship.

We had no major conflicts with the Bush administration; to the contrary, as recently as October 2002, the president had praised Raines and Fannie Mae publicly. Snow, not Summers, was Treasury secretary. And Baker seemed to have moderated his demands. He held only two hearings on the government-sponsored enterprises in 2002, and his April 2003 inquiries to Treasury and HUD indicated that the focus of his GSE concerns had narrowed to regulation and governance. Both were issues in which we had an interest as well. We had reached the end of our rope with OFHEO and were eager to consider alternatives. We believed that a strong, capable, and credible regulator would be better for our investors, as long as that regulator was objective and not politicized. And ambiguities in our charter and governance lay at the heart of our battles with large lenders. Clarifications in some of these areas, including selected concessions on our part, had the potential to lower the competitive temperature to everyone's benefit.

Weighing these factors, Raines made a crucial decision. Eleven years had passed since the landmark GSE legislation in 1992, and during that time many of the issues thought settled then had been put back into play. There now seemed to be an opportunity to achieve, as Raines put it, another "10 years of peace" politically for Fannie Mae. He did not want to let that opportunity slip by. Having resisted efforts at GSE legislation since the beginning of his chairmanship, Raines would change tack and work with Snow and Treasury to produce a bill Congress could pass.

Baker introduced HR 2575 on June 24, 2003. His bill abolished OFHEO and shifted safety and soundness regulation of Fannie Mae and Freddie Mac to the Office of Thrift Supervision (OTS), under Treasury. The bill contained a number of new GSE regulatory powers for the OTS, but it did not revoke Treasury's $2.25 billion GSE backstop as his 2000 legislation had done. Baker said he had discussed his legislation informally with Treasury but had no understanding with Snow about any of its provisions, and that he had introduced his bill merely "to stake out a proposal." House Financial Services Committee Chairman Mike Oxley said he would hold hearings on the Baker bill in September, when representatives of the government-sponsored enterprises and the administration would be invited to present their views on it.

Raines and Snow spent the summer in discussions over the content of a bill both could support. They agreed that OFHEO should be replaced with a new safety and soundness regulator, housed within the Treasury Department. They also agreed on removing the budget of the new regulator from the appropriations process and on giving HUD enhanced powers for enforcing the GSEs' affordable housing goals. Raines made a major concession on risk-based capital, in which he was willing to allow flexibilities in the standard that we had been unwilling to concede in 1992. (OFHEO's failures in implementing the 1992 version made this concession easier.) But he took firm stances against allowing the new safety and soundness regulator to change our minimum capital requirement and against moving program approval authority from HUD to the new regulator.

By the time of the Oxley hearings, Raines and Snow had reached agreement on all of the principal provisions of the proposed legislation, and they had a handshake deal on what each would say in their respective testimonies. Following established procedure, Snow submitted his written testimony to the National Economic Council (NEC)—the economic policy coordination office of the White House—for review by the Bush administration's economic policy team. At that point, things began to go badly awry.

The Administration Rises in Opposition

When Snow appeared before Oxley's committee on September 10, he said in both his written and oral testimonies that Treasury supported the proposed new safety and soundness regulator being given the authority to oversee existing as well as new government-sponsored enterprise activities to ensure they were consistent with our charters. That was contrary to what had been agreed to with Raines, and it was a provision Fannie Mae could not accept. Raines made that clear when he testified to Oxley's committee on September 25. Oxley was hoping to draft consensus legislation, but with Treasury and Fannie Mae on opposite sides, he was forced to admit that the program approval issue was "still kind of out there." The committee, he said, would have to make a call on it before the revised version of HR 2575—the Secondary Mortgage Market Enterprises Regulatory Improvement Act—was marked up in early October.

Markup never took place. The administration learned that Oxley and Baker had agreed to leave program approval with HUD to make HR 2575 more palatable to Democrats, and on October 7, the day before markup was scheduled, it withdrew its support of the bill. A spokesperson for the administration, Treasury Assistant Secretary Wayne Abernathy, was quoted as saying that HR 2575 was "not a credible bill," and that the administration "doesn't support sending the legislation to the House floor in its current form because it isn't strong enough to achieve the goal of making the markets safer and more secure."

It was revealing that the administration's about-face on the GSE legislation was announced and explained not by Secretary Snow or Treasury Undersecretary of Domestic Finance Peter Fisher but by Abernathy. Abernathy had been assistant secretary for financial institutions, under Fisher, only since December 2002. He had come to Treasury after 20 years on the staff of the Senate Banking Committee, where he had been a protégé of Senator Gramm. Gramm said at Abernathy's nomination hearing, "For all practical purposes, when I was chairman, Wayne Abernathy was chairman of the committee." Senator Sarbanes commented at that same hearing, "The Republican economist of the committee—I always thought it was Senator Gramm, but it was really Wayne Abernathy," adding, "Wayne has been involved in every major piece of legislation which has been considered by the committee since 1981." That legislation of course included the Gramm-Leach-Bliley repeal of Glass-Steagall in 1999—and the 1992 GSE legislation.

Abernathy's sudden appearance as the official administration spokesman on GSE issues spoke volumes about the internal politics at the White House. Snow's draft testimony, when circulated broadly by the NEC among economic policy types within the administration, had set off alarm bells. Fannie Mae was threatening to repeat what we had done in 1992: convince Congress to pass legislation that would simultaneously make us stronger and close off the most promising avenues our opponents had for curtailing our influence. None of the top economic officials in the Bush administration at the time—Snow and Fisher at Treasury, Steve Friedman at the NEC (who as a former Fannie Mae board member had recused himself from GSE issues), or Josh Bolten at the OMB—had particularly strong views on Fannie Mae. But many people within and outside their organizations did, as did FM Watch, its members, and supporters. When those people made their arguments to White House Chief of Staff Andy Card for why opposing us would be good politics as well as policy for the Bush administration, Card came down forcefully on their side. Minority home ownership notwithstanding, opposing Fannie Mae would be a White House priority going forward.

The administration's opposition to the Oxley bill effectively killed it. Both sides maintained publicly that their remaining differences could be worked out, but in reality we were moving further apart. The focus of the administration's efforts already had shifted to the Senate, where Banking Committee Chairman Shelby was putting together his own version of a GSE bill.

As late as September 17, Charles Gabriel of the Washington Research Group—who widely was viewed as the best-informed and most savvy observer of the GSE political scene—had written to his subscribers, "The Bush Administration has given no public or (I believe) private hints that it feels the GSEs should be throttled (particularly before Election Day 2004)." The ink was barely dry on that statement when it no longer was true. Right around that time, the White House formed a working group on GSE issues, headed by Card. That group sanctioned and served as the focal point for a now much more aggressive and visible set of anti-GSE activities that extended beyond the administration to include the spectrum of our opponents and critics.

Abernathy appeared at an event at the Heritage Foundation, a conservative think tank long critical of Fannie Mae, on October 22. Joining him there was Peter Wallison of the American Enterprise Institute, another prominent Fannie Mae critic. Wallison called for Fannie Mae privatization, and Abernathy acknowledged in his speech that the White House would lose a vote in Congress on its top priorities for GSE regulation but said it would not back away from them. Then, responding to a reporter's question, he said the administration would be open to discussions about removing Treasury's $2.25 billion backstop. News of this statement roiled the market for Fannie Mae debt, and given the reaction to a similar comment by Gary Gensler in 2000, it seemed to have been a deliberate provocation. Later that day, Raines wrote Snow a letter expressing his disappointment with the episode and saying to Snow that he "hope[d] we can change course."

But the course had been set, and more members of the administration were following it. In early November, the chairman of the President's Council of Economic Advisers, Greg Mankiw, gave a speech to the Conference of State Bank Supervisors about GSE reform. After running through the now-standard talking points about Fannie Mae and Freddie Mac's charter benefits, size, and risk, Mankiw detailed the authorities the administration wanted for the new government-sponsored enterprise regulator. He noted three that were familiar—permanent funding, broad authority to set risk-based and minimum capital standards, and authority to reject new activities—and then added an element not in the Oxley legislation but about to be requested in the Shelby bill: "receivership powers necessary to wind down the affairs of a troubled GSE." Mankiw dismissed the impact the proposed GSE reforms might have on the housing market, saying, "If the housing GSEs were to lose some of their implicit subsidies, private financial institutions would eagerly step in."

Senator Shelby said in January that before producing a final version of his bill, he wanted to hold hearings in February to solicit a range of views on GSE reform and regulation. He specifically mentioned Fed Chairman Greenspan as one of the people he wanted to hear from. A spokesperson for Shelby said, "[Greenspan] has already made it clear that he has some important viewpoints on this matter. He's a recognized expert in many areas, and it would be important to get his input." Greenspan had made numerous comments about the government-sponsored enterprises and GSE reform since the first Baker bill in 2000, all of them carefully crafted to indicate support for restraining Fannie Mae and Freddie Mac while avoiding endorsement of any specific action. His Senate Banking Committee testimony would be different. Since the administration had taken off the gloves with the GSEs, he would as well.

Greenspan's Senate testimony was scheduled for February 24, and the day before, he went out of his way in a speech to the Credit Union National Association to question the wisdom of consumers' preference for financing their homes with 30-year fixed-rate mortgages—the loan type that comprised over 90 percent of Fannie Mae's mortgage portfolio and mortgage-backed security guarantees. He told his audience, "Homeowners pay a lot of money for the right to refinance and for the insurance against increasing mortgage payments," adding, "Recent research within the Federal Reserve suggests that many home owners might have saved tens of thousands of dollars had they held adjustable-rate mortgages rather than fixed-rate mortgages during the past decade." (In hindsight, yes; interest rates had fallen for the last 20 years.) He went on to counsel, "American consumers might benefit if lenders provided greater mortgage product alternatives to the traditional mortgages."

Reading about these comments at the time, I was astonished. The new "alternative" mortgage products Greenspan was touting already were flooding into the market, and many of them we either wouldn't finance because we thought they were too risky or we couldn't finance because the private-label securities market was underestimating their risk and outbidding us for them. Greenspan's comments about adjustable and fixed-rate mortgages, I thought, were so wildly off base economically that they must have had a purpose politically.

They did. They were the first of the three-part litany developed by FM Watch four years earlier: the GSEs don't do much for housing, they're risky, and something must be done about it. Greenspan added the rest in his Senate Banking Committee testimony. He framed the risk issue this way:

> Given their history of innovation in mortgage-backed securities, why do Fannie and Freddie now generate such substantial concern? The unease relates mainly to the scale and growth of the mortgage-related assets held on their balance sheets. That growth has been facilitated, at least in part, by a perceived special advantage of these institutions that keeps normal market restraints from being fully effective.

The "special advantage" was our federal charter and the implicit guaranty accorded to our debt by investors. What to do about it? Greenspan dismissed the possibility of disciplined risk management as a solution to his concern with the overstated claim that "the current system depends on the risk managers at Fannie and Freddie to do everything just right." Instead, his prescription was, "Our financial system would be more robust if we relied on a market-based system that spreads interest rate risks, rather than on the current system, which concentrates such risk with the GSEs."

To no one's surprise, Greenspan's primary recommendations for government-sponsored enterprise reform were the same the White House was advocating: "In sum, Congress needs to create a GSE regulator with authority on a par with that of banking regulators, with a free hand to set appropriate capital standards, and with a clear process sanctioned by the Congress for placing a GSE in receivership." But he had a further recommendation of his own:

> However, if the Congress takes only these actions, it runs the risk of solidifying investors' perceptions that the GSEs are instruments of the government, and that their debt is equivalent to government debt . . . Thus, the GSEs need to be limited in the issuance of GSE debt and in the purchase of assets, both mortgages and nonmortgages, that they hold.

With that, his secret was out. Effective risk management could not overcome Greenspan's objections to us, and even "bank-like regulation" would not be enough. There had to be federally mandated limits on the size of our portfolio.

Greenspan's testimony stripped away the pretense that there could be any such thing as consensus GSE legislation. What the Bush administration, the members and supporters of FM Watch, and Greenspan all wanted from the Shelby bill were mechanisms that could be used to our disadvantage. Having begun the legislative process in the spring of 2003 in good-faith negotiations with Secretary Snow on the content of the Baker-Oxley bill, in early 2004 we found ourselves furiously playing defense to stop provisions we opposed from being put into the Shelby bill against our will. And the provision being pushed the hardest by the administration was the one we objected to the most—receivership. For us, receivership was a poison pill. A safety and soundness regulator housed in Treasury, under Treasury control, and with receivership powers could liquidate Fannie Mae for any reason. We couldn't possibly agree to that.

Receivership was an idea that began with Treasury and had been endorsed by the administration and Greenspan. It never had been on the FM Watch agenda. None of our competitors were pushing for it. They wanted Treasury to have more control over us—so they could earn more profits at our or consumers' expense—but they wanted us to remain in business. Talk of a receivership provision also worried the rating agencies. Standard & Poor's, Moody's, and Fitch all were watching the Shelby bill closely for signs of a change in the relationship between the GSEs and the government, and all warned that evidence of such a change could trigger a downgrade on our debt. Fitch and S&P specifically singled out receivership as a source of concern. S&P's Mike DeStefano stated the obvious: "Giving the regulator that kind of power over the GSEs is not a good thing for debt holders."

Receivership became the battleground in the Shelby bill. To get a bill through his committee, Shelby was forced to accept an amendment by Republican Bob Bennett of Utah (whose son headed Fannie Mae's Utah partnership office) requiring that the new regulator give Congress up to 45 days to reverse any decision it made to place a GSE in receivership. With that amendment, on April 1 Shelby's bill passed narrowly, 12 to 9, on a near party-line vote. Only Democrat Zell Miller from Georgia voted with the Republicans.

The bill would have faced a bitter partisan fight on the floor, but it never got there. Once again, the Bush administration pulled its support from the legislation. In a joint statement, Secretary Snow and HUD Secretary Alphonso Jackson said the amended bill "is now unworthy of the reform efforts." The administration was walking away from GSE legislation over a provision that had not even been contemplated in the Oxley bill six months earlier, from which it also had walked away. The goalposts were moving, and Shelby was not happy about it. He badly wanted to get a bill done. Shelby said he would continue to press for GSE reform in the Senate, but he did not sound optimistic about its prospects. "It's on the calendar," he said. "We'll see what happens."

Operation Noriega

The administration already had decided on a different approach. Its next move was spelled out with remarkable candor in a front-page article on April 28 in the *Wall Street Journal* titled "Regulators Hit Fannie, Freddie with New Assault." The article began, "Frustrated by its inability to win congressional approval to tighten regulation of mortgage giants Fannie Mae and Freddie Mac, the government is pursuing the same goal through regulatory fiat." It explained:

> The administration still sees a need for legislation to clamp down on Fannie and Freddie but thinks regulatory steps will help constrain them in the meantime. By effectively parking more tanks on the companies' lawns, officials also hope to persuade them that they won't be able to avoid tougher regulation by resisting the administration's initiatives in Congress.

The administration had an internal nickname for these efforts, Operation Noriega. It was a reference to the harassment strategies the U.S. military used against former Panamanian strongman Manuel Noriega, in which it blasted loud rock music at him nonstop to dislodge him from his refuge at the Vatican embassy and get him to surrender. The administration's GSE version ranged from minor harassments to major onslaughts. Included among the harassments were an inquiry by the Internal Revenue Service into possible misuse of the Fannie Mae Foundation, an examination by the Department of Labor of the structure and investments of our 401(k) plan, and a review by HUD of whether the consulting work done by our International Housing Finance Services Group—a five-person operation in existence for 15 years, which took on many of its assignments at the request of the State Department—was within the scope of our charter. The more serious and consequential actions were taken by Treasury, by HUD on affordable housing, and by OFHEO.

Fannie Mae's charter act contained a provision that said, "The corporation is authorized to set aside any mortgages held by it . . .

and, upon approval of the Secretary of the Treasury, to issue and sell securities based upon the mortgages so set aside." For all of Fannie Mae's history, we and Treasury had interpreted this provision as giving Treasury what we both referred to as "traffic cop" authority—making sure our planned debt issues did not interfere with theirs. Abernathy began telling the press that the approval provision in our (and Freddie Mac's) charter could be interpreted as giving Treasury the ability to set absolute limits on our debt issuance. We disagreed with that interpretation. Everyone consulted with their lawyers, and in July Treasury said that the Justice Department had given them a legal opinion that they could limit our debt issues for safety and soundness reasons or to protect the financial markets.

Treasury did not act on this opinion, however. Perhaps that was because they intended to use the threat of limiting our debt issuance as negotiating leverage in future legislation. But it also may have been that reality had intervened. Our portfolio—which critics insisted would grow uncontrollably unless the government did something to restrain it—was in fact three percent smaller in July 2004 than it had been in September 2003. Away from the political world, financial market conditions had changed drastically since our legislative discussions began the past spring. We were losing share to the private-label securities market, and spreads between mortgages and our debt costs had tightened to the point where there were many fewer portfolio purchase opportunities than there had been previously. Our critics, including the Fed chairman, might not have accorded much importance to our risk disciplines, but they were having a pronounced effect on our business.

HUD's major contribution to the regulatory assault was significantly higher affordable housing goals for Fannie Mae and Freddie Mac for the years 2005 through 2008. In May, HUD proposed a series of increases in the percentage of our business we were required to do with low- and moderate-income borrowers, from 50 percent in the 2002–2004 period to an eventual 56 percent in 2008. Even greater relative increases were proposed for our underserved area and special affordable housing goals, and a new set of home purchase subgoals was added as well. We were not an originator and could buy or guarantee only what our lenders offered to us. HUD's proposed affordable housing percentages were well above the percentages our lenders were originating (although HUD claimed they were not). I believed at the time that one of the rationales for boosting the goals so much was to force us to cut back on the amount of the business we did that was not goals-eligible. Many of my colleagues agreed with this assessment; they called it "using the numerator to control the denominator."

The White House had tried to replace Armando Falcon as director of OFHEO in 2003, but the nomination of his proposed successor, Mark Brickell, had stalled in the Senate. That was a fortunate break for them. On January 21, 2004, the White House withdrew Brickell's nomination without telling him, leaving Falcon in place. OFHEO was in the best position of anyone to make our lives difficult, and Falcon was perfect for the job. His dislike of Fannie Mae had gone beyond the institutional; he felt Raines and other company executives, including me, did not respect him. (We thought he was a very poor regulator, but it was never personal.) For Falcon, allying with the administration's crusade against the GSEs was a path not only to getting himself and his agency back in its good graces but also to settling a score. He eagerly followed it. When the administration abandoned its efforts on the Shelby bill over its compromise receivership clause, Falcon began working on a regulation that used an existing OFHEO authority to create what he called a "liquidating conservatorship" for us and Freddie Mac that he contended could have the same effect as receivership. Falcon also had launched a review of Fannie Mae's accounting and was saying publicly that he believed this review would find irregularities that would require us to restate our earnings.

Faced with the bleak prospect of unrelenting opposition from the Fed, the Treasury, HUD, and OFHEO, in the spring of 2004 we again undertook a serious study of potential changes to our business structure, including full privatization. We retained Goldman Sachs for this project, which I led. Our efforts focused on the portfolio business, the bête noire of our critics. With Goldman we looked at a large number of restructuring possibilities, including spin-offs, nonagency subsidiaries, changing the portfolio to a REIT, and breaking the portfolio into smaller independent units. We also considered Sallie Mae–style privatization. We had a full discussion of all of these alternatives with our board in July of 2004, but as was the case with the Maxwell privatization efforts in the 1980s, we could not come to agreement that any one of them would be better for our stakeholders—home buyers and our shareholders—than our current structure.

As the year came to a close, we knew we had to do something to appease our critics. We did not want to give in on minimum capital because that was a slippery slope that could lead to our business becoming uneconomic, but we were increasingly open to a negotiated limit on the size of the portfolio.

The parallel worlds of Fannie Mae never were more divergent than in 2004. In our political world, we were desperately trying to fend off legislative and regulatory assaults by critics who claimed that the interest rate risk of our mortgage portfolio—which had been kept well under control for the past two decades and just reduced further through our 2003 risk disciplines—posed grave threats to the financial system. At the same time, in our business world, we were scrambling to protect ourselves against the greatly increased credit risk of the new mortgage products and risk combinations now prevalent only because they could be financed through the private-label MBS mechanism promoted and supported by the very group of critics attacking us in our political world.

Our political critics never raised the size and credit risk of our MBS guaranty business as issues. To the contrary, Greenspan had concluded his February Senate Banking Committee testimony by saying:

> Fannie and Freddie should be encouraged to continue to expand mortgage securitization, keeping mortgage markets deep and liquid while limiting the size of their portfolios. This action

will allow the mortgage markets to support home ownership and home building in a manner consistent with preserving safe and sound financial markets of the United States.

For years, Fannie Mae's adversaries, including Greenspan, had convinced themselves that GSE interest rate risk was the only mortgage risk that posed any danger. Now there was a real risk looming right in front of them, largely of their own making, and they simply didn't see it.

PART FOUR

Countdown to
the Meltdown

CHAPTER 14

Allegations of Fraud:
The Special Examination

I N THE FALL OF 2002, FRANK RAINES AND I RECEIVED IDENTICAL anonymous letters containing allegations of serious accounting, financial reporting, and internal control irregularities at Freddie Mac between 1999 and 2001. We turned them over to our general counsel, Ann Kappler, who faxed a copy of the letter Raines received to Freddie Mac's chairman and CEO, Leland Brendsel. This seemingly innocuous action began a lengthy and complex chain of events that became entangled in the mortgage wars, intensified the mortgage crisis, and ultimately led to the demise of both Freddie Mac and Fannie Mae as public companies.

Freddie Mac Stumbles

Brendsel informed his board of directors of the letter, and on December 10, 2002, Freddie Mac's Audit Committee retained the outside law firm of Baker Botts L.L.P to look into its allegations. Baker Botts quickly concluded that the allegations were unfounded, but during their investigation, their team found other issues they said they "believed required further inquiry." Baker Botts shared the findings of their investigatory work with Freddie Mac's new auditor, PriceWaterhouse Coopers (PwC). Freddie Mac had hired PwC in

March 2002 to replace their former auditor, Arthur Andersen, after questions arose about Andersen's role in the collapse of Enron in the fall of 2001. In the course of its audit of Freddie Mac's 2002 financial statements, PwC also had found accounting treatments it questioned and that it suspected might involve more than simple accounting error.

On January 22, 2003, the Freddie Mac board issued a press release saying it would publish unaudited financial statements for 2002 that would be subject to change as PwC completed its audit. It also revealed that "management expects to restate its financial results for 2002, 2001, and possibly 2000." The board noted that the reaudit involved "accounting policies previously used by management and approved by the company's prior auditor, Arthur Andersen," having to do with the "hedge accounting treatment of certain transactions including those occasioned by the implementation of FAS 133."

The Office of Federal Housing Enterprise Oversight followed the Freddie Mac press release with a statement from Falcon, which given the circumstances was surprisingly mild. Freddie Mac generally stayed in the background on political issues—allowing Fannie Mae to take the lead (and the heat)—so at OFHEO as on Capitol Hill, they were considered the good GSE. Falcon's statement neutrally described Freddie Mac's reaudit as "the result of accounting interpretations and the resulting uncertainty associated with the timing of their income recognition" and called it "prudent and appropriate." It did not mention the earnings restatement at all. Falcon praised Freddie Mac as a "well-capitalized institution with sound internal controls and prudent risk management," while pledging, "OFHEO will remain fully engaged with Freddie Mac as the reaudit progresses."

Freddie Mac put out its unaudited 2002 earnings on January 27. That same day, the Freddie Mac board retained Baker Botts to investigate the circumstances surrounding the transactions under review by PwC. PwC continued its reaudit during the winter and spring of 2003, as Baker Botts conducted their investigation of the accounting issues. On June 4, the Baker Botts investigators learned that Freddie

Mac's president and chief operating officer, David Glenn, had altered entries and in one case removed pages from a notebook he kept and had been asked to produce in connection with the investigation. Baker Botts immediately informed the Freddie Mac board of this discovery. The board's reaction was swift and severe. On Monday, June 9, Freddie Mac announced the retirement of their chairman and CEO, Leland Brendsel; the resignation of their chief financial officer, Vaughn Clarke; and the termination of Glenn. Brendsel's job was split in two. Outside director Shaun O'Malley was elected nonexecutive chairman of the board, and Greg Parseghian—Freddie Mac's chief investment officer and the head of its mortgage portfolio business—was made president and CEO.

Falcon was caught flat-footed by these developments. Only a few days earlier, OFHEO had released their 2003 annual report to Congress on Fannie Mae and Freddie Mac. The report included a discussion of the Freddie Mac reaudit that ended with the statement, "We remain satisfied that the Board of Directors and executive management are taking the appropriate action." The Freddie Mac board informed Falcon of its decision concerning the three executives, and the rationale behind it, on June 6. Scrambling to appear to be on top of the situation, Falcon sent the board a letter on June 7 in which he attempted to front-run the announcement the board told him it would be making on June 9. In that letter, released to the media, Falcon said in part, "I have become increasingly concerned about evidence that has come to light of weakness in controls and personnel expertise in accounting areas and the disclosure of misconduct on the part of Freddie Mac employees." He added, "The removal of members of the management team only goes a part of the way toward correcting serious problems—concerns surrounding management practices and controls remain." That same day, Falcon ordered a special OFHEO examination of Freddie Mac, and he put Steve Blumenthal in charge of conducting it.

The Freddie Mac accounting restatement and executive turmoil came at an extremely bad time for Falcon. A strong consensus already existed in Congress that OFHEO was feckless and not up to the task of regulating either Fannie Mae or Freddie Mac. Falcon's clumsy attempt to play catch-up with the Freddie Mac situation only served to reinforce that view. On June 24, Richard Baker introduced HR 2575, abolishing OFHEO and shifting safety and soundness regulation of Fannie Mae and Freddie Mac to the OTS, inside the Treasury Department. The following month, Congressman Ed Royce of California introduced a bill creating a new regulator for Fannie Mae, Freddie Mac, and the Federal Home Loan Banks, also inside Treasury, and on July 31 and September 25, two more bills abolishing OFHEO were introduced in the Senate.

Facing sharp criticism for having missed the severity of the problems at Freddie Mac—one of only two companies he regulated—and with his agency in danger of being eliminated, Falcon knew he had to respond decisively. On July 14, he announced in a letter to the Senate Banking and Appropriations Committees that he intended to conduct a special examination of Fannie Mae, similar to the one he had announced in early June for Freddie Mac. Then he got tough on the good GSE.

Baker Botts released its "Internal Investigation of Certain Accounting Matters" to Freddie Mac's board and the general public on July 22. One revelation that attracted attention was that Freddie Mac's newly appointed president and CEO, Greg Parseghian, had as the company's chief investment officer approved many of the transactions PwC found to have been accounted for improperly. Shaun O'Malley, Freddie Mac's new chairman, and James Doty, the Baker Botts partner who led the accounting investigation, each said they were fully aware of Parseghian's involvement with the transactions at the time the board proposed him as CEO and that they continued to support him. But a number of observers were troubled by Parseghian's connection to the accounting difficulties, and some were saying the company would have been better served with a different choice for CEO.

Critics' reaction to the Baker Botts report gave Falcon a second chance to exert his regulatory authority in the Freddie Mac situation, and he did not miss it. He directed the Freddie Mac board to replace

Parseghian as president and CEO and to commence a search for his successor. Falcon had no statutory authority to require the Freddie Mac board to dismiss Parseghian (or Freddie Mac's general counsel, Maud Mater, whom he also wanted replaced), so in an August 22 letter, he made a thinly veiled reference to the potential consequences of the board's not acceding to his wishes: "The Board understands that OFHEO has continuing supervisory authority with regards to the matters addressed in this letter and that OFHEO is committed to the safe and sound operation of Freddie Mac," he said. He added, "The actions outlined here should assist in meeting that end. The Board's compliance signals a commitment to cooperation and to ensuring the continued safe and sound operation of the Corporation."

Directing the board to oust Parseghian may have made sense for Falcon politically, but it resulted in the near complete replacement of Freddie Mac's top management in a very short period of time. Parseghian had been at the company since 1996, and with Brendsel gone, he was the most seasoned and experienced risk manager Freddie Mac had. In December 2003, the Freddie Mac board chose Richard Syron as Parseghian's successor. Syron had been president of the Federal Reserve Bank of Boston between 1989 and 1994, but his most recent positions had been as chairman of the American Stock Exchange and as chairman of the Thermo Electron Corporation, a provider of scientific instruments. Syron lacked the in-depth mortgage experience of either Brendsel or Parseghian. The extensive turnover of Freddie Mac's top management, coupled with the choice of Syron to replace Parseghian as CEO, came just as mortgage credit standards were being relaxed dramatically and would have profound impacts on the company's response to the worsening credit environment in the months and years immediately ahead.

Falcon Sets His Sights on Fannie Mae

OFHEO issued their report on the special examination of Freddie Mac in December 2003, the same month Syron became CEO. In the report, OFHEO noted that most of the accounting judgments

PwC found to be incorrect were related to the implementation of FAS 133 in 2001. OFHEO said, "It is clear that management went to extraordinary lengths to transact around FAS 133 and push the edge of the GAAP envelope," adding, "Freddie Mac cast aside accounting rules, internal controls, disclosure standards, and the public trust in the pursuit of steady earnings growth."

I took careful note of OFHEO's analysis of the causes of the Freddie Mac accounting errors. If OFHEO were looking for any of the same issues at Fannie Mae, there was a simple reason they would not find them. We and Freddie Mac had approached FAS 133 very differently. Our response had been to work with the FASB to improve the standard, to avoid using derivatives that did not qualify for hedge accounting, and to publish a simple and understandable supplemental non-GAAP earnings measure that eliminated the distorting effects of FAS 133. Freddie Mac's approach to dealing with the FAS 133 distortions involved trying to offset them with what OFHEO claimed were accounting treatments that were inconsistent with GAAP and transactions OFHEO believed had little or no business purpose. Freddie Mac's accounting problems stemmed directly from their choice of how to implement FAS 133. We had none of those problems because we had made a different choice.

OFHEO officially launched their special examination of Fannie Mae in November 2003, in a letter to us containing an extensive request for documents. That December OFHEO was granted $7.5 million in additional funding to pay for their special examinations of both Fannie Mae and Freddie Mac, and in February of 2004, OFHEO contracted with Deloitte & Touche to serve as consultants for the Fannie Mae examination. By March the Fannie Mae examination was well under way.

On the business side of Fannie Mae's parallel worlds, I was confident we would acquit ourselves well in the OFHEO exam. But I also was keenly aware of what was being said on the political side. Led by FM Watch (which by this time had renamed itself FM Policy Focus), the anti–Fannie Mae forces were filling the media with their version of what was about to unfold. The storyline they were pushing was that Fannie Mae would turn out to have even worse accounting problems than had been found at Freddie Mac. Like them we would be forced to restate our earnings—possibly in conjunction with changes in top management as had been the case at Freddie Mac—and in response, Congress finally would agree on long-overdue legislation to toughen the regulation of both companies.

In the Fannie Mae special examination, Falcon had a path to redemption. If he could force an earnings restatement, he would be a hero to Fannie Mae's critics and also do more than just prevent OFHEO from being replaced as a regulator; he could come away with more power for his agency.

The special examination was barely under way before Falcon trumpeted his objective. One day prior to the March 31 issuance of a routine OFHEO press release announcing our fourth quarter 2003 capital classification, Falcon directed his public relations staff to include the following sentences in the release:

> In addition, Fannie Mae's capital calculation is based on financial information and the application of accounting policies currently under review by OFHEO. The outcome of the review may result in a restatement of prior period results and a revision of the respective capital calculations.

We vehemently protested this addition. We knew of nothing we had done or that OFHEO was reviewing that would warrant their alarming our investors with such an explicit warning in advance of any actual finding. Moreover, it was the second time in barely a month that Falcon had used the media to convey a message about our accounting that was without a basis in fact. On February 24, he had provided the *Wall Street Journal* with an advance copy of a letter he was about to send to Frank Raines, directing Fannie Mae to submit a "remediation plan" for some 70 manual systems we used in our accounting processes. The Raines letter was sent against the advice of Falcon's own accounting and examination staffs, who told him they had not even looked at most of the systems he was asserting Fannie

Mae needed to fix, let alone concluded they were deficient. Falcon sent the letter anyway and gave a copy to the *Journal* to ensure that Raines would be questioned about it at a Senate Banking Committee hearing scheduled for the following day.

These blatantly political actions led us to ask Missouri Senator Kit Bond to request an investigation of the circumstances behind both the disclosure of the February 24 letter to the *Wall Street Journal* and the March 31 news release mentioning a possible restatement. Bond agreed to do so. In an April 20, 2004, letter he asked the HUD inspector general to look into the matters as well as to "assess whether these disclosures reflect any inappropriate or undue political influence in the examination process."

The HUD inspector general did not make the report of its investigation public until October, after OFHEO had released their preliminary findings in the Fannie Mae examination. The inspector general's report was replete with testimony from named and unnamed witnesses alleging that Falcon and Blumenthal harbored animus toward Fannie Mae and that they undertook the special examination to promote their public image and do harm to the company. It cited testimony from a confidential witness who said that after the March 31 press release, Blumenthal was "watching the movement in the stock, in the equity price, to see what kind of damage had been done to the Enterprise," and that he "was almost gleeful that it was going down." It also quoted a Blumenthal e-mail that "after discussing the drafting of what would become the Raines letter of February 24, 2003, concludes, 'THE PRODUCT OF OUR COMPANY IS REGULATION, government is the institutionalized use of force. Make them do something.' [original caps]." OFHEO's chief accountant told the inspector general that she believed the goal of the examination was "to force a financial restatement."

The summary of the report concluded:

Testimony and evidence indicate that the "corporate culture" and "tone at the top" at OFHEO have been significantly affected since June 2003, by the following key developments:

perceived "humiliation" in the Freddie Mac affair, the abortive attempt to remove the present Director, ongoing legislative efforts designed to eliminate OFHEO, and the transition to a "New OFHEO" culture. This evidence and testimony raises questions about the substance and credibility of certain OFHEO enforcement actions, and the motivation behind such actions.

The HUD inspector general made a criminal referral of Falcon to the Department of Justice, but the U.S. attorney for the District of Columbia declined prosecution in favor of administrative remedies. HUD Secretary Alphonso Jackson—an enthusiastic participant in Operation Noriega—took no action in response to the report's findings. We were, and would continue to be, on our own.

In late April, OFHEO told us they believed our accounting for impairments on the private-label manufactured housing securities we owned was incorrect. I was not surprised that they would challenge us on this issue; it echoed the claim of a persistent critic of Fannie Mae named Peter Eavis. Through the end of 2003, we had taken $155 million in write-downs on our then $8 billion in manufactured housing securities (which at one point totaled $10 billion). Eavis frequently cited the $183 million write-down by the Federal Home Loan Bank of New York on a much smaller portfolio of manufactured housing securities as support for his contention that we should have written off more than $1 billion on our holdings and that our failure to do so was improper. OFHEO had decided to take essentially that same position.

They picked the wrong issue. Manufactured housing was our "canary in the coal mine" on the risks of private-label securities. When the manufactured housing market collapsed, we realized how little we actually knew about that business. In late 2002, I led a multidisciplinary team to assess our loss exposure on our investments in manufactured housing securities and to determine what actions we could take to minimize it. We quickly concluded that the key to controlling our ultimate losses was the servicing on the delinquent loans backing our securities. To further our interests, we went as far as to make a bid to purchase the servicing rights of a large company in bankruptcy, Conseco Finance, which had issued many of the securities we owned. While we lost the bid, our involvement in the process gave us leverage to negotiate more favorable servicing terms from the entity that won it.

Over the course of our work with the Conseco servicing portfolio, we became highly knowledgeable about the factors that influenced the delinquencies, defaults, and loss severities of manufactured housing loans. Using this knowledge, we built loss models for each of the manufactured housing securities we owned. Virtually all of our holdings were AAA-rated senior tranches, so in order for us to take credit losses on these securities, the tranches junior to them had to be wiped out first. When we did our detailed models, we found that even using conservative assumptions (that is, ones not very favorable to us), our projection was that we would not experience losses on most of the tranches we owned if we held them to maturity.

GAAP permits a company with the ability and intent to hold a security to maturity to use a "loss-based," rather than a price-based, methodology in determining whether the security in question is impaired and must be written down. That is what we did. We believed our loss-based method was more accurate than a price-based method would have been, since the manufactured housing securities market was illiquid and as a consequence, the pricing for most securities did not reflect their economic value. Our outside auditor KPMG concurred with our accounting, but just to be on the safe side as a new registrant, we also consulted with the SEC. The SEC concurred with our accounting as well.

OFHEO was unaware we had taken our manufactured housing accounting to the SEC, and when Falcon found out, he was furious. He accused us of attempting to interfere with OFHEO's examination. And he didn't change his position—at least not publicly. Privately he backed off his contention that our manufactured housing accounting was not GAAP compliant, since the SEC had opined that it was. Falcon's public claim became that our accounting was not "best in class." He directed us to change it to a method that resulted in a higher level of impairments and also pushed for a restatement. We went back to the SEC for guidance. The SEC did not require a change in our accounting, nor did they require a restatement, but they did counsel us that getting into a battle over accounting methods with our regulator would not be our wisest course of action. We agreed to adopt the OFHEO impairment accounting, only to have our auditor, KPMG, tell us that *it* was not GAAP compliant. A flurry of work by all parties over a weekend finally produced a method everyone could live with. This method generated an additional $265 million in impairments, which we committed to record prospectively with our second quarter results.

OFHEO and Fannie Mae's critics were upset and frustrated that the manufactured housing accounting episode did not force the earnings restatement they were seeking. We had won the first round, or at least not lost it. We heard nothing more from OFHEO about the special examination for four months. As late as mid-August, in response to a due diligence inquiry from KPMG related to the filing of our second quarter 2004 financial results with the SEC, OFHEO informed us they did not know of "any material errors or misstatements" in our financials.

If that were true, they discovered quite a bit very quickly. On Friday, September 17, Falcon requested a meeting with the independent members of Fannie Mae's board of directors the following Monday, to present what OFHEO called its "findings to date" in the Fannie Mae special examination. We had no idea what to expect. On Monday morning, we read in the *Wall Street Journal* that "OFHEO found evidence of a pattern of decisions by [Fannie Mae] executives aimed at manipulating earnings," and that Richard Baker and the SEC already had been briefed on OFHEO's findings. But no one at Fannie Mae knew anything else about the OFHEO report until OFHEO officials provided us with copies just prior to meeting with our independent directors in the company's boardroom that day.

The 211-page report was withering. It claimed not just that we had gotten the accounting wrong but that we had done so intentionally and fraudulently. The report alleged deliberate violations of GAAP in two areas: accounting for derivatives (FAS 133) and accounting for the amortization of mortgage purchase premium and discount (FAS 91). It also asserted that in 1998, we had fraudulently deferred $200 million in amortization expenses in order to reach an earnings level that met analysts' expectations and triggered maximum executive bonuses. In a stinging transmittal letter to the Fannie Mae board accompanying the report, Falcon wrote, "These findings cannot be explained as mere differences in interpretation of accounting principles, but clear instances in which management sought to misapply and ignore accounting principles for the purposes of meeting investor analyst expectations [and] reducing volatility in reported earnings." He went on to say, "We must consider the accountability of management and whether we have sufficient confidence in management" to remedy the problems OFHEO claimed to have found. Falcon's letter made clear that he, at least, did not have such confidence.

When the interim OFHEO report was released to the public on Wednesday, September 22, it had the effect OFHEO and Fannie Mae's critics intended. OFHEO's allegations were almost universally accepted as matters of fact, and they elicited uniform and harsh condemnation. Long-time Fannie Mae critics attempted to outdo one another in their expressions of outrage, with most adding some version of "I told you so." In an editorial, the *Wall Street Journal* went directly to its end game: "This news gives new urgency to the need to reform, and ultimately to privatize, these two 'government sponsored enterprises.'" Baker issued a scathing press release calling the claims in the OFHEO report "inexcusable" and a "disgusting revelation," and he announced his intention to hold a hearing on the report in early October.

Baker set his hearing for October 6. Raines and I were invited to testify, as were Falcon and Fannie Mae's presiding director, Ann Korologos. Because of pending litigation, I had been advised by my personal counsel to assert my Fifth Amendment rights at the hearing, but along with Raines I chose to testify under oath.

The two most serious allegations in the OFHEO report were that we had improperly deferred 1998 amortization expenses and that we had knowingly accounted for our derivatives incorrectly. Raines and I flatly denied OFHEO's claims about the 1998 expenses. We had asked Fannie Mae's outside counsel to investigate the allegations, and they found nothing to support them. Questioned about the OFHEO accusation, Raines responded unequivocally: "There were no facts in the OFHEO report—none. We looked into the facts of what happened six years ago—we found no facts that would support the allegations in the report."

We defended our derivatives accounting as well. Raines and I both noted that FAS 133 was an extraordinarily complex standard, with experts differing widely on many of its implementation issues. We testified that we believed we had applied FAS 133 in a GAAP-compliant manner, and we stressed that our outside auditor, KPMG, concurred with our accounting and had not withdrawn its opinion of our financial statements. Raines said he found it highly unusual that OFHEO had not raised any accounting concerns with either Fannie Mae's management or KPMG before going to our board and the public with their allegations of impropriety, adding, "I don't believe there has been an adequate explanation of why they have followed this path." Raines told the committee that the SEC "ultimately has the final authority over GAAP" and said we would be submitting our FAS 133 accounting (and our FAS 91 accounting) to them for their review and final determination.

OFHEO's supporters on the committee were caught off guard by the vigorous defense Raines and I mounted. Committee members' reactions to it split along party lines, with Republicans supporting Falcon and challenging Raines and Democrats doing the opposite. The hearing ended in a standoff, which was viewed as a victory for Fannie Mae. (The company's stock rose 4.5 percent over the ensuing two days.) Everyone understood that it now would come down to the SEC, who either would agree with OFHEO or with us on the accounting issues.

The Chief Accountant's Surprise

OFHEO had challenged us on nine specific FAS 133 applications. On October 18, we made a 47-page written submission to the SEC, formally requesting guidance from their Office of the Chief Accountant on each one of them. For each application, we gave the rationale for the approach we took and discussed why we believed it was correct. KPMG concurred with the entirety of our submission, and on November 5, our accounting policy staff met with SEC staff to discuss it. Bill McLucas—a senior lawyer with our outside counsel, Wilmer, Cutler & Pickering, and a former head of the SEC's enforcement division—was present at the meeting. He later described it to Raines and me as a cordial and professional discussion in which both sides made reasonable arguments over complex technical aspects of the standard. McLucas told us that he left the meeting thinking it was very unlikely the SEC would take a harsh stand against our FAS 133 implementation. His experience, he said, was that the SEC reserved its most severe penalties for companies that either did not know an accounting rule they should have known or knew it but chose not to follow it. It seemed obvious to McLucas that Fannie Mae fell into neither category.

On the afternoon of December 15, Raines received a request to come to the office of the SEC's chief accountant, Don Nicoliasen, at 6 p.m. that evening. I was not asked to accompany him, nor were any of Fannie Mae's accountants. Falcon already was in Nicoliasen's conference room when Raines arrived. Also present at the meeting were officials from the Justice Department, lawyers from Wilmer, Cutler & Pickering, accountants from KPMG and Deloitte & Touche, and three outside Fannie Mae directors—Steve Ashley, Joe Pickett, and Tom Gerrity.

As described in a press release issued later that evening, Nicoliasen informed Raines that "Fannie Mae's accounting practices did not comply in material respects with the accounting requirements in Statement Nos. 91 and 133." Regarding FAS 133, he said:

Fannie Mae internally developed its own unique methodology to assess whether hedge accounting was appropriate. Fannie Mae's methodology, however, did not qualify for hedge accounting because of deficiencies in its application of Statement No. 133. Among other things, Fannie Mae's methodology of assessing, measuring and documenting hedge ineffectiveness was inadequate and not supported by the statement.

Nicoliasen directed us to restate our financials for FAS 133 to eliminate the use of hedge accounting and to restate for FAS 91 if the correction proved to be material.

I learned of Nicoliasen's ruling shortly after the meeting concluded. I was stunned by it and even more astonished when I read the SEC press release the next day. Nicoliasen had not ruled on a single one of the nine issues we addressed in our FAS 133 submission. His statement was extraordinarily vague. He did not say where or how we had gotten FAS 133 wrong, just that we had. KPMG was equally shocked by the ruling and was as perplexed as we were by its lack of specificity. KPMG had a larger share of major financial institutions as clients than any of the other top accounting firms. If it had gotten FAS 133 wrong for Fannie Mae—its largest and most prominent financial institution client—might not it have done the same thing for all its other clients? KPMG repeatedly sought clarification from Nicoliasen on the rationale for his Fannie Mae ruling but never was able to obtain any.

The disallowance of hedge accounting forced Fannie Mae to immediately recognize approximately $9 billion in derivatives losses we otherwise would have recorded over the lives of the hedges in question. This $9 billion was not an economic loss, nor was it unknown to our investors. We fully disclosed our deferred hedge losses on our balance sheet. Taking them right away would increase our income in the future by almost exactly the same amount. Where the problem arose was that, unless we could somehow offset it, a $9 billion book loss would push our regulatory capital below our statutory minimum.

Any minimum capital shortfall allowed OFHEO to classify Fannie Mae as "significantly undercapitalized" and under the terms of the 1992 statute gain greatly enhanced powers over us. This, of course, was precisely the outcome OFHEO, our critics, and our opponents were seeking.

A Trip to Omaha to See Mr. Buffett

Raines made a final attempt to salvage the situation. On Friday, December 17, he came into my office and said, "We're going to Omaha." I knew exactly what he had in mind. Warren Buffett was rumored to have been sitting on over $20 billion in Treasury securities. If we could convince him to do a private placement of capital in Fannie Mae, there still would be time for him to sell some of those Treasuries and settle a capital transaction with us before the end of the year.

We flew to Omaha on Saturday morning and after landing at Eppley Airfield went to a small room in the private services terminal where Buffett wanted to meet. He came alone (which surprised me), and he had done his homework. He told us he was prepared to do a private placement of preferred stock in Fannie Mae in whatever amount we needed, provided we met his terms, which he said were not negotiable. They included an interest rate and a minimum non-call period he specified. In addition, he said, the preferred stock had to be cumulative (meaning any missed or suspended dividends would accumulate and be paid later), and OFHEO would have to declare us adequately capitalized as of September 30, 2004, which they had not yet done. Finally, he told us that if word of the transaction got out before it was settled, the deal would be off. We told Buffett that we would agree to his terms but that it would be up to OFHEO to agree to his conditions.

Buffett walked us out to the plane we were taking back to Washington, a Falcon 2000 from NetJets, a company he owned. As I settled into my seat, that day's *New York Times* was on the table beside it. My picture was on the front page of the business section under the caption, "Fannie Mae Board to Meet." Inside was another picture with a caption that said, "J. Timothy Howard of Fannie Mae helped certify financial statements that violated accounting rules," along with an article speculating on the fates of Raines and me. The gist of it was that I was almost certainly going to be forced out, but there was a chance Raines would be able to convince the board to keep him on. With the possibility of getting a capital deal done before year-end, I still held out hope that both of us might be able to stay.

Our plane was just approaching its cruising altitude when its left engine began to make a loud revving noise, rising and falling in amplitude, and the plane shook violently sideways. Raines and I looked at each other and had the same thought: "No one is going to believe this." After the moment of immediate danger had passed—and after what seemed like several minutes but probably was less than one—the pilot opened his door and said, "I'm sure you've noticed we're having some engine trouble. I've shut down our left engine, and we're diverting to an alternate airport." Air traffic control had given him the choice of Springfield or Peoria, Illinois, and he picked Peoria.

The runway at the Peoria airport was lined with emergency vehicles, all with their lights flashing. There was a strong crosswind, so the pilot had to bring the plane in with its nose up unusually steeply, but he got us down safely. After we deplaned—and thanked our pilot—Raines called his office to arrange for a new plane to take us to Washington. While we waited for that plane to arrive, I had ample time to reflect that as bad as it was to have your name and reputation trashed in the media and possibly lose your job, worse things could happen.

We had survived the Falcon in the air, but there still was a Falcon on the ground. We did not fare as well with that one. He did not accept the terms Buffett required in order to do a capital placement with us. This had never been about capital or safety and soundness; it was about institutional power and control. Whether we could cover our capital shortfall by year-end was irrelevant to Falcon; OFHEO had not yet completed their official classification of Fannie Mae's capital adequacy for the previous quarter. We had submitted our September 30 capital data—showing a surplus of $6 billion compared with our minimum requirement (and more than a $20 billion surplus compared with our risk-based requirement)—to OFHEO in November, but they had not yet acted upon it. By applying Nicoliasen's ruling disallowing our hedge accounting retroactively, Falcon could create a $3 billion minimum capital shortfall as of September 30 and declare us significantly undercapitalized whether we covered the shortfall by year-end or not. And that is exactly what he intended to do.

The September 30 capital shortfall gave Falcon the leverage he needed with the Fannie Mae board to force out Raines and me. I was the first to go. On Sunday evening, December 19, I received a call at home from Korologos informing me that the board had determined it would be in the company's best interest if I were to step down. I agreed to do so. I expected my resignation to be announced on Monday, but a complication arose with my employment contract that we were unable to resolve that day. While I was attempting to iron out my contract issue, the board was meeting to discuss Raines's fate.

Falcon was insistent that Raines leave. As had been the case with Freddie Mac's Parseghian, Falcon lacked the statutory authority to dismiss him. But Fannie Mae's new condition of being significantly undercapitalized gave Falcon additional powers he could use against the company. In the end, Raines's many supporters on the board concluded that the cost of a protracted fight with OFHEO would be too great, and reluctantly they agreed to ask Raines to leave. His and my departures were made public simultaneously. On December 21, 2004, Frank Raines announced his retirement from Fannie Mae, and I announced my resignation.

CHAPTER 15

Sorting Out the Facts

REACTIONS IN THE POLITICAL AND BUSINESS WORLDS TO Nicoliasen's ruling on Fannie Mae's accounting were strikingly different.

The Office of Federal Housing Enterprise Oversight and the *Wall Street Journal* pronounced the $9 billion earnings restatement a worse accounting scandal than Enron, WorldCom, or Tyco. Fannie Mae's investors (and Warren Buffett) concluded otherwise. The company's stock barely moved in the days following the ruling. Investors understood that the restatement had no effect on Fannie Mae's economic value. There was no "phantom income." OFHEO admitted that our hedges were effective; their objections were limited to the timing of when the expenses associated with those hedges should be recognized. The restatement was huge, but that was because we did so much hedging to reduce our interest rate risk; had we hedged less, the restatement would have been smaller. And the reason removing hedge accounting resulted in a loss was that we hedged our debt and interest rates had fallen; had interest rates risen, those same hedges would have produced a gain. In the business world, there was no "scandal" at all. As one security analyst noted in a research report, "Fannie Mae didn't hide deferred hedge losses. They were right there in the financial statements, reducing equity in the GAAP numbers. Everyone could see them and debate how they should be treated. The restatement will be a monumental effort that will simply move them from one place in the statements to another."

Business World Repercussions

A week after the meeting between Raines and Nicoliasen at the SEC, reporters from the *Wall Street Journal* drew on interviews with attendees to present an account of what had taken place there. The *Journal* reported that on hearing Nicoliasen's ruling that "Fannie hadn't taken the steps needed to qualify for hedge accounting" and would have to restate its financials, Raines protested that if Fannie Mae and KPMG could not get the standard right, nobody could. The *Journal* quoted Nicoliasen as telling Raines, "Many companies can and do comply with the rules. Sir, hedge accounting is a privilege, not a right. [It] is applied only under strict circumstances, and you did not comply." The *Journal* said that when Raines asked how far off Fannie Mae's FAS 133 implementation had been, "Mr. Nicoliasen held up a sheet of paper and told Mr. Raines that if it represented the four corners of the rule, 'you were not even on the page.'"

The *Journal*'s account was universally accepted as the definitive recounting of the episode. In the political world, it may have been. There, all that mattered was that OFHEO had won, and Fannie Mae had lost. Nicoliasen had ruled against Fannie Mae, and to the media and in Washington, how he arrived at that verdict was of no interest or consequence whatsoever. But in the business world, it was.

At the Baker hearing, Falcon had said flatly about FAS 133, "We feel very strongly these are black-and-white accounting issues," and, "These are not issues that reasonable people will disagree on." At the time he was so confidently making those statements, hundreds of financial institutions along with their outside auditors were grappling with the ambiguities of the standard. One of the more vexing was the application of what was called the "assumption of no ineffectiveness," or ANI. For certain types of transactions under FAS 133, ANI allowed a company to qualify for hedge accounting without having to do detailed calculations of the effectiveness of its hedges each quarter. For Fannie Mae, which had some 30,000 individual hedge transactions, ANI was a great operational benefit, and working with KPMG, we sought to use it for as many types of hedges as we believed the standard permitted.

To qualify for hedge accounting in general, FAS 133 required a hedge to be "highly effective"—that is, the gains or losses on the hedge had to closely offset the losses or gains on the hedged item. Unfortunately, however, nowhere in FAS 133 was there a precise definition of hedge effectiveness. To the contrary, FAS 133 seemed to go out of its way *not* to give clear guidance, stating, "The appropriateness of a given method of assessing hedge effectiveness can depend on the nature of the risk being hedged and the type of hedging instrument used." That left the determination of when and how to use hedge accounting to the judgment of a company and its outside auditor, based on the types of hedges in question.

FAS 133 provided even less guidance for when it was appropriate to rely on the assumption of no ineffectiveness. We, KPMG, and many others interpreted FAS 133 as permitting something less than an exact match of the terms of a hedge transaction—what accountants called "minimal ineffectiveness"—to be the basis for the use of ANI in hedge accounting. OFHEO challenged this interpretation in their special examination. They took the position that under FAS 133, a hedge had to be "perfectly effective" for a company to use ANI. OFHEO claimed that because our hedges were not perfectly effective (and we agreed that they were not), the fact that we did not do quarterly calculations of effectiveness for several different categories of our hedges was a GAAP violation, carrying the consequence that we should have to restate our financials to eliminate the use of hedge accounting.

In the political world, the question Nicoliasen was being asked to address was, "Is OFHEO right, or is Fannie Mae right?" In the business world, that same question was, "Is 'perfect effectiveness' or 'minimal ineffectiveness' the requisite criterion for employing the assumption of no ineffectiveness in hedge accounting?" Leading up to the ruling, I thought it was highly unlikely that Nicoliasen would say a hedge had to be perfectly effective for a company to use the assumption of no ineffectiveness. That was why I was so confident we would not be forced to restate our earnings. It never occurred to me that Nicoliasen would respond to the political question without responding to the business one. His statement to Raines that Fannie Mae's application of FAS 133 was "not even on the page"—which was fully satisfactory and convincing to everyone from the media waiting breathlessly for the chief accountant's ruling on the matter—pointedly avoided any description of what *was* on the page.

Nicoliasen's refusal to answer the very clear accounting question put directly in front of him puzzled me at the time and still does. I could come up with no better explanation than that he had succumbed to the pressure from OFHEO—and quite likely from others within the Bush administration—to give OFHEO the political victory they were seeking, but that he sought to do so in a way that minimized the business effect on other companies. If that was the case, he was too clever by half. Unlike in the political sphere, the vagueness of his opinion on our derivatives accounting did not go unnoticed in the world in which the rest of the country's financial institutions had to operate.

In the continued absence of clarification from either Nicoliasen or the SEC commissioners on what Fannie Mae had done incorrectly, the only logical inference anyone could draw from the ruling on our FAS 133 implementation was that something very close to a perfect match *must* be required for the assumption of no ineffectiveness to be used in hedge accounting. Between the end of 2004 and the end of 2006, nearly three hundred companies—including Citicorp, Bank of America, and GE—restated their financials for FAS 133. This left little doubt that a very large number of the companies Nicoliasen claimed "can and do comply with the rules" had in fact been interpreting them much the way we had. Tellingly, no CEO or CFO at any of those companies was accused by regulators of deliberate misstatement or earnings manipulation, nor were any forced to resign their positions.

Nicoliasen left the SEC in November 2005. The SEC chief accountant position remained vacant until August 2006, when a man named Conrad Hewitt, formerly with Ernst & Young, was appointed to fill it. Early in 2007, Hewitt invited the four major accounting firms to address what he called the "confusion" over the requirements for electing hedge accounting under FAS 133. Hewitt asked the firms to submit a white paper on the issue to the FASB's Emerging Issues Task Force (EITF), a body that includes the SEC chief accountant and whose judgments serve as authoritative guidance on implementing FASB standards. On March 15, 2007, the EITF responded to the white paper by giving a definitive answer: GAAP did *not* require an exact match for the assumption of no ineffectiveness to be used in hedge accounting. The EITF advised that under FAS 133, a company using ANI could apply hedge accounting even when "the terms of the hedge and the hedged item do not exactly match," as long as testing showed that a hedging relationship was "highly effective and that any ineffectiveness was *de minimis*."

Nearly two and a half years after our FAS 133 submission to the SEC, the EITF provided the clarity we had sought but not received, and it supported our implementation. The EITF's clarification was welcomed by the industry, but it came too late for Fannie Mae. And it garnered no media attention at all. The circus had decamped long ago, and the crowds had drifted off.

The Wheels of Justice Grind Slowly

The severity and high profile of OFHEO's allegations, together with the size of the Fannie Mae restatement, made me the subject of eight actual or threatened legal actions. The most serious were possible criminal charges from the Justice Department, possible charges of securities law violations by the SEC, a regulatory lawsuit by OFHEO, and a class action civil suit in which I was a named defendant.

In a very short period of time, I had morphed from a respected financial executive—whom the *New York Times* described in an

October 2004 article as "the architect of Fannie Mae's recent success"—into a caricature of "the CFO gone bad," pursued by a host of governmental entities bent on retribution. It was Kafkaesque. I didn't even think we had gotten the accounting wrong, yet here I was defending myself against accusations that we had done so deliberately and fraudulently. I knew the charges were fictitious—invented to try to turn public opinion against my former company—but few others agreed with me. Nor would they be likely to. The reality of these situations is that while you are charged in public, you have to defend yourself in private. Knowing that, my lawyers and I buckled down and got to work.

The Justice Department investigation ended without much involvement on our part. After releasing their interim examination report in September 2004, OFHEO repeatedly made statements to the media that they were "sharing [their] findings with the Justice Department for possible criminal prosecution." These statements were worrying Fannie Mae's investors, and after almost two years of them, the company's new general counsel, Beth Wilkinson, asked Justice Department officials to clarify the status of their inquiry. Somewhat surprisingly, they did. On August 25, 2006, Fannie Mae announced that the Justice Department had informed them that its criminal investigation of Fannie Mae had come to an end, and that it would not be filing any charges. A Justice Department spokesman noted that Raines and I still were under scrutiny, but this was in response to a request made by Richard Baker, who had asked for a perjury investigation in response to his claim that we had lied in our testimony before his subcommittee. Nothing came of that inquiry.

OFHEO released its final *Report of the Special Examination of Fannie Mae* on May 23, 2006. That same day, the SEC filed a complaint against the company, based on the OFHEO report, alleging that Fannie Mae "engaged in a financial fraud involving multiple violations of Generally Accepted Accounting Principles." Simultaneous with the release of the OFHEO report and the SEC complaint, Fannie Mae entered into a consent agreement with OFHEO in which it agreed to pay a $350 million civil penalty to the SEC and

$50 million to Treasury to settle the fraud charges. In agreeing to the settlement, the company neither admitted nor denied guilt. Officials at OFHEO and the SEC were not similarly constrained. At a press conference announcing the settlement, SEC chairman Chris Cox said, "Those whose actions led to the accounting fraud you've heard described today will be vigorously pursued."

I was fairly certain I knew who Cox was referring to as "those," and in June 2007, my lawyer received what is called a Wells notice from an official in the SEC's enforcement division, informing him of the SEC's intent to file charges against me for fraud. Normally one does not respond to a Wells notice, since it rarely persuades the SEC to change their mind and often provides material that strengthens their case. But I did want to respond, because I was convinced the SEC had been exposed only to OFHEO's side of the story, and I thought that seeing the full picture might cause them to think twice about initiating an action against me in spite of the spotlight chairman Cox had shone on the case.

In response to the Wells notice, we sent the SEC what is called a Rule 408 letter, in which we offered arguments against the charges we believed the SEC intended to bring. Their main focus was on OFHEO's claim that in 1998, we had improperly deferred expenses to meet earnings goals and compensation targets. That section of the OFHEO report cited only selected documents, and I believed misstated the record. The goal of our letter was to make the SEC aware of the full range of documents relevant to the issue (most of which OFHEO had ignored) as well as the fact that witness testimony (none of which OFHEO cited) did not support OFHEO's interpretation of the event they alleged was improper. After sending our Rule 408 letter to the SEC in September 2007, we did not hear from them again.

OFHEO filed a "Notice of Charges" against Raines, Fannie Mae's former controller, Leanne Spencer, and me on December 16, 2006. New OFHEO director James Lockhart—a personal friend of President Bush who assumed his position in May 2006 after Falcon stepped down in May 2005—said in a press release, "The 101 charges reveal how the individuals improperly manipulated earnings to maximize their bonuses, while knowingly neglecting accounting systems and internal controls, misapplying over twenty accounting principles and misleading the regulator and the public." OFHEO said it would seek more than $100 million in civil money penalties and disgorgement of bonuses exceeding $115 million through an administrative law procedure as mandated in our regulatory statute. Under that procedure, the case was to be argued before a U. S. administrative law judge (ALJ). The ALJ would provide a recommended decision to the OFHEO director, who could accept, modify, or reject it, and then could levy penalties and make demands for disgorgement of bonuses at his sole discretion.

Notwithstanding the overwhelming procedural bias in their favor, OFHEO chose to settle the case in April 2008, just as it was about to be heard. Their timing was curious, and I thought it had a simple explanation. OFHEO had been able to present their case against Raines, Spencer, and me to the media unchallenged. The administrative law procedure would have been open to the public and the press, and we were prepared to mount a vigorous defense. OFHEO was not eager for our side of the story to be publicized; indeed, they recently had been held in contempt of court in the Fannie Mae civil suit for failing to make available to the defense documents favorable to it even after having been directed to do so by the judge. OFHEO had settled their suit against Raines, Spencer, and me, I believed, to try to prevent the weakness of their case from becoming known.

OFHEO put a dollar value on the settlement of $31.4 million, but it was widely reported that they in fact settled for next to nothing. For Raines and me, the settlement involved a $2 million cash payment to the Treasury that was covered by insurance, the forfeiture of some old and near-worthless stock options, and the donation to a housing-related charity of shares of Fannie Mae stock we had not yet received. OFHEO derived their dollar amount for the settlement by valuing the forfeited stock options at their grant prices, which ranged between $71 and $81, rather than at the actual $28 stock price at the time. In an ironic way, it was a fitting climax: a suit that began with

OFHEO accusing us of deliberate fraud ended with OFHEO putting a deliberately fraudulent value on what we paid to settle it.

The class action civil suit was the only legal action against me to run its full judicial course. Typically in a class action suit, the plaintiff and lead defendant agree to settle it fairly quickly, for a sum acceptable to both parties. That did not happen in this instance. Plaintiffs' initial settlement demands were in the billions of dollars, which was astronomically more than Fannie Mae considered reasonable to dispose of a suit it deemed to be without merit. With no clear prospects for settling, the case dragged on for years. During that time, nearly 67 million pages of documents were reviewed, 123 fact witnesses were interviewed, and lawyers on both sides received written and oral testimony from another 35 expert witnesses. Through all of this fact finding, or in legal terms discovery, no direct evidence emerged that anyone at Fannie Mae had knowingly falsified the company's accounting.

Raines, Spencer, and I were the individual defendants in the civil suit, and once discovery was completed, we were allowed to file motions with the presiding judge in the case, Richard J. Leon, dismissing us from it, in what is called summary judgment. The requirements for a grant of summary judgment are straightforward but highly stringent: after reviewing all available evidence and drawing "all justifiable inferences" in favor of the plaintiffs, the judge must agree that "no genuine issue of material fact is in dispute" and that there is no basis for putting the case before a jury. The three of us filed summary judgment motions in August 2011, nearly seven years after the OFHEO report was made public.

A hearing on our summary judgment motions was held on June 6, 2012. The first motion slated for discussion was the one filed by Raines. Raines's lawyer, Kevin Downey, was given 45 minutes to make his argument, which he was allowed to split between an initial presentation and a reply to the response of plaintiffs' counsel. Downey talked for about 25 minutes and sat down. Counsel for the plaintiffs, Paul DeMarco, then rose to speak.

After establishing that in the absence of direct evidence against Raines, all evidence plaintiffs would be presenting against him was circumstantial, Judge Leon got right to the point. "What," he asked DeMarco, "is your best single piece of circumstantial evidence that Franklin Raines intended to defraud the public, the investing public?"

DeMarco replied, "I think the best piece of evidence is . . . a statement made on the *Kudlow & Cramer* show on CNBC on July 24 [2003]."

Leon could not mask his incredulity. "On a TV show?" he exclaimed. "A statement on a TV show?"

DeMarco explained that the statement was incriminating because it was made in spite of a memo Raines had received from Spencer in November 2001 that addressed income planning for 2002 and 2003. DeMarco claimed that this memo discussed activities that were in violation of generally accepted accounting principles, making Raines's statement on *Kudlow & Cramer* false.

Leon began quizzing DeMarco about the Spencer memo. He specifically wanted to know which witnesses had opined that there was anything improper about its contents. It quickly became apparent that the plaintiffs deliberately had elected not to ask either the author of this document or its recipients any questions about it in their depositions. Leon was not pleased about that. After several minutes of very tough questioning—and unmistakably skeptical responses to the answers he was getting—Leon expressed his exasperation at how DeMarco could consider the Spencer memo a relevant piece of evidence ". . . if [Raines] wasn't confronted with it, if he wasn't questioned about it, if he was never asked if he even read it, or if there ever was any discussion about it, if there is no evidence Ms. Spencer ever discussed it with him."

To anyone listening in the courtroom, there could be no doubt that the plaintiffs' "single best piece of circumstantial evidence" against Raines was going down in flames. This was a disaster for them. When they first filed their case, they had visions of a multibillion dollar payday at the end of it. Now it was starkly apparent they might walk away with nothing at all.

Attorney DeMarco must have sensed that as well. I was sitting behind him and could not see his face. But his voice started to waver. He said, "I am sorry." He continued speaking but stopped in midsentence. He seemed to stiffen, wobbled a bit, then suddenly pitched forward, hit his head on the podium in front of him, and collapsed to the floor.

There was an audible gasp in the courtroom. My lawyer, Steve Salky, who is a trained emergency medical technician, leaped up and dashed to DeMarco's side. As court personnel rushed to get help, Salky checked DeMarco's breathing and pulse rate. He was unconscious but otherwise not in danger. As Salky explained to me later, DeMarco had had a rush of adrenaline and simply blacked out.

Judge Leon called a recess, and we all went into the hall outside the courtroom. Between Fannie Mae, its outside auditor KPMG, and the individual defendants, the defense had more than a dozen lawyers present at the hearing. I asked whether any of them had ever seen that sort of thing happen before. One of the lawyers spoke for the group, saying, "No, I've never experienced anything like this in my life." He could have said exactly the same thing about the entire case.

Raines was dismissed from the civil suit on September 20, 2012, and I was dismissed a month later, on October 16. In ruling in my favor, Judge Leon cited "the overwhelming evidence of Howard's good faith" before going on to assert that the "plaintiffs offer no evidence from which a reasonable juror could conclude that any of Howard's statements concerning Fannie Mae's accounting practices or internal controls were made with an intent to deceive, or were otherwise made without any reasonable basis." Spencer was dismissed on November 20.

The outcomes of the Justice Department inquiry, the SEC investigation, and the OFHEO lawsuit all made clear that OFHEO's allegations against Raines, Spencer, and me had no merit at the time they were made. Had any doubts remained, Judge Leon's opinions in the civil suit removed them. But in the greater scheme of things, none of that mattered. In the politicized maelstrom of 2004, OFHEO didn't need merit to achieve their objectives; all they needed was a story. This they certainly had, and it had been enough to decapitate Fannie Mae.

CHAPTER 16

Baseless Demand, Fateful Results

O N SEPTEMBER 27, 2004, THE FANNIE MAE BOARD ENTERED INTO a written agreement with OFHEO that addressed a number of the issues raised in the interim report presented to it the week before. The eight-page document included items on accounting, capital, organization, and corporate governance. Among them was the requirement that "[the Fannie Mae] Board shall direct the appointment of a chief risk officer, to be independent of other corporate responsibilities and to have duties crafted in consultation with OFHEO."

Adding a Chief Risk Officer Adds Risk

The appointment of a chief risk officer echoed a recommendation OFHEO had made for Freddie Mac. In its special examination of that company, OFHEO claimed that "certain problems at Freddie Mac can be attributed to imbalances of power within the structure of the Enterprise." OFHEO believed that an independent chief risk officer reporting directly to Freddie Mac's CEO would have "the stature to deal effectively with the business units" and for that reason recommended one.

Stature and imbalances of power were not issues with the risk management functions at Fannie Mae. During his chairmanship,

Raines had carefully configured Fannie Mae's organization to create a balance between the company's marketing, affordable housing, and risk management objectives that, if anything, put a thumb on the scale on the risk management side. Raines's organizational structure had all operational and customer-oriented activities reporting to him through one of his two vice chairmen, Dan Mudd, who carried the title of chief operating officer. All financial risk-related activities reported to Raines through his other vice chairman, me. I had the formal title of chief financial officer but also served informally as the company's chief risk officer.

In this configuration, Raines had strong and capable advocates for Fannie Mae's business volume and affordable housing objectives in Mudd and his staff, and strong and capable advocates for our financial and risk management objectives in my staff and me. In title, Mudd and I were equals. The thumb went on the scale in the Risk Policy Committee. One of the purposes of Risk Policy was to "serve as [the] primary forum for raising and resolving all issues relating to the extent to which business unit activities or strategies are achieving defined corporate risk management objectives." I chaired that committee. For any judgment I made there to be altered or overturned, Mudd or his officers had to appeal it to Raines, who as chairman and CEO had ultimate responsibility for finding the right balance among our competing objectives. It was a sound and workable structure, one that, as Raines put it, "made it harder to make bad decisions."

The interim OFHEO report had noted the variety of responsibilities I had and then stated, in bold print, "The combination of these responsibilities does not provide the independence necessary for an effective Chief Risk Officer function." That was all the report said on the subject. It cited no shortcomings of our risk management processes and made no recommendations for their improvement; indeed the special examination focused exclusively on accounting and internal control issues and did not address risk management at all. OFHEO simply asserted that Fannie Mae's risk management organization was not effective, and in the September 27 agreement, the board consented to change it in the manner OFHEO directed, including by appointing an independent chief risk officer.

As it happened, early in 2004 I had seriously considered adding a chief risk officer (CRO) position when our chief credit officer, Adolfo Marzol, informed me in February that he wished to step down from his job later on in the year. I saw his impending move as an opportunity to investigate incorporating a CRO into our financial risk organization, and I worked with Marzol and the head of Fannie Mae's portfolio business, Peter Niculescu, to try to devise a CRO job description and organizational structure that would be practical at Fannie Mae. I was not successful. The problem I encountered was that the best organizational models for managing credit risk and interest risk were opposites. In the credit guaranty business, credit risk assessment was most effective when it was done independently of the product acquisition function. In the portfolio business, risk assessment and portfolio decisions—whether for asset acquisition, funding, or rebalancing—took place interactively and simultaneously; they could not be separated functionally, so it made little sense to separate them organizationally. The contrasting models of risk management for Fannie Mae's two businesses made it almost impossible to design a CRO organization that did not create more coordination and integration challenges than it added benefits. I gave up on the idea.

When Marzol left his chief credit officer job in August 2004, I kept the mortgage portfolio business management structure as it was and created the position of senior vice president–credit finance as a replacement for the chief credit officer. I put Credit Policy's research, modeling, loan performance analysis, and finance functions in the new Credit Finance group and reorganized them, and I moved Credit Policy's transactions-related functions into the business units. I asked a senior officer of the Credit Policy department to take the SVP–credit finance position on an interim basis, while I conducted a national search for the best person to fill it.

One month later, I was back looking at the chief risk officer model again—this time with a number of other people and in response to

OFHEO's directive that we implement it whether it suited Fannie Mae or not. Our board of directors had created a Compliance Committee to manage and report on all of the undertakings in our OFHEO agreement, and that committee had contracted with Mercer Consulting to help "develop for Fannie Mae a blueprint for creating a gold standard finance and risk management organization that will also be responsive to recent OFHEO guidance." The Compliance Committee formed an advisory group that included former Comptroller of the Currency Gene Ludwig and former SEC Chairman Richard Breeden as outside experts, along with Raines and me as experts on Fannie Mae, to work with Mercer on this task.

For as long as Raines and I remained at the company, the "preferred option" in the Mercer project was for the chief risk officer to have lead responsibility for both financial and operational risk management. Under this option, the head of Credit Finance would have reported to the CRO, and other credit risk-related duties and interactions would have remained essentially as they were, pending changes by the CRO, once hired, at his or her discretion. This produced minimal disruption to the credit risk management organization and business processes we had just put in place—and were relying on for protection in the high-risk market environment we faced—and I thought it was as good a result as we were likely to obtain.

Upon Raines's departure, Dan Mudd was named interim chief executive officer. (The board elected him CEO in June 2005.) Steve Ashley, an outside board member and former mortgage banker, was named nonexecutive chairman. Raines had been heavily involved in financial risk issues throughout his Fannie Mae career, and I had been the company's top risk management executive for close to 20 years. But in January 2005, both of us were gone. It was up to Mudd and Ashley to implement OFHEO's directive to add a CRO to the company's risk functions, and the way in which they did so drew more on the customer orientation they brought from their old jobs than on the risk management orientation required in their new ones.

Barely a month after Raines and I left, in February 2005, the head of the Mercer project informed the members of the Compliance

Committee that the CRO now "would have an oversight role, rather than a controlling role over individual transactions." The functions of all the groups within the CRO organization were changed from "management" to "oversight," and lead responsibility for "identifying, measuring, and managing key risks" in the credit guaranty business was moved from groups independent of the business to executives *within* the business. With these changes, a discipline that had existed since the Maxwell years—where an independent credit officer could exercise "terminal authority" over decisions made by marketing executives—disappeared. The chief risk officer and his or her staff could set broad policies for interest rate and credit risk taking and observe and report to the CEO and the board on the risks taken by business unit management, but they would have no decision-making authorities themselves.

The changes in credit risk accountability under Mudd quickly led to the dismantling of the credit risk management organization and business processes put together under Raines. The Credit Finance Department—which contained groups and personnel with complementary skill sets and responsibilities and was designed to work as a unit—was split up and dispersed throughout the company. With Credit Finance gone, the search to find an SVP-credit finance (whose job description included the responsibility for "ensuring that all mortgage credit risk borne by the company is properly assessed, graded, and valued") was suspended and the job eliminated. The SVP-credit finance had been the successor position to the chief credit officer, but a new chief credit officer was not appointed either. The Risk Policy Committee, which under Raines had the ability to limit business-unit risk taking, was replaced by a succession of management and board committees with only advisory and oversight authorities. And with neither a Credit Finance group nor a Risk Policy Committee to enforce them, the corporate financial disciplines adopted by the board in 2003—which had been quantitative, specific, binding on the company, and subject to third-party review—were replaced in September 2006 by a set of corporate risk tolerance *principles*, which were qualitative, vague, nonbinding, and of insufficient substance to warrant any sort of review at all.

At the time of the OFHEO report, Fannie Mae bore almost a trillion dollars of interest rate risk and over two trillion dollars of credit risk. We had been building and refining our interest rate and credit risk management capabilities to world-class levels since the beginning of the Maxwell era. It is beyond ironic that this 20-year arc of progress was being reversed because of an action by Fannie Mae's "safety and soundness" regulator. Armando Falcon had only the most superficial knowledge of how Fannie Mae's financial risk management operations were set up and operated, and he had no idea at all of what was required to make them successful. His demand that the company revamp its risk management organization to add a chief risk officer had a purely political motive—to enhance the impression he wished to create that Fannie Mae was out of control and required OFHEO intervention to right it. That the new CRO would have "duties crafted in consultation with OFHEO" was an empty promise. OFHEO stood mutely by as their mandated CRO position was stripped of any actual authority over Fannie Mae's risk taking and as the company's existing credit risk management processes and disciplines were replaced by ones any credible regulator immediately would have recognized as markedly inferior.

Fannie Mae Loses Its Way

In the final year of Raines's chairmanship, Fannie Mae was losing business to the private-label market both because of pricing and because of our unwillingness to purchase or guarantee many of the riskier loan types and features that were being put into private-label securities. Adherence to our underwriting and pricing disciplines had outsized impacts on the business we did with two companies that previously had been our biggest customers.

Since the late 1990s, Fannie Mae's largest single customer, by far, had been Countrywide Financial; from 2000 through the middle of 2003, we had either purchased or guaranteed over 80 percent of their prime conventional loans. By the end of 2004, however, only about 30 percent of Countrywide's (now much riskier) business was coming to us. The situation was even worse with Washington Mutual (WAMU). In the early 2000s, we had financed virtually all of WAMU's prime conventional loans, but when WAMU switched the bulk of their production to pay-option ARMs—which we would not buy or guarantee—our business with them dropped off to next to nothing.

Fannie Mae maintained its credit discipline in the initial months after Raines and I left, with the consequence that their total book of business shrank by a little over 1 percent during the first half of 2005. But executives were growing restless about their continued loss of market share, and they were being pressured by their largest customers to be more accommodative. A company can make two types of credit mistake: accepting loans that turn out to be bad, and rejecting loans that turn out to be good. To many at Fannie Mae, it began to appear as if they might not have the balance right between the two. They were losing business to the private-label market at an alarming rate, and in each of the five years Dan Mudd had been at the company, their credit losses had been minuscule—less than one basis point of total mortgages and MBS.

Fannie Mae's risk appetite had been the primary topic of the company's 2003 strategic retreat, and at that time we had elected to scale back our risk taking and impose stricter disciplines on ourselves. In 2005, however, Fannie Mae had new top leadership and a different management group. They decided to do their own risk appetite assessment at their next strategic retreat in June. By the time of the June retreat, the restructuring of Fannie Mae's risk organization had been completed, and its "enhanced corporate risk framework" included "delegating to the business units primary responsibility for the management of the day-to-day risks inherent in the activities of the business unit." As a practical matter, that meant it would be the head of Fannie Mae's single-family mortgage business, Tom Lund, rather than the interim chief risk officer, who would be responsible for doing the analysis for and leading the discussion on the company's credit risk alternatives.

Lund prepared a presentation in which he reviewed the changes in mortgage product mix and risk characteristics over the past two years. "The risk in the environment has accelerated dramatically," he observed. He told his colleagues, "We are at a strategic crossroad" at which "[w]e face two stark choices." Lund labeled these choices "Stay the Course" and "Meet the Market Where the Market Is." To stay the course, he explained, the company would "maintain our strong credit discipline" and "protect the quality of our book." To meet the market, they would "participate in volume and revenue opportunity/current growth areas" and "accept higher risk and higher volatility of earnings."

Lund's list of "potential implications" for the two alternative strategies reflected his 10-year background on the marketing and product acquisition side of the company: all five of the implications he identified for staying the course were negative, whereas he had an equal mix of positive and negative implications for meeting the market. That left little doubt as to what the company ultimately would do. But it wouldn't happen immediately. Lund noted, "Realistically, we are not in a position to 'meet the market' today." He recommended that the company "stay the course" for the moment, while at the same time dedicating resources to what he called "underground" efforts to develop the capabilities and infrastructure to assess and acquire "higher risk alternative mortgage products" and subprime loans.

Having determined two years earlier that it was worth sacrificing some business and potential revenue to maintain Fannie Mae's financial strength, now in 2005, in a vastly more threatening credit environment, the company was concluding the opposite: it was a better choice to sacrifice financial strength for more business. The difference had everything to do with who was making the assessment. In 2005 Fannie Mae no longer had a chief credit officer, and their interim chief risk officer had been shunted to the sidelines. The head of the single-family business, Tom Lund, was being asked to balance the credit and marketing perspectives of his business himself. I knew Lund well and had great respect for him. He was conservative by instinct, and he knew credit, but not in the depth required to stay out of trouble in as treacherous an environment as Fannie Mae had found itself. Lund had been given a task by his leadership that he simply was not equipped to perform, even drawing on the credit analytic resources still in the company and available to him. He would do as well as he knew how, but he was in an impossible position.

The 2006 objectives submitted to the Fannie Mae board in January included the explicit goal of increasing the company's share of new conventional conforming mortgage originations financed to 35 percent, with no attached credit conditions. The Financial Crisis Inquiry Commission (FCIC) reported that at the same board meeting, Fannie Mae's chief business officer Rob Levin "proposed a strategic initiative to 'increase our penetration into subprime.'" In June 2006, Fannie Mae hired Enrico Dallavecchia to be their permanent chief risk officer. Introducing him at the company's strategic retreat that month, board chairman Ashley said, "We have to think differently and creatively about risk, about compliance, and about controls," and then he made his expectations for the CRO unmistakable by adding, "Enrico Dallavecchia was not brought onboard to be a business dampener." Fannie Mae's new credit posture was summarized succinctly in a memo communicating the results of the June retreat: "Single-family's strategy is to say 'yes' to our customers by increasing purchases of subprime and Alt-A loans." (Alt-A, or "Alternative-A," loans were mortgages with reduced or no documentation of the income or the assets of the borrower.) The memo omitted one crucial fact. Fannie Mae would be taking the credit risk on these loans, which neither their customers nor private-label securities issuers were doing themselves.

To have any hope of success, a risk-taking company choosing to compete with entities *not* taking risk absolutely must have its own independent view of what those risks are worth. But in 2006, Fannie Mae no longer did. By then management had convinced itself that the combination of a shrinking market share and extremely low credit losses meant their credit risk evaluation tools were unreliable. Credit staff who knew that the low loan losses were attributable to sharply rising home prices rather than faulty model predictions—and that their credit models were looking ahead to a time when home prices might fall—were too junior in the new organizational hierarchy for their views to be accorded much weight. Wrongly mistrustful of their credit analytics, Fannie Mae's leadership concluded they could protect themselves against the increased risks of the subprime and Alt-A loans they intended to acquire by drawing a line at what they thought were the worst products and features in the private-label securities market and accepting the rest. For a company with more than $2 trillion in credit exposure, that approach was woefully naive. And while it might have stood a chance of working in an earlier period, at the height of a housing bubble and with the toxic set of mortgage products and risks then prevalent, it was doomed at the outset.

Private-label securities issuance continued to exceed the combined issuance of Fannie Mae, Freddie Mac, and Ginnie Mae MBS in 2005 and 2006. With the GSEs' credit standards remaining irrelevant and with financial regulators on the sidelines, the rating agencies were the only potential disciplinarians of lenders' underwriting practices. Unfortunately, the rating agencies' risk assessment process encouraged, rather than penalized, high-risk lending.

The riskiest mortgage types—such as interest-only or pay-option ARMs—and the most aggressive types of risk layering had been in the market only since mid-2003. There were no available data on the performance of these products and risk characteristics during past national or regional downturns, because they didn't exist then. Between June 2003 and June 2006, average U.S home prices rose by more than 40 percent. Literally *any* mortgage type or risk combination will perform well in a housing bubble. So when the rating agencies put high-risk loans and features into their rating models, none had much impact on the default probabilities the models produced, and the rating agencies as a consequence did not require much additional credit subordination to protect against them.

The rating agencies did have extensive historical data on credit scores, and during the 2004 to 2006 period, credit scores became by far the most important determinants of private-label ratings. Lenders quickly figured that out. The average credit score for private-label securities issued between 2004 and 2006 was some 10 points higher than for similar securities issued earlier in the decade, but nearly all of the other risk attributes—product type, documentation, investor properties, and the presence of "piggy-back" or simultaneous second mortgages—were markedly worse. (This was eerily similar to what had occurred with manufactured housing securities in the 1990s: giving the rating agencies what they were looking for, then slipping in risks they couldn't properly evaluate.) Because the rating agencies were not charging remotely accurate risk premiums, lenders found that the most profitable mortgages to put into private-label securities were the riskiest ones, for which they could charge the highest interest rates. Perversely, this gave them an incentive to find even less qualified borrowers willing to pay even higher rates. So-called NINJA (No Income, No Job, or Assets) loans flourished in this environment, and the housing bubble continued to inflate.

It is extraordinarily difficult for any company to maintain risk management discipline in the midst of a speculative bubble. Pressures from customers and shareholders to stay in the game are intense, and while the bubble is in progress and everyone is making money, being on the sidelines seems to all the world to be the wrong decision. I often have wondered how Fannie Mae would have dealt with those pressures had Raines and I remained at the company. That, of course, is impossible to know. Yet I do believe, to a virtual certainty, that because of the risk monitoring systems and disciplines we had developed and put in place, Fannie Mae would not have failed.

The history of finance is replete with instances of companies failing because their business producers overrode the objections of their risk managers. The lure of immediate volume-related income is very hard to resist when the only restraint is the possibility of distant risk-related losses. For that reason, the best companies do not rely on judgment alone; they supplement their judgment with organizational checks and balances and business processes that help management avoid mistakes. That was one of the purposes of our 2003 risk disciplines.

In 2004 we were acutely aware of the problem the rating agencies and private-label issuers had wished away: that the new risky loan types and layered-risk combinations that were flooding the market had been subjected only to environments in which home prices had risen rapidly. Our response was to set dollar exposure limits for categories of loans for which we had determined that "pricing reliability is substantially uncertain," and then to have the Credit Finance group closely track these loans and risk types and conduct analyses on them to try to draw from the data that did exist information about their probable performance under more adverse conditions. Unless and until we gained sufficient confidence in our ability to predict that performance, we would maintain our exposure limits. For loans we did believe we could assess and price, our 2003 risk disciplines required that the present value of any shortfall between the guaranty fees we charged and our model-generated fees be added immediately to capital.

As mortgage credit quality continued to worsen in 2005 and 2006, and home prices rose ever higher, a larger and larger percentage of our lenders' new loans would have fallen short of our loss predictability standards. Any proposal to continue to purchase or guarantee these loans—let alone to begin acquiring even riskier ones—would have come to the Risk Policy Committee for approval and would have been subjected to a full risk analysis by Credit Finance. Under the 2003 disciplines, a decision to take on more risk or to accept more performance uncertainty, had one been made, automatically would have required a compensating increase in capital. There would have been similar capital constraints on our pricing. In 2006 Fannie Mae was having to price some of their credit guarantees more than 25 basis points below the model-generated fee to win back market share; adherence to the risk disciplines would have required the addition of so much capital to offset the fee reductions as to make those transactions uneconomic.

But neither the monitoring systems nor the risk disciplines survived Raines's and my departures and the OFHEO-mandated restructuring of Fannie Mae's risk organization. And instead of cutting back on its risk taking, the company did the opposite, at the worst possible time. Fueled by the torrent of cheap mortgage credit funneled into the market by private-label securities issuers over the previous three years, by the summer of 2006 new home sales, existing home sales, and home prices all had been pushed to unsustainably high levels. New and existing home sales actually had peaked in 2005, and home prices were peaking just at the time Fannie Mae was dropping its last vestige of resistance to the lending frenzy and moving aggressively to join it.

Loans from Fannie Mae's 2006 and 2007 books of business began to default almost immediately. The company reported a $3.6 billion loss for the fourth quarter of 2007, driven by $3 billion in credit-related expenses. It lost another $2.2 billion in the first quarter of 2008. For the first time since early in the Maxwell era, Fannie Mae's investors and security analysts had reason to be seriously concerned about the company's financial prospects.

CHAPTER 17

The Market Melts Down: Fannie Mae Is Nationalized

W ITHIN A FEW MONTHS OF FANNIE MAE'S DECISION TO MOVE more heavily into the subprime and Alt-A markets, a number of hedge funds and investment banks turned negative on the private-label securities market the company was trying to win business from. Had it been Fannie Mae or Freddie Mac who were negative on that market—as they should have been had they been paying attention to what was going on there—they would have not only pulled back from it but also warned borrowers and investors of its dangers. The government-sponsored enterprises had a public mission, and because their business was limited to the residential mortgage market, they had strong incentives to protect it. (Fannie Mae had contemplated going public with concerns about interest-only ARMs in 2004, only to decide against it for fear of a backlash from our lenders.) Investment banks and hedge funds, in contrast, were free-market institutions with free-market incentives. And rather than pour water on the private-label securities fire, their response was to add gasoline to it in the hopes of making money from the conflagration.

The Beginning of the End

The vehicle they employed for that purpose was yet another Wall Street innovation, the synthetic collateralized debt obligation (CDO).

A synthetic CDO was an even more contrived invention than the CDO itself. Synthetic CDOs used credit default swaps—derivative agreements that caused one counterparty to pay another in the event of a default or other "credit event" on a specifically referenced loan or security—in conjunction with CDOs from earlier transactions to create an investment that existed only on paper. Stripped to its core, the synthetic CDO was a bet on the performance of the actual CDOs referenced in the synthetic structure; if those CDOs did poorly, the seller of the synthetic CDO made money at the expense of the buyer. The profits available from selling synthetic CDOs to still-eager buyers of high-yielding mortgage securities gave the hedge funds and savvy Wall Street firms anticipating poor performance from subprime and other risky mortgage types a powerful incentive to prolong the mortgage bubble for as long as they possibly could.

Private-label mortgage security and synthetic CDO issuances stayed strong through the middle of 2007, but the fundamentals were working against them. As 2007 began, both housing starts and new home sales were down by more than 30 percent from their highs in the summer of 2005, and home prices were falling in most regions. Delinquencies and early payment defaults on subprime loans had turned sharply higher in the second half of 2006, and they were continuing to shoot up in 2007. Subprime lenders were reeling. New Century Financial announced in February 2007 that it would restate its financials to correct errors in past statements, and on April 2 it declared bankruptcy. By then more than two dozen smaller subprime lenders also had gone out of business, and several large subprime lenders had stopped making new loans.

The Federal Reserve and Treasury were slow to grasp the import of these developments. In 2007 both institutions had new leadership: Ben Bernanke had succeeded Alan Greenspan at the Fed in February 2006, and Hank Paulson had succeeded John Snow at Treasury in July of that year. Bernanke had been head of the economics department at Princeton before being appointed to the Fed's board of governors in 2002. President Bush asked him to chair his Council of Economic Advisers in June 2005 and made him Fed chairman less than a year later. Paulson, like Bob Rubin, led Goldman Sachs before becoming Treasury secretary. (Rubin had been cochairman with Steve Friedman, a Fannie Mae board member from 1996 to 2002, when Goldman was a partnership; Paulson was Goldman's CEO after it became a public company in 1999.) Bernanke had done extensive studies of the Great Depression as an economics professor, and he looked at the economy and financial markets from a broad and theoretical perspective. Paulson, in contrast, was a pragmatic Wall Street deal maker who made decisions based on experience and instinct rather than theory. Despite their differences in background and orientation, Bernanke and Paulson formed a close partnership that was furthered by the weekly breakfast meetings they held, just as Rubin and Greenspan had done.

Yet neither Bernanke nor Paulson knew or understood what had been happening in the private-label MBS market their two institutions had nurtured. Both viewed the spike in mortgage delinquencies as a "subprime" problem—rather than one that had infected the $11 trillion mortgage market as a whole—and perhaps because the first subprime collapse had so few effects on the economy or the financial markets, they believed the same would be true this time. In any event, as late as May 2007, Bernanke told the audience at a Chicago Fed financial conference, "We believe the effect of the troubles in the subprime sector on the broader housing market will likely be limited, and we do not expect significant spillovers from the subprime market to the rest of the economy or to the financial system." Paulson was saying at around the same time that he believed the subprime mortgage problems were "largely contained." Both were badly mistaken.

Investors were slow to react to the problems as well. While prices of private-label securities experienced episodic bouts of weakness during the first half of 2007, they held up surprisingly well in light of soaring subprime delinquencies and the failures of subprime lenders. One reason was that investors still had confidence in the ratings of these securities, and those ratings had not changed. In the summer of 2007, however, they finally did. On July 10, Moody's downgraded 399 tranches of subprime mortgage-backed securities, and shortly afterwards Standard & Poor's downgraded 498 tranches. Both agencies placed more tranches on watch for future downgrades. Private-label MBS prices plummeted.

On July 31, two hedge funds run by Bear Stearns Asset Management—which had invested heavily in subprime MBS and CDOs—filed for bankruptcy. Then on August 8, the largest bank in France, BNP Paribas, suspended redemptions on three funds holding U.S. mortgage securities, triggering a liquidity crisis that required $130 billion in loans from the European Central Bank to quell. In October, Moody's and Standard & Poor's downgraded thousands more private-label security tranches. Subsequently, Merrill Lynch announced $6.9 billion in CDO losses on October 24, and six days later their CEO, Stan O'Neal, resigned. A week after that, the CEO of Citigroup, Chuck Prince, resigned after his company disclosed it owned over $50 billion in subprime mortgages and would write off close to a fifth of them.

These and other developments threw the private-label securities market into turmoil. New private-label MBS issuance began to dry up in the third quarter of 2007, and by the end of the year, it had virtually ceased. It had taken more than four years, but investors finally had figured out how badly stacked against them these securities were. Private-label financing had fueled the rapid run-up in home prices between 2003 and 2006; now the abrupt withdrawal of that financing would make the mortgage market even more treacherous for those who remained in it.

Almost overnight the government-sponsored enterprises found they were again the primary providers of residential mortgage credit and now essentially the *only* providers of credit. Fannie Mae saw opportunity, rather than danger, in this situation. With no effective means of gauging the dramatically higher risks that now characterized the market, they took comfort from their still-low delinquencies and loan losses and believed that their newfound ability to raise guaranty fees, together with their "avoid the worst" loan screening strategy, would adequately protect them from losses in the future. Freddie Mac was in no better position. Their CEO, Richard Syron, had fired his chief risk officer in 2005 over disagreements about the riskiness of the loans they were buying, and his new CRO no longer was part of his senior management team.

The GSEs were eager to do more business, and Congress wanted them to do more as well. Congress' most pressing priority was helping borrowers of what were called "jumbo" loans—loans in amounts above the Fannie Mae–Freddie Mac limit. These loans relied heavily on private-label financing, and when that financing disappeared, jumbo loan rates skyrocketed. Toward the end of 2007, several members of Congress proposed a temporary increase in the GSE loan limit, from $417,000 to $759,750, to help stabilize the jumbo market. The administration and Treasury said they would oppose a loan limit increase unless it was tied to GSE reform, but in the face of overwhelming Congressional support for the measure, they dropped that condition. The loan limit increase was included in the Economic Stimulus Act of 2008 that passed on February 13. With it, Fannie Mae and Freddie Mac had access to a larger share of new residential mortgages than at any time in their history.

Fannie Mae's Final Chapter

The Bush administration, the Treasury, and the Federal Reserve faced a dilemma. The private-label securitization mechanism they had promoted as the best and safest means of financing U.S. housing had imploded, a victim of its own excesses. To prevent a complete collapse of the housing market, their only realistic option was increased reliance on financing from the GSEs, whom they bitterly opposed. Congress knew that, and Treasury secretary Paulson knew it too. As he told the FCIC two years later, "[The GSEs] were the only game in town . . . They, more than anyone, were the engine we needed to get through the problem."

A battle that had been waged for decades between the supporters and opponents of GSE financing—which had intensified greatly in the last several years—finally seemed to have been decided, and the GSEs were the ones left standing. But that was not the outcome the administration, the Treasury, and the Federal Reserve intended, and it was not too late to change it.

Fannie Mae's business, political, and ideological opponents were masters at using the media to paint a picture of the GSEs and put out information about them that suited their purposes and advanced their objectives. So it was that on March 8, 2008, an article titled "Is Fannie Mae the Next Government Bailout?" appeared in *Barron's* magazine. The article began, "It's perhaps the cruelest of ironies that in the U.S. housing market's greatest hour of need, the major entity created during the Depression to bring liquidity to housing, Fannie Mae, may itself soon be in need of a bailout." The article cited the company's recent credit losses, risky loan acquisitions, and four accounting treatments it questioned—for deferred tax assets, low-income housing tax credits, the company's MBS guaranty obligation, and the valuation of its nonagency MBS holdings—as reasons for speculating that "a bailout of Fannie, in effect a nationalization," might be required.

The basis for the *Barron's* article was a paper titled "Fannie Mae Insolvency and Its Consequences" that had circulated inside the administration beforehand. On the day the article appeared, a copy of the paper was sent by Jason Thomas, a senior staffer at the National Economic Council, to Robert Steel, Treasury's undersecretary for domestic finance. Steel was a 28-year veteran of Goldman Sachs, a trusted friend and advisor of Paulson, and Paulson's point person on Fannie Mae and Freddie Mac issues. Thomas's brief transmittal memo to Steel read, "Attached is the document used as the sourcing for today's *Barron's* article on the potential collapse of Fannie Mae. This is for your eyes only. I send it only to help inform potential internal Treasury discussions about the potential costs and benefits of nationalization."

Five days later, Steel rushed into Paulson's office to tell him that Bear Stearns was having difficulty rolling over its short-term debt. Bear Stearns was the smallest of the big five investment banks, after Goldman Sachs, Merrill Lynch, Morgan Stanley, and Lehman Brothers, and it had been heavily involved in subprime mortgages.

Paulson knew what Bear Stearns' liquidity problems meant, and it wasn't good. The Treasury and the Federal Reserve would have to act quickly. After three days of frenzied activity, on Sunday, March 16, they succeeded in averting a Bear Stearns bankruptcy by arranging for the company to be taken over by JP Morgan, for $2 a share (later increased to $10). To make the rescue work, the Fed had to agree to extend a $30 billion loan to an entity named Maiden Lane that would hold and manage a like amount of Bear Stearns assets JP Morgan did not want. If the Maiden Lane loans did not perform well, the Fed would not get all its money back.

Paulson was worried about the market's reaction to the news of the Bear Stearns rescue, and according to his memoir, *On the Brink*, he thought a positive announcement about Fannie Mae and Freddie Mac might have a calming effect. For months, Fannie Mae CEO Mudd and Freddie Mac CEO Syron had been negotiating with Steel, OFHEO director Lockhart, staff from the Fed, and key members of Congress and the administration over the terms under which OFHEO might reduce the 30 percent capital surcharge it had imposed on the two companies. Congress wanted more GSE lending, and the GSEs wanted it as well, but the GSEs were constrained by capital. Steel and Lockhart had proposed reducing their surcharge provided they raised $1.50 to $2 in new capital for every dollar in existing capital a lower percentage surcharge freed up. Mudd and Syron had been holding out for better terms when Paulson intervened.

A few hours before the Bear Stearns news was made public, Paulson asked Steel to arrange a conference call with Lockhart, Mudd, and Syron to resolve the capital issue. During this call, Paulson convinced Lockhart to lower the GSEs' capital surcharge from 30 percent to 20 percent in exchange for nothing more than vague promises from Mudd and Syron to raise "significant capital" at some point in the future. (Freddie Mac never would raise any.) Lockhart was very unhappy with this development. Shortly afterwards, he wrote an e-mail to Steel, Mudd, and Syron in which he fretted, "The idea strikes me as perverse, and I assume it would seem perverse to the markets that a regulator would agree to allow a regulatee to increase its very high mortgage credit risk leverage (not to mention increasing interest rate risk) without any new capital." He added, "We seem to have gone from 2 to 1 right through 1 to 1 to now 0 to 1."

What Lockhart failed to guess was that Paulson almost certainly had made a decision. His action to not just allow but actually encourage Fannie Mae and Freddie Mac to add new mortgages with no firm commitment to raise capital to back them is understandable only if by then he had concluded that Treasury would be able to use the road map from the GSE insolvency paper given to Steel to put the GSEs into receivership or conservatorship—by writing down the value of their tax assets and private-label security holdings and greatly boosting their loss reserves to exhaust their capital. On the day of the Bear Stearns rescue, there can be little question that Paulson already was thinking of the GSEs as instrumentalities of the government.

The GSEs' reduced capital surcharge was announced on March 19. At a press conference to publicize it, the Treasury, the Fed, and OFHEO all touted the fact that the capital freed up by the lower surcharge would enable the GSEs to purchase or guarantee an additional $200 billion in mortgages. Paulson voiced no concern about adding to the GSEs' credit exposure. Instead he emphasized the positive, saying, "Fannie Mae and Freddie Mac are significant participants in the mortgage market, and I am encouraged that today's announcement will make more financing available in this area." Given Treasury's history of antagonism to the GSEs and their extreme sensitivity to GSE risk taking, this was a dog that wasn't barking. Unaware of Treasury's intentions, Lockhart echoed Paulson's seeming optimism. He said, "The companies are safe and sound, and they will continue to be safe and sound," and he called talk of a potential GSE bailout "nonsense."

In fact, their end was not far off. On Monday, July 7, a report from a Lehman Brothers security analyst erroneously claiming that an imminent regulation might require Fannie Mae and Freddie Mac to add $75 billion in new capital sent the companies' stocks into free fall. That gave Treasury the opening they needed. Four days later, on Friday, July 11, the *New York Times* carried a front-page story claiming "Senior Bush administration officials are considering a plan to have the government take over one or both of the companies and place them in a conservatorship if their problems worsen." The story had all the earmarks of a deliberate leak.

The companies' stocks plunged again when the *Times* story appeared. That afternoon Paulson had Treasury issue a statement in his name, saying, "Today our primary focus is on supporting Fannie Mae and Freddie Mac in their current form as they carry out their important mission." Paulson needed Congressional backing for any actions Treasury or the Fed might take to aid the GSEs, and on Saturday, July 12, he called Mudd and Syron to ask for their cooperation on GSE legislation that would enable Treasury to offer that aid. Both CEOs promised it. With those assurances, Paulson scheduled a press conference for Sunday afternoon, before the opening of the financial markets in Asia. In front of a throng of reporters on the west steps of the Treasury Building, he declared, "Fannie Mae and Freddie Mac play a central role in our housing finance system and must continue to do so in their current form as shareholder-owned companies." He added, "In recent days, I have consulted with the Federal Reserve, OFHEO, the SEC, Congressional leaders of both parties, and with the two companies to develop a three-part plan for immediate action." The second part of that plan, Paulson revealed, was "temporary authority for Treasury to purchase equity in either of the two GSEs if needed."

Forty years after Fannie Mae's 1968 charter had given GSE securities what investors viewed as an implicit government guarantee, this statement by Paulson made the government's support explicit. And in doing so, it sealed the companies' fates. Two and a half weeks later, with Paulson's strong advocacy and Fannie Mae and Freddie Mac's acquiescence, Congress passed and on July 29 President Bush signed into law the Federal Housing Finance Agency Reform Act of 2008, creating a new regulator for the two companies—the Federal Housing Finance Agency, or FHFA—as a successor to OFHEO and giving it authority to place them into conservatorship or receivership.

Tucked within the new law was a one-sentence clause that read: "The members of the board of directors of a regulated entity shall not be liable to the shareholders or creditors of the regulated entity for acquiescing in or consenting in good faith to the appointment of the Agency as conservator or receiver for that regulated entity." This clause was not there by accident. It gave FHFA extremely broad latitude to put the company into conservatorship or receivership for virtually any reason. Fannie Mae's board and top executives—who represented the company's shareholders—knew about the clause but had not objected to it because they naively believed the government would never use it unless absolutely necessary.

They could not have been more wrong. Treasury had no intention of allowing Fannie Mae and Freddie Mac to operate as shareholder-owned companies with the government standing behind their securities, particularly given their newly expanded market roles. And it would be easier to poison the GSEs' shareholders now that their directors had been given an antidote.

Before the GSEs could be taken over, however, Treasury needed both a public rationale and the cooperation of FHFA. The public rationale was the easy part. Paulson notes in *On the Brink* that the Federal Reserve, the Comptroller of the Currency, and the advisor hired by Treasury, Morgan Stanley, all analyzed the two GSEs' books and "agreed that the organizations were sorely undercapitalized . . . and [that] the quality of their capital was suspect." If the findings of those groups seemed familiar, it was because they aligned remarkably closely with the contentions made in the source document for the *Barron's* article sent to Treasury six months earlier—repeated, conveniently, in another *Barron's* article appearing on August 16, which also contained an accurate description of the senior preferred stock agreement that would be imposed upon the companies the following month.

FHFA was nothing more than OFHEO renamed (Lockhart still ran it), and OFHEO consistently had been saying that Fannie Mae and Freddie Mac were safe and sound and adequately capitalized. Paulson and Bernanke had to push Lockhart hard to get him to agree to change his agency's posture on the two companies. He did, and it then became his job to convince his staff to make the same reversal. For any agency except the former OFHEO, this might not have been possible. But they had done it once before. In 2004 their special examination of Fannie Mae had blatantly ignored and contradicted the previous findings and opinions of their examination staff and had been sent directly to the company's board as OFHEO's final regulatory conclusions without management having the opportunity to respond to or dispute them. The new OFHEO, FHFA, would do exactly the same thing in 2008.

On September 4, FHFA sent both companies extremely harsh midyear review letters, chronicling alleged serious deficiencies in their management, business practices, credit quality, and accounting. The letter to Fannie Mae concluded that "the critical unsafe and unsound practices and conditions" documented in the letter "likely require recapitalization of the Enterprise." Mudd objected that neither FHFA nor OFHEO ever had communicated any of the criticisms of their September 4 letter before and that the letter was not fair. That may have been true, but given the regulator's past history, it should not have come as a surprise. Perhaps Mudd felt betrayed. He had publicly repudiated what he called Raines's arrogant approach to OFHEO and done everything he could to be conciliatory, first to OFHEO then to FHFA. Yet in the end, FHFA treated Mudd no differently from how OFHEO treated Raines.

Three days after the supervisory letters were sent to the two companies, and less than six weeks after the GSE regulatory reform act was passed, on September 7, 2008, Treasury made FHFA conservator of Fannie Mae and Freddie Mac. At the same time, Treasury entered into a senior preferred stock agreement with both GSEs under which each could borrow up to $100 billion (later raised to $200 billion) from Treasury, at a 10 percent annual interest rate, in order to maintain a positive net worth. In exchange for this agreement, both GSEs were required to give Treasury $1 billion in senior preferred stock and warrants to purchase 79.9 percent of their common stock at a negligible price.

Fannie Mae had $47 billion in regulatory capital and was in full compliance with all of its statutory capital requirements on the day it was put into conservatorship and the senior preferred stock agreement was signed. But that was irrelevant. Treasury always had believed the company's capital was inadequate, and they finally had the power to make their view the only one that counted. Fannie Mae's shareholders had no say in the matter, and their investment in the company was all but wiped out.

After 40 years as a shareholder-owned institution, Fannie Mae—the foundation of what just five years earlier had been the most successful housing finance system in the world—was gone. What had weakened the company to the point where Treasury could put it into conservatorship was not what its critics had been opposing and warning about so unrelentingly for the previous three decades: its outstanding debt and the interest rate risk of its mortgage portfolio. The portfolio performed quite well throughout the mortgage crisis. Instead, it was Fannie Mae's credit guaranty business, which critics had grudgingly tolerated as its only defensible activity, that had fallen prey to excessive risk—credit risk that came into the company only after it and Freddie Mac had lost their standard setting role to the private-label securities market championed by those same critics, and after Fannie Mae's credit risk management had become ineffective as a consequence of politically motivated acts by its safety and soundness regulator.

A Full-Blown Crisis

Putting Fannie Mae and Freddie Mac into conservatorship when they did was a policy choice by Treasury. In his memoir, Paulson said that they wanted to do it before Lehman Brothers announced "a dreadful loss" for the second quarter of 2008, which it was scheduled to do in mid-September. Lehman had been a concern of investors—and of Treasury and the Fed—ever since the Bear Stearns failure. They were the weakest of the remaining four major investment banks, with over $50 billion in mortgage assets that many analysts believed were worth far less than the value Lehman put on them. Like other investment banks, Lehman was heavily dependent on short-term debt for financing and needed the confidence of investors to remain solvent. In an attempt to maintain that confidence, they had been working to shed risky assets and to raise additional capital since March.

Paulson and Bernanke expected the Fannie Mae and Freddie Mac takeovers to calm the financial markets and buy time for Lehman, but they had the opposite effect. With the benefit of hindsight, it is not hard to understand why. To justify the takeovers, Treasury had to maintain that the GSEs' mortgage problems were far worse than anyone had realized as recently as July, when Paulson famously said he did not intend to use the "bazooka" of unlimited authority to invest in the GSEs that he had just asked Congress to grant him. Well, if things could have gotten that much worse that quickly for the mortgages owned by the GSEs—whose regulator on August 25 had deemed them to be adequately capitalized—why would the same not also be true at Lehman Brothers?

Lehman came under immediate pressure, and now Paulson and Bernanke had an even bigger problem on their hands. Treasury had just committed $100 billion in taxpayer money as the price for their decision to put the GSEs into conservatorship. Already this was being called a "bailout," and it came on top of the $30 billion the Fed had committed in the acquisition of Bear Stearns by JP Morgan six months earlier. More federal money in a rescue of Lehman would be out of the question. No one expected Lehman to survive on its own, so Paulson and Bernanke faced the daunting task of finding an acquirer who would take them without the benefit of government assistance. Despite the most concerted efforts of the Fed, the Treasury, and the entire Wall Street community (who feared the ramifications of a Lehman failure), they were unsuccessful. Lehman held on for as long as they could, but on Monday, September 15, they filed for bankruptcy.

The Lehman bankruptcy opened the floodgates. Virtually all of the major U.S. financial institutions had been caught up by and participated in the excesses of the last several years (JP Morgan was the main exception). The Lehman failure seemed to make clear that at least some companies who found themselves in trouble would not have the benefit of a federal safety net. Investors and creditors were not inclined to wait to see which would be saved and which allowed to fail; their reaction was to get out of any that were even remotely vulnerable. The chairman of Merrill Lynch, John Thain, saw what was coming and arranged to be acquired by Bank of America the weekend of the Lehman bankruptcy. Others were not as prescient or fortunate. In rapid succession, AIG, Washington Mutual, Wachovia, and Morgan Stanley all faced intense selling of their equity and life-threatening runs on their debt. It was a classic financial panic.

With the entire U.S. and global financial systems on the verge of collapse, the Federal Reserve and Treasury threw all the rules out the window. The Fed flooded the financial markets with liquidity—purchasing assets and loaning hundreds of billions of dollars to banks and securities dealers as well to purchasers of corporate commercial paper and asset-backed securities—to keep them functioning. Treasury sought, and after an initial rebuff received, authority from Congress for a Troubled Assets Relief Program (TARP) that gave them $700 billion to use to keep troubled banks from failing. Armed with these funds, Treasury put capital into over 700 banks and in conjunction with the FDIC and the Fed guaranteed massive numbers of assets to facilitate mergers or stem runs on markets or financial institutions.

These extraordinary actions worked. But the carte blanche the Treasury and the Federal Reserve were granted to stabilize the financial system also allowed them to reshape it in a way that reflected their institutional and ideological viewpoints. Given the opportunity to eliminate Fannie Mae and Freddie Mac as private entities—which always had been their objective—they eagerly had taken it. Given an opportunity to break up or nationalize the large commercial banks and investment banks, they did not. Nor did Treasury or the Fed attach any significant conditions or penalties to the lifelines they extended to the institutions they viewed as too systemically important to fail. The mantra of "private gains and public losses" so frequently used to describe the GSEs did indeed have validity, but only for entities favored by the banking regulators. The GSEs were not among them.

The Fed and the Treasury were able to save the financial system, but by the time they finally grasped what was happening with the mortgage crisis, it was far too late to save its ultimate victims, U.S. home owners. The time to have rescued them was before the mortgage and housing bubbles inflated. Then, however, both regulators were focused less on mortgage borrowers and the products they were being offered than on who their lenders should be.

The battle for control of the U.S. mortgage system occurred at a unique time for the global financial markets. Nearly two decades earlier, the collapse of communism had brought a number of countries with low costs of production into the market economy in a very short time. U.S. consumers purchasing goods from these countries sent large amounts of dollars overseas to holders who invested rather than spent them. Record international dollar liquidity helped keep global interest rates low and credit freely available in the late 1990s and early 2000s, and that in turn triggered a rise in worldwide asset prices, including U.S. housing. Low U.S. mortgage rates made it tempting for individuals to use debt to purchase more house (and in some cases, more homes) than they needed, while rising home prices gave lenders comfort that they could extend this credit and still get repaid.

Some of this was normal cyclical behavior. What was *not* normal was the extreme relaxation in underwriting standards that began in the summer of 2003. That was what set the mortgage crisis in motion, and it occurred because U.S. financial regulators allowed, and indeed encouraged, the private-label mortgage-backed securities market to develop in a way that allowed its participants to profit from making loans their borrowers never could repay. Home owners relied on the mortgage finance system to safely finance the largest purchase most of them would ever make, their homes, and here the stewards of that system failed them utterly. Dramatically easier and widely available credit brought an avalanche of new buyers into the market who would not have been able to qualify for a mortgage under traditional underwriting, and by the time these buyers had pushed housing starts, home sales, and home prices to unsustainably high levels, there was nothing anyone could have done to prevent the ensuing collapse.

The magnitude of that collapse mirrored the intensity of the bubble that preceded it. Housing starts and new home sales fell by a staggering 75 percent between 2005 and 2011. Home prices fell by more than 30 percent nationwide, and in some regions they fell by over 60 percent. The total value of American homes dropped by $5.6 trillion before it finally hit bottom. Millions lost their homes to foreclosure, and nearly one-quarter of home owners owed more on their homes than those homes were worth. Sharp cutbacks in spending by families affected by the crisis triggered the worst recession since the Depression, with real GDP falling by 5.1 percent in 18 months. Between February 2008 and February 2010, nearly nine million people lost their jobs, and the unemployment rate more than doubled, hitting 10 percent at its peak. The recession officially ended in June 2009, but the vast amount of household wealth lost during the meltdown made the ensuing recovery the weakest in modern history. The aftereffects of the mortgage wars pervade both the U.S. economy and the financial markets to this day.

Aftermath

I N THE FIRST YEAR AND A HALF AFTER ITS CONSERVATORSHIP, Fannie Mae reported a staggering $127 billion in losses, exhausting its capital and causing it to draw $75 billion under its senior preferred stock agreement with Treasury in order to maintain a positive net worth. The size of these losses left little doubt in anyone's mind about the severity of the company's financial problems or the wisdom of Treasury and the Federal Housing Finance Agency in putting it into conservatorship when they did.

It only seemed that way. During that 18-month period, Fannie Mae's actual credit-related losses—its loan charge-offs and foreclosed property expense—were just $16 billion. Virtually all the rest of its losses were accounting entries made by the company's conservator, FHFA, that pulled into Fannie Mae's 2008 and 2009 financial statements over $100 billion in expenses that otherwise would have been incurred in the future, if they were incurred at all.

Following the script from the paper "Fannie Mae Insolvency and Its Consequences," FHFA took a $21 billion charge to set up a reserve against the company's deferred tax assets, arguing that it would not earn enough in the future to realize their full value, and gave a similar reason for writing off $8 billion in low-income housing tax credits. FHFA also took $17 billion in impairments on the company's private-label security holdings and put $56 billion into its reserve for future loan losses, increasing that to $66 billion on December 31, 2009.

FHFA and Treasury engineered these large and early losses deliberately. Fannie Mae's senior preferred stock agreement required a 10 percent dividend on all draws against it and had the unique feature that once a draw was made, it never could be repaid, even if the company returned to profitability. The structure of this agreement made it possible for Fannie Mae to be kept permanently insolvent by quickly pushing its losses to a high enough level that annual dividend payments on the resulting nonrepayable Treasury draws would exceed what it ever could hope to earn.

Treasury already had acted to limit Fannie Mae's earning power. Even though the mortgage portfolio had not been the cause of the company's losses—it was a source of income helping to offset them—Treasury included in the preferred stock agreement a provision reducing the portfolio by 10 percent per year until it fell to $250 billion. Shrinking Fannie Mae's portfolio made it that much harder for the company to earn its way back to health at the same time as it accomplished a longstanding ideological goal.

During 2010 and 2011, Fannie Mae incurred a further $42 billion in credit-related losses and added another $11 billion to its loss reserve. With these losses and expenses, the company's Treasury draws rose to $116 billion at December 31, 2011, obligating it to make $11.6 billion in dividend payments for every year in the future. That was more than Fannie Mae had earned in any single year in its history. Seemingly it was a death sentence.

But then in 2012, a surprising thing happened. Home prices had hit bottom, and with asset values rising and Fannie Mae's loan losses falling, the company began to make money again. The demise of the private-label securities market had left Fannie Mae, Freddie Mac, and the Federal Housing Administration as the financing source for over 90 percent of all new home mortgages, and since the conservatorship, Fannie Mae had put on almost $1.5 trillion in highly profitable credit guaranty business.

In the first quarter of 2012, Fannie Mae earned $2.7 billion—almost as much as its $2.9 billion dividend payment to Treasury. Then in the second quarter, it earned an astonishing $5.1 billion and was able to add $2.2 billion to its net worth even after the quarterly dividend payment. That was not supposed to have been possible.

Treasury reacted almost immediately. Less than 10 days after the August 8 release of Fannie Mae's second quarter earnings, on August 17 Treasury and FHFA amended the senior preferred stock agreement. Effective January 1, 2013, Fannie Mae would be required to remit to Treasury all of its retained earnings in excess of an applicable "capital reserve amount" (initially set at $3 billion, dropping to zero in 2018). Incredibly, a 10 percent dividend on nonrepayable draws pushed artificially high by conservative accounting had not been enough to keep Fannie Mae from beginning to rebuild its capital. To ensure that it could not continue to do so, Treasury changed the already crushingly punitive terms of its senior preferred stock agreement to make them confiscatory: in the future, the required dividend on the $1 billion in senior preferred stock the company had been given in 2008 would be "everything you ever earn."

Treasury knew what was coming. A substantial portion of the $100 billion in accounting losses recorded on Fannie Mae's books in 2008 and 2009 was about to be reversed. With Fannie Mae again making money, the company's management revisited the 2008 decision to set up a valuation reserve for their deferred tax assets, which by the first quarter of 2013 had grown to over $50 billion. Those assets now had value, so Fannie Mae released the reserve on them. Added to other income, this produced $59 billion in first quarter 2013 earnings. The earnings were remitted to Treasury, and just that quickly, the total of Fannie Mae's Treasury payments—its previous senior preferred stock dividends plus the first quarter's payment—soared to $95 billion, approaching the $116 billion the company had drawn since the conservatorship.

Fannie Mae still had a $60 billion loan loss reserve, which almost certainly was far more than it needed. Its first quarter 2013 credit losses were only $1.5 billion, or $6 billion annualized. A typical financial institution might have two to three years' worth of losses in its reserve; Fannie Mae appeared to have at least a 10-year reserve and arguably much more. Were it to return to the average credit loss rate of the Maxwell, Johnson, and Raines years, its annual credit losses would be less than $1 billion. If and when Fannie Mae concluded that much of its $60 billion loss reserve was not necessary, the excess would be brought into income. Then, if not before, it would have paid more to the Treasury than Treasury paid to it. Whether Treasury chooses to call that a repayment or not, it will be.

Fannie Mae's financial resurgence adds to the growing weight of evidence refuting the assertion of the company's opponents and critics that it was the poster child of poor lending practices during the mortgage crisis. The loss data never have supported that claim. Fannie Mae's average credit loss rate during the years 2008 through 2012 was 58 basis points per year. While that is astronomically higher than the 4 basis point average of the Maxwell-Johnson-Raines years, it still is less than half the single-family mortgage loss rates of commercial banks during the 2008–2012 period and less than one-quarter of the loss rates experienced on private-label securities issued during the bubble years.

Nor do the loss data or the historical record support the contention made by a few vocal commentators that the mortgage crisis was caused by the government pushing Fannie Mae and Freddie Mac to acquire risky loans to meet their statutory housing goals. Of the $76 billion in single-family credit losses Fannie Mae recorded between 2008 and 2012, some 87 percent, or $66 billion, came from loans purchased or guaranteed after 2004—when the private-label market was setting the standard for the types of loans being originated. Only 13 percent of those losses, or $10 billion, came from loans acquired prior to 2005.

Moreover, the main culprits in Fannie Mae's 2008–2012 credit losses were not high loan-to-value ratios and low credit scores—the features most characteristic of affordable housing loans—but rather they were reduced or no documentation (Alt-A) mortgages and interest-only (I/O) ARMs. I/O ARMs accounted for less than 2 percent of Fannie Mae's loans prior to 2005, and the company's decision to ramp up its Alt-A business in 2006 came not because of the housing goals but in spite of them. The great majority of Alt-A loans did not have available income information; if counted at all, they counted against the goals, making it harder for the company to hit them.

Indeed, developments since 2008 have made it unmistakably clear that the dramatic differences in the current circumstances and conditions of commercial and investment banks and the government-sponsored enterprises are attributable not to economic or financial factors that existed prior to the meltdown but to governmental and regulatory policies that were followed during and after it. To ensure that banks emerged from the financial crisis with as little lasting damage as possible, the Treasury and the Federal Reserve threw them lifelines—including the Fed's aggressively reducing the federal funds rate to lower banks' cost of funds and Treasury's providing them with access to repayable preferred stock at only 5 percent interest. In an attempt to ensure that Fannie Mae and Freddie Mac would not emerge from the crisis at all, Treasury and FHFA threw them anchors. Yet even with those anchors, the GSEs somehow were struggling back to the surface.

*   *   *

In the late 1990s, the U.S. mortgage finance system was envied throughout the world. As Fannie Mae's CFO, I met regularly with officials of private financial firms and governmental institutions in Europe and Asia, and a frequent refrain I heard from them was, "I wish we had a Fannie Mae in our country." It was not hard to see why. The United States was one of only two countries to make the consumer-friendly 30-year fixed-rate mortgage widely available to its citizens—Denmark was the other—and we did so while providing better protection against the inherent risks of fixed-rate mortgage lending than any other mechanism yet devised in any other time or place.

But the very success of this system was the source of its undoing. Financial services deregulation during the 1980s and 1990s led to mortgage lending being concentrated among a small number of large bank and nonbank institutions. These lenders had national ambitions and viewed the dominant positions of Fannie Mae and Freddie

Mac in the largest credit market in the world—the U.S. residential mortgage market—as an impediment to those ambitions. It became a priority for them to turn a housing finance system built around the GSEs into one in which neither the government nor market regulation played significant roles. They found ready allies in that quest in the Federal Reserve and Treasury, who opposed the GSEs for both ideological and regulatory reasons. As discussed earlier in this book, Fannie Mae and Freddie Mac fought to maintain their roles, and the mortgage wars began.

The mortgage wars were fought not over reducing risk to the taxpayer or providing the lowest-cost and safest types of home loans to consumers, but over ideology, market power, and money. Consumers were well served before the wars began, and the mortgage finance system was safer than it had ever been. The widely held notion to the contrary—that Fannie Mae and Freddie Mac were operating with dangerous levels of risk and needed to be "reined in" legislatively—was the product of a highly aggressive disinformation campaign waged by the GSEs' opponents and competitors, who sought to supplant them with products and lending mechanisms that in fact put very few limits on risk at all.

Replacing the GSEs involved two parallel efforts: creating a private-market alternative to GSE mortgage securitization and trying to impose legislative or regulatory restraints on the GSEs' business. Both efforts were pursued aggressively and produced results at around the same time. In 2004, issuance of private-label MBS exceeded issuance of GSE mortgage-backed securities, enabling private-label securities issuers and the credit rating agencies to wrest from the GSEs the role of conventional mortgage standard-setter. That same year, Fannie Mae's safety and soundness regulator, OFHEO, emboldened by the anti-GSE zeal of the Bush administration, launched an all-out attack on the company that succeeded in pressuring its board to oust its top management. Subsequently, highly risky loans financeable through private-label securitization became the norm, and Fannie Mae's new management, fearing it was becoming irrelevant, talked itself into relaxing its credit standards to try to win back market share.

The private-label securities market imploded in 2007. Fannie Mae and Freddie Mac became the only major sources of financing for a rapidly weakening housing market, but both companies were losing money because of their ill-advised acquisitions of high-risk loans during the bubble. Unwilling to see the GSEs emerge as the victors in the mortgage wars, Treasury took advantage of their weakened conditions and put them into conservatorship in September 2008.

The global financial environment provided fertile ground for the mortgage crisis to develop, and the battle between the GSEs and their opponents resulted in very poor credit judgments on both sides, but the overriding cause of the crisis was a catastrophic failure of the regulatory process. There was far too little regulation of primary market mortgage originators and the private-label securities market, and there was excessively adversarial and incompetent regulation of the GSEs.

The Federal Reserve and Treasury were driven by their strong free-market orientation and fierce opposition to the GSEs to downplay the importance of curbing unsound subprime lending practices, and to be blind to the obvious conflicts of interest embedded in the private-label securitization process they promoted as the preferred alternative to GSE securitization. Even after private-label securitization fueled a late-1990s boom in manufactured housing followed by a spectacular collapse in the early 2000s, the Fed and Treasury ignored the episode—thereby allowing exactly the same process to engulf the entire financial system half a dozen years later.

Under the directorship of Armando Falcon, OFHEO allowed their political and personal agendas to supersede their regulatory responsibilities. Falcon forced out experienced risk managers at both companies he oversaw—Greg Parseghian at Freddie Mac and Frank Raines at Fannie Mae—at the very time mortgage credit conditions were deteriorating, and Fannie Mae was further required to change its risk management organization in the midst of the bubble. Compounding that error, although OFHEO regulated just two companies taking only two types of risk on one type of asset, they never noticed the tremendous amounts of credit risk both began building up after their previous CEOs were removed.

For all of that, Fannie Mae and Freddie Mac might still have survived had the 1992 risk-based capital standard been implemented by a competent regulator. The "Volcker standard" had been designed to detect any major increase in risk taken by the two companies and automatically require them to hold more capital, but the version of the standard implemented by OFHEO sacrificed regulatory considerations for political ones and did neither.

Critics' claims notwithstanding, the "GSE model" for the secondary mortgage market was not flawed; it was sabotaged by hostile and inept regulation. And the alternative free-market model proved to be an unqualified disaster.

* * *

Today, over 90 percent of the mortgages made in America are financed in the secondary market by a government-controlled entity—either Fannie Mae, Freddie Mac, or the FHA. No one views this as a permanent arrangement.

Numerous proposals have been made for reforming the housing finance system going forward. Almost all start with the premises that the GSEs must be eliminated and that the private sector must play an enhanced role in the provision of mortgage credit. As I wrote in this book, however, neither of these premises is consistent with a proper reading of our experience in the mortgage crisis. There are aspects of the GSE model that should be retained in the future as well as aspects of the private-market model it will be essential to avoid.

Any responsible proposal for mortgage reform must begin with specific objectives for the exercise. Based on my two decades of managing mortgage risk at Fannie Mae, I would offer these three:

First, *we must maintain the broad availability of the 30-year fixed-rate mortgage*. There appears to be a consensus in favor of this objective, as there should be. By removing the unpredictability from a home owner's monthly mortgage payments, the 30-year fixed-rate mortgage contributes importantly to economic stability. Substituting adjustable-rate or balloon mortgages for 30-year fixed-rate loans would have negative effects on both household budgets and the U.S. economy as a whole.

Second, if the 30-year fixed-rate loan is our primary mortgage instrument, *the mortgage finance system must be designed to tap the international capital markets as efficiently as possible.* Because of their heavy reliance on short-term funding, commercial banks are not natural holders of long-term fixed-rate mortgages. Capital markets investors are able and willing to bear fixed-rate mortgage prepayment risk, but they will not invest in individual mortgages directly. Tapping these investors as a funding source requires a credit guaranty. Mortgage finance reformers should seek to develop a guaranty mechanism that attracts international capital at the lowest achievable interest rate. It is possible that some form of structured security—with investor-paid rather than issuer-paid credit ratings—might be able to accomplish this, but an entity-based guaranty, similar to that used by Fannie Mae and Freddie Mac, seems much more likely to be successful on a broad scale.

Third, *the mortgage finance system should provide maximum benefits to consumers rather than to financial institutions.* It will be tempting for policy makers to try to devise a system that gives roles to several different groups of private sector companies. To hold down costs for consumers, however, the credit guaranty system of the future should be kept as simple as possible, consistent with high taxpayer protection standards. Financial firms today enjoy unprecedented market power and do not need more government assistance. Faced with choices in the new mortgage finance system between adding revenues to the financial sector and reducing costs for consumers, policy makers should opt for the latter.

Given these objectives—and drawing on the lessons from the wrenching experience of the recent crisis—I believe the best structure for the mortgage finance system of the future is an amended version of what worked so well in the 1990s: a capital markets–based system with some form of government-sponsored (or guaranteed) entity, or entities, as its centerpiece. These entities could be *de novo* companies, or rechartered versions of the existing GSEs.

The previous system failed not because of risk or a lack of effectiveness, but because of the consequences of unwavering opposition to Fannie Mae's and Freddie Mac's portfolio businesses. The GSEs' portfolios always will be controversial, and for that reason I believe that in spite of the fact that they performed well throughout the mortgage crisis, they should be wound down over time, at a pace dictated by the ability of capital markets investors to absorb the loans they contain. Without their portfolios, Fannie Mae and Freddie Mac could be given new charters as private companies, with regulated returns and limited to providing credit guarantees only on loans below a certain dollar amount and within defined credit parameters. They could be regulated either by the Fed or the Treasury, and their relationship to the government either could remain implicit or be made explicit through payment of a catastrophic risk reinsurance fee.

A straightforward entity-based mortgage credit guaranty, with government backing, is the most effective and efficient way to channel fixed-rate mortgage funds to housing. It produces the lowest possible MBS yield required by capital markets investors, avoids the subjective judgments of credit rating agencies, and converts a pool of unrated individual mortgages to securities of the highest quality for a cost to home owners of only the amount of the guaranty fee (plus, for high loan-to-value-ratio mortgages, the cost of borrower-paid private mortgage insurance), which for my time at Fannie Mae averaged around 20 basis points.

Whether the support is implicit or explicit, and whether or not a rechartered Fannie Mae and Freddie Mac are the mortgage guarantors, the government can offer credit support for residential mortgages at very little risk of loss. With prudent underwriting, professional management, national diversification, and competent regulation, residential mortgage lending is extremely safe. During the 15 years I was chief financial officer at Fannie Mae, the company's credit loss rate averaged less than 2 basis points, and prior to 2008, the highest it ever got when Fannie Mae was shareholder-owned was 12 basis points in 1987. Setting capital requirements or guaranty fees high enough to cover the loss rates experienced in the 2008–2012 period in my view is neither necessary nor desirable. Those loss rates resulted from lending practices, a financing mechanism, and a hands-off regulatory approach that should not be possible in the system being contemplated for the future.

Many may resist this model because it relies on "the government." Yet it does so with results that are matched by few other programs that government can offer. Implied or direct mortgage guarantees will enable millions of families to save hundreds of dollars per year on their mortgage payments at little if any risk or cost to the taxpayer. Moreover, most other proposals offered for mortgage finance reform also involve government in some form—just not as obviously and typically in ways that benefit corporate entities more than home buyers. Before rejecting the government-sponsored guarantor model, policy makers should ask themselves: how do the proposed alternatives differ in terms of the mortgage rates paid by home buyers, the revenues earned by the financial institutions providing the services, and the risks borne by taxpayers? Honest answers to these questions, in conjunction with clearly specified objectives, will point the right way forward.

The history of U.S. mortgage finance is replete with failure. Mutually owned building and loan societies failed in large numbers during the Great Depression, as did the balloon mortgages made by commercial banks. The thrift industry spawned by the Depression was built on a mismatch between asset and debt maturities that could not survive the high interest rates of the late 1970s. The deregulated thrift industry lasted less than a decade before it blew up. The unregulated private-label securities market fell prey to unmanageable conflicts of interest in a similar amount of time. And for Fannie Mae and Freddie Mac, opposition to their portfolio businesses, present from their origins, culminated in a regulatory assault that weakened both to the point that they were unable to survive as shareholder-owned entities.

Ignoring the lessons of the meltdown of the manufactured housing market in the early 2000s doomed the entire single-family mortgage market to a repeat of that experience six years later. We must at all costs avoid the similar mistake of basing the mortgage finance system of the future on a politicized interpretation of what happened in the past. The new system must incorporate the lessons of what really *did* happen in the 2008 crisis and be based on a hard-nosed understanding of how the financial markets actually work. In addition, it must have broad support, not be controversial, and be capable of providing reliable, low-cost, fixed-rate financing in amounts sufficient to sustain an $11 trillion market essential to the economy's well-being.

If we can succeed in devising such a system, something positive will have come out of the mortgage wars after all.

Glossary of Key Acronyms

ARM   adjustable-rate mortgage

CBO   Congressional Budget Office

CDO   Collateralized debt obligation—a form of structured mortgage-backed security backed by lower-rated pieces of existing structured securities

CMO   collateralized mortgage obligation

FASB   Financial Accounting Standards Board—a private organization that sets accounting standards and defines generally accepted accounting principles (GAAP)

FDIC   Federal Deposit Insurance Corporation—the federal agency that guarantees the deposits of member banks

FHFA   Federal Housing Finance Agency

GAAP   Generally accepted accounting principles

GAO   Formerly General Accounting Office, now Government Accountability Office

GSE   Government-sponsored enterprise—a term frequently used to describe the two housing-related GSEs, Fannie Mae and Freddie Mac

HOEPA   Home Ownership and Equity Protection Act

HUD   Department of Housing and Urban Development

LTV Loan-to-value ratio—the amount of a mortgage loan compared with the purchase price or the appraised value of the home the loan is financing

MBS Mortgage-backed security—a debt instrument backed by a group of mortgages

NEC National Economic Council

OCC Office of the Comptroller of the Currency—an independent regulatory agency within the Treasury Department charged with regulating national banks

OFHEO Office of Federal Housing Enterprise Oversight—the safety and soundness regulator of Fannie Mae and Freddie Mac created by Congress in 1992

OMB Office of Management and Budget

OTS Office of Thrift Supervision—created in 1989 as the successor to the Federal Home Loan Bank Board to regulate the savings and loan industry

REMIC real estate mortgage investment conduit

SMMEA Secondary Mortgage Market Enhancement Act—a law passed in 1984 to enhance the marketability of private-label mortgage-backed securities

TARP Troubled Assets Relief Program

Notes on Sources

The foundation of *The Mortgage Wars* is my knowledge and experience from 30 years in the financial services industry and 23 years as a senior executive at Fannie Mae. What made it possible for me to write it, however, was the fact that for eight years after I left Fannie Mae in 2004, I was enmeshed in litigation that caused me to delve deeply into many of the issues and areas that I focused on in this book. My review of hundreds if not thousands of documents during this process was of immeasurable value in refreshing my memory as I reconstructed the situations, circumstances, and events I relate in the book. In addition, in writing the narrative of the mortgage wars, I was fortunate to be able to draw on a wealth of publicly available information to give immediacy to the story and bring it to life.

A major theme of the book is the divergence between what was happening with Fannie Mae as a business and what was happening to it politically. Virtually all of the data cited in the book for the Fannie Mae business story come from information put out by the company in annual or monthly reports or from other public sources. The nuances on and insights into those data—including the discussions of Fannie Mae's risk management practices—draw on my personal experience, in many cases confirmed by internal documents accumulated while at the company.

Fannie Mae was the subject of numerous studies by government agencies, going back to the early 1980s. The Congressional Budget Office did studies of Fannie Mae in 1983, 1991, 1996, and 2001; the General Accounting Office did Fannie Mae studies in 1985, 1990, 1991, and 1996; the Department of Housing and Urban Development's Fannie Mae studies were in 1991 and 1996; and Treasury did studies of Fannie Mae in 1990 and 1996. Collectively, these studies are a treasure trove of historical facts about Fannie Mae and its business environment.

In telling the Fannie Mae political story, I benefited greatly from access to a large set of articles from major newspapers and magazines that I began clipping and retaining shortly after the formation of the lobbying group FM Watch in 1999. Material from those articles proved invaluable in recreating the political dynamic that played out during the years of Frank Raines's chairmanship. Where there were gaps, contemporaneous articles from the *Wall Street Journal*, *Washington Post*, *New York Times*, *American Banker*, and other sources generally were available through my online research. A number of former Fannie Mae executives also shared their recollections and insights in interviews I conducted as I wrote the book.

The 2008 financial crisis and the events leading up to it have been covered extensively, and I tapped a number of sources to help tell that aspect of the story. Particularly valuable were the report of the Financial Crisis Inquiry Commission published in January 2011 and materials released by the House Oversight Committee in December 2008. Of the many books written on the financial crisis, I found *All the Devils Are Here* by Bethany McLean and Joe Nocera and *On the Brink* by former Treasury Secretary Hank Paulson to be especially useful.

At several points in the book, I relied on specific reference sources to refresh or supplement my knowledge of the topics I was writing about.

For information on the evolution of the mortgage finance industry following the Depression in Chapter 3 ("Birth, Trial, and Turnaround") and for my brief discussion of the thrift crisis of the

1980s in Chapter 5 ("The Volcker Standard Gives Fannie Mae an Edge"), I drew on material from three books—*The Fateful History of Fannie Mae* by James Hagerty, *From Buildings and Loans to Bailouts: A History of the American Savings and Loan Industry 1831–1995* by David L. Mason, and *An Examination of the Banking Crises of the 1980s and Early 1990s* from the Federal Deposit Insurance Corporation—along with a paper by Kenneth A. Snowden titled "Anatomy of a Mortgage Crisis: A Look Back to the 1930s," prepared for *The Panic of 2008* conference at George Washington University Law School in June 2009.

Chapters 7 and 8 ("Conflicts with Fast-Growing Lenders" and "A Surprise from the Treasury Department") address the deregulation and consolidation of the financial services industry in the 1980s and 1990s. I found useful facts and information on these topics in three publications from different Federal Reserve district banks: "Investigating the Banking Consolidation Trend" in the spring 1991 *Federal Reserve Bank of Minneapolis Quarterly Review*; "Explaining the Rising Concentration of Banking Assets in the 1990s" in the August 2000 edition of *Current Issues in Economics and Finance* from the Federal Reserve Bank of New York; and "Changes in the Size Distribution of U.S. Banks: 1960 to 1995" from the fall 2006 *Federal Reserve Bank of Richmond Economic Quarterly*. Also helpful were a September 2011 article from the *Journal of Business and Economics Research* titled "Consolidation in the U.S. Banking Industry Since Riegle-Neal" and a July 2009 publication from the Center for Economic Policy Research called *A Short History of Financial Deregulation in the United States*.

Finally, I found good background material for my discussions of subprime mortgage lending in Chapter 9 ("Private-Label Mortgage-Backed Securities") and Chapter 12 ("Private Label Takes Center Stage") in the July 20, 2000, report of the joint HUD-Treasury Task Force on Predatory Lending and in "The Evolution of the Subprime Mortgage Market" from the January/February 2006 edition of the *Federal Reserve Bank of St. Louis Quarterly Review*.

While I have taken great care to verify and confirm all of the factual information contained in this book, it is possible that some errors may have gone undetected. For any such instances, I am solely responsible.

Index

Veterans Administration (VA), 21, 94
Volcker, Paul, 23, 51–55, 59, 106
Volcker standard, 55–56, 59–62, 159,
    266
Voluntary initiatives, 112–116, 141, 152

Wachovia, 7, 9
Wall Street
  bailout, 6
  GSE MBS and, 174
  manufactured housing and private-
      label MBS, 129
  subprime lenders, 127
Wall Street Journal, 145–148, 192,
    205–206, 209, 217, 218
Wallison, Peter, 187
WAMU. *See* Washington Mutual

Warehouse lines, 127
Washington Mutual (WAMU), 6, 235
Washington Post, 80
Washington Press Club, 102
Washington Research Group, 187
Weill, Sandy, 106
Welch, Jack, 92
Wells Fargo, 9, 88, 95
Wells notice, 223
Wilkinson, Beth, 222
Wilmer, Cutler & Pickering, 212
Wolfensohn, Jim, 51, 52, 54, 65, 80
World Bank, 104

Yield spread premium, 169

Zoellick, Bob, 73, 76